Oracle ADF 11gR2 Development Beginner's Guide

Experience the easiest way to learn, understand, and implement rich Internet applications using Oracle ADF 11gR2

Vinod Krishnan

PUBLISHING

BIRMINGHAM - MUMBAI

Oracle ADF 11gR2 Development Beginner's Guide

First published: April 2013

Production Reference: 1180413

Published by Packt Publishing Ltd.
Livery Place
35 Livery Street
Birmingham B3 2PB, UK.

ISBN 978-1-84968-900-7

www.packtpub.com

Cover Image by Suresh Mogre (suresh.mogre.99@gmail.com)

Credits

Author

Vinod Krishnan

Reviewers

Frank Nimphius

Sten E. Vesterli

Acquisition Editor

Grant Mizen

Lead Technical Editor

Azharuddin Sheikh

Technical Editors

Chirag Jani

Veena Pagare

Project Coordinator

Amey Sawant

Graphics

Ronak Dhruv

Valentina Dsilva

Copy Editors

Brandt D'Mello

Insiya Morbiwala

Sajeev Raghavan

Laxmi Subramanian

Aditya Nair

Proofreaders

Katherine Tarr

Maria Gould

Indexer

Tejal R. Soni

Production Coordinator

Manu Joseph

Cover Work

Manu Joseph

About the Author

Vinod Krishnan has over eight years' experience in the Information Technology industry this exposed him to a wide range of technologies that include Java, J2EE, WebLogic, Fusion Middleware, SOA, and Webcenter.

He has been working with Oracle ADF Technologies since 2005, and enhanced his affinity towards ADF after he joined Oracle India. For the last five years, Vinod is actively involved in large implementations of next-generation enterprise applications, utilizing Oracle's JDeveloper and Application Development Framework (ADF) technologies. He holds a B.Tech. in Information Technology from Anna University, Chennai, India.

He is currently responsible for building and deploying applications using the Oracle Fusion Middleware technology stack as a Project Lead in Oracle America.

He is an `Oracle Certified Specialist`, and the technologies he has worked on include Oracle ADF, SOA, Webcenter, and Identity Management. His contribution towards `Jdeveloper and ADF` discussion forums is immense. With his experience, he has learned many tips and techniques that will help a new user to learn this technology without any hassles. He writes his own blog (`http://vtkrishn.com`) that discusses the tips and tricks with using Oracle technologies.

Vinod has had a multifaceted career, he has worked in positions such as Senior Consultant, Senior Applications Engineer, Software Engineer, and Solution Architect for MNCs such as Oracle, Capgemini, and Keane. Currently he is working as a Project Lead in Oracle America.

I would like to express my gratitude to the people who saw me through this book, to all those who provided support, talked things over, read, wrote, offered comments, allowed me to quote their remarks, and assisted in the editing, proofreading, and design.

I want to thank my wife, Sandhya, who supported and encouraged me in spite of all the time it took me away from her. It was a long and difficult journey for her.

I would like to thank Grant Mizen, Stephanie Moss, Ameya Sawant, and Poonam Jain for helping me with the process of selection and editing.

Thanks to Packt Publishing for giving me the opportunity to help and guide new users of ADF with my book.

About the Reviewers

Frank Nimphius is a Senior Principal Product Manager in the Oracle application development tools group at Oracle Corporation, specializing in Oracle JDeveloper and Oracle Application Development Framework (ADF).

In his current position, Frank represents and evangelizes the Oracle JDeveloper and Oracle ADF products worldwide as a speaker at user group and technology conferences as well as in various publications. Frank runs the ADF Code Corner website, the "OTN Forum Harvest" blog, and is the co-author of the *Oracle Fusion Developer Guide* book published in 2009 by *McGraw-Hill*.

Sten E. Vesterli took up Oracle development as his first job after graduating from the Technical University of Denmark, and hasn't looked back since. He has worked with almost every development tool and server Oracle has produced in the last two decades, including Oracle ADF, JDeveloper, WebLogic, SQL Developer, Oracle Portal, BPEL, Collaboration Suite, Designer, Forms, Reports, and even Oracle Power Objects.

He started sharing his knowledge with a conference presentation in 1997 and has since given more than 100 conference presentations at Oracle OpenWorld and at ODTUG, IOUG, UKOUG, DOAG, and other user group conferences around the world. His presentations are highly rated by the participants, and in 2010 he received the ODTUG Best Speaker award.

He has also written numerous articles, participated in podcasts, and has written *Oracle Web Applications 101*, *McGraw-Hill*, and *Oracle ADF Enterprise Application Development – Made Simple*, *Packt Publishing*. He is currently writing his third book on Oracle ADF Essentials.

Oracle has recognized Sten's skills as an expert communicator on Oracle technology by awarding him the prestigious title of Oracle ACE Director, which is carried by less than 100 people in the world. He is also an Oracle Fusion User Experience Advocate and sits on the Oracle Usability advisory board, and he is part of the Oracle WebLogic Partner Council as well.

Based in Denmark, Sten is a partner in the Oracle consulting company Scott/Tiger, where he works as a Senior Principal Consultant. When not writing books or presenting, he helps customers choose the appropriate technology for their needs, teaching, mentoring, and leading development projects. In his spare time, Sten enjoys triathlon and completed his first Ironman in 2012.

www.PacktPub.com

Support files, eBooks, discount offers and more

You might want to visit www.PacktPub.com for support files and downloads related to your book.

Did you know that Packt offers eBook versions of every book published, with PDF and ePub files available? You can upgrade to the eBook version at www.PacktPub.com and as a print book customer, you are entitled to a discount on the eBook copy. Get in touch with us at service@packtpub.com for more details.

At www.PacktPub.com, you can also read a collection of free technical articles, sign up for a range of free newsletters and receive exclusive discounts and offers on Packt books and eBooks.

http://PacktLib.PacktPub.com

Do you need instant solutions to your IT questions? PacktLib is Packt's online digital book library. Here, you can access, read and search across Packt's entire library of books.

Why Subscribe?

- ◆ Fully searchable across every book published by Packt
- ◆ Copy and paste, print and bookmark content
- ◆ On demand and accessible via web browser

Free Access for Packt account holders

If you have an account with Packt at www.PacktPub.com, you can use this to access PacktLib today and view nine entirely free books. Simply use your login credentials for immediate access.

Table of Contents

Preface

Application Development Framework (ADF) 11gR2 is the next-generation JEE framework from Oracle for building robust and scalable enterprise applications. ADF 11gR2 provides out of the box infrastructure solutions that simplify application development and end user experience. Application development using ADF 11gR2 is fun as it provides a visual and declarative development experience. Some of the noted features offered by ADF 11gR2 are rich and powerful components support for rich Internet applications, Page Flow 2.0 support, drag-and-drop support for data bindings, ADF business components support, mobile development support, security implementation support, declarative development support, runtime customization, reusability support, and so on.

Oracle ADF 11gR2 Development Beginner's Guide aims to provide step-by-step instructions for designing, developing, and deploying a highly scalable, secured, and rich Internet application. This book will help any user with basic programming skills to quickly learn what options are available, and how to develop web applications using ADF 11gR2. This book has been designed to help you learn basics and have fun while developing practical applications using ADF 11gR2.

In this book, you will learn about developing web-based applications using ADF 11gR2 in a simple and easy way. Screenshots and practical instructions are included to make the book more interactive. This book will serve as a faithful friend to its readers.

What this book covers

Chapter 1, *Installing and Configuring JDeveloper IDE* will teach you how to install and configure the JDeveloper IDE, and how to work with the IDE.

Chapter 2, *Getting Started with ADF* will teach you the basics of the Model-View-Controller architecture, how ADF fits into the MVC pattern, the components of ADF, and how to build a simple ADF application.

Chapter 3, *Understanding the Model Layer* will teach you about ADF Business Components, how they work, and it will help you familiarize with the components.

Chapter 4, *Validating and Using the Model Data* describes how to write business logic declaratively. Learn groovy expressions, and how to manage transactions and expose the data.

Chapter 5, *Binding the Data* teaches you how to use the data controls and bind the data for the user interface.

Chapter 6, *Displaying the Data* shows how to display the data in the UI using layers and components.

Chapter 7, *Working with Navigation Flows* describes how to use page flows and activities, pass parameters, and about the ADF life cycle.

Chapter 8, *Layout with Look and Feel* will teach you how to style the page and make it presentable.

Chapter 9, *Implementing Security* will help in securing the page that you have created, and show how to allow and restrict access for different roles and groups.

Chapter 10, *Deploying the ADF Application* will help you deploy the application to the server.

Chapter 11, *Advanced Features of ADF* delves into the Advanced features of the ADF 11*g*R2 framework.

What you need for this book

You will need a computer running either the Windows or Linux or Mac operating system with a minimum of 2 GB of RAM. A minimum of 1024 x 768 resolution is desired for development. It will be good if you have a minimum of 3 GB of hard drive space in your machine. These requirements are detailed in *Chapter 1*, *Installing and Configuring JDeveloper IDE*. An Internet connection is required to download the files. You should have modern browsers such as Internet Explorer, Firefox, or Chrome installed on your machine to test the application.

Who this book is for

The book is intended for beginners who know a little bit of HTML and Java programming and would like to learn how to develop rich web applications using Oracle ADF 11*g*R2.

Conventions

In this book, you will find a number of styles of text that distinguish between different kinds of information. Here are some examples of these styles, and an explanation of their meaning.

Code words in text are shown as follows: " Accept the prompt to save `jdevstudio11123install.exe` on your machine "

A block of code is set as follows:

```
<context-param>
    <param-name>org.apache.myfaces.trinidad.CHECK_FILE_MODIFICATION</
param-name>
    <param-value>true</param-value>
  </context-param>
  <context-param>
    <param-name>org.apache.myfaces.trinidad.DISABLE_CONTENT_
COMPRESSION</param-name>
    <param-value>true</param-value>
  </context-param>
```

When we wish to draw your attention to a particular part of a code block, the relevant lines or items are set in bold:

```
[default]
exten => s,1,Dial(Zap/1|30)
exten => s,2,Voicemail(u100)
exten => s,102,Voicemail(b100)
exten => i,1,Voicemail(s0)
```

Any command-line input or output is written as follows:

```
# cp /usr/src/asterisk-addons/configs/cdr_mysql.conf.sample
    /etc/asterisk/cdr_mysql.conf
```

New terms and **important words** are shown in bold. Words that you see on the screen, in menus or dialog boxes for example, appear in the text like this: "clicking the **Next** button moves you to the next screen".

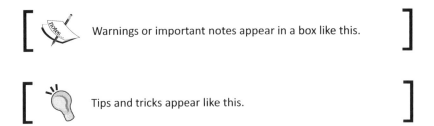

> Warnings or important notes appear in a box like this.

> Tips and tricks appear like this.

Reader feedback

Feedback from our readers is always welcome. Let us know what you think about this book—what you liked or may have disliked. Reader feedback is important for us to develop titles that you really get the most out of.

To send us general feedback, simply send an e-mail to feedback@packtpub.com, and mention the book title via the subject of your message.

If there is a topic that you have expertise in and you are interested in either writing or contributing to a book, see our author guide on www.packtpub.com/authors.

Customer support

Now that you are the proud owner of a Packt book, we have a number of things to help you to get the most from your purchase.

Downloading the example code

You can download the example code files for all Packt books you have purchased from your account at http://www.packtpub.com. If you purchased this book elsewhere, you can visit http://www.packtpub.com/support and register to have the files e-mailed directly to you.

Errata

Although we have taken every care to ensure the accuracy of our content, mistakes do happen. If you find a mistake in one of our books—maybe a mistake in the text or the code—we would be grateful if you would report this to us. By doing so, you can save other readers from frustration and help us improve subsequent versions of this book. If you find any errata, please report them by visiting http://www.packtpub.com/submit-errata, selecting your book, clicking on the **errata submission form** link, and entering the details of your errata. Once your errata are verified, your submission will be accepted and the errata will be uploaded on our website, or added to any list of existing errata, under the Errata section of that title. Any existing errata can be viewed by selecting your title from http://www.packtpub.com/support.

Piracy

Piracy of copyright material on the Internet is an ongoing problem across all media. At Packt, we take the protection of our copyright and licenses very seriously. If you come across any illegal copies of our works, in any form, on the Internet, please provide us with the location address or website name immediately so that we can pursue a remedy.

Please contact us at copyright@packtpub.com with a link to the suspected pirated material.

We appreciate your help in protecting our authors, and our ability to bring you valuable content.

Questions

You can contact us at questions@packtpub.com if you are having a problem with any aspect of the book, and we will do our best to address it.

1
Installing and Configuring JDeveloper IDE

Developing a web application using ADF is fun, and the most interesting part is to work in an integrated development environment such as JDeveloper IDE. JDeveloper IDE imparts a declarative environment and supports an end-to-end development life cycle for an enterprise application using ADF. JDeveloper has been designed to interact efficiently with most of the technologies.

JDeveloper has undergone several phases of changes/versions, and it is now the prominent, most preferred IDE for developing web applications using Oracle technologies, especially ADF. The latest version of JDeveloper available in the market is 11*g*R2 with the release Version 11.1.2.3.0. The advantage of the JDeveloper 11*g*R2 release 11.1.2.3.0 is that it supports the development of mobile applications for iOS and Android mobile devices.

In this chapter, we will learn how to:

- ◆ Install JDeveloper on Windows
- ◆ Work with the IDE
- ◆ Get familiar with the IDE components

System requirements for Windows

JDeveloper 11*g*R2 is supported to run on the following operating systems:

- ◆ Windows
- ◆ Linux
- ◆ Mac OS X

The recommended system requirements for Windows are as follows:

- ◆ **Operating system version**: Windows 7 and Windows XP with service pack 3 on both 32-bit and 64-bit systems
- ◆ **Minimum system memory**: 2 GB for 32-bit and 3 GB for 64-bit machines is desirable
- ◆ **Display settings**: Minimum of 1024 x 768 resolution for ADF development
- ◆ **JDK requirement**: Java 6.0 Update 24 and above

 When writing this book, the author used JDeveloper 11*g*R2 (11.1.2.3.0) on Windows 7 professional, a 32-bit operating system with 3 GB of system memory.

Installing JDeveloper

Installing JDeveloper 11*g*R2 on Windows is an easy task. Following the steps will ensure a smooth installation.

The installation process involves:

- ◆ Downloading the installer from OTN
- ◆ Installing the software in Windows

Time for action – downloading the installer

JDeveloper 11*g*R2 Studio Edition is free for development and is licensed under the OTN JDeveloper license agreement. JDeveloper 11*g*R2 (11.1.2.3.0) has a free runtime license for applications deployed to GlassFish using the ADF Essentials feature. Perform the following steps for downloading the installer:

1. On the OTN website (`http://www.oracle.com/technetwork/developer-tools/jdev/downloads/index.html`), click on the **Downloads** tab, read the terms, and accept the license agreement.

2. Select the **Windows Install** drop-down option for **Studio Edition: 11.1.2.3.0** and click on the **Download File** button.

3. Accept the prompt to save `jdevstudio11123install.exe` on your machine.

What just happened?

You have downloaded the installer from the OTN site to install the JDeveloper 11.1.2.3.0 Studio edition on Windows.

This installer is an executable that will run only on Windows. The installer and the installation procedure differ from platform to platform. You will have to download a Linux install for a Linux platform, and there is an option to download a generic, platform-independent installer for MAC. Refer to the following URL for more information on how to use a generic installer:

```
http://www.oracle.com/technetwork/developer-tools/jdev/documentation/
index.html
```

Have a go hero – researching the optional components for JDeveloper

Ok, now it's your turn to research more on the optional components that can be downloaded for JDeveloper 11*g*R2. There are other components that support adding more features for JDeveloper IDE.

Ask yourself the following questions and find the answers on the **Downloads** page:

◆ We have different development teams to work with. What are the options to collaborate for increased productivity?

◆ How can you find out more about the previous versions of JDeveloper before starting with 11*g*R2?

◆ Can I install my ADF application on any other JEE servers?

◆ Where can I see the ADF framework components in action?

◆ I want to develop my own custom theme for the ADF components. Where can I find a user-friendly editor for customizing the components?

Studio edition

For a start, installing JDeveloper 11*g*R2 in Windows is straightforward and will not include any other extra steps. We will now move on to the installation of JDeveloper 11*g*R2 on Windows.

Time for action – installing JDeveloper Studio Edition

Let's perform the following steps to install the JDeveloper 11gR2 Studio Edition:

1. Double-click on the `jdevstudio11123install.exe` file to launch the installer. The Oracle installer starts preparing for the installation, and a screen with a progress bar appears.

2. Once the preparation is completed, a **Welcome** screen is displayed. Click on the **Next** button to proceed with the installation process.

3. The next screen will ask you to choose the middleware home directory for the installation. The **Middleware Home Type** section will have two options to choose from. One is **Use an existing Middleware Home** and the other one is **Create a new Middleware Home**.

> When we select **Use an existing Middleware Home**, the existing middleware installation paths get enabled, and the installation of the additional component depends on the user selection.

4. Select **Create a new Middleware Home** and locate the directory where you want to install JDeveloper Studio and other additional components. The installers will display an error message if the path already exists. The directory that you specify here will be your middleware home, and a common practice is to refer to the directory as `MW_HOME`.

5. Click on the **Next** button to choose the installation type on the next screen.

6. On this screen, you will select how you want to install the product. You will see two options, namely **Typical** and **Custom**.

    ❑ The **Typical** installation will install JDeveloper Studio, application development framework runtime, and WebLogic Server on your system

    ❑ The **Custom** installation will allow you to choose the product and components to install

7. We will select the **Typical** option this time; it will install all the related components necessary to run the application.

8. The next screen will display the installation directories for different components. Following are the default directories:

    ❑ For JDeveloper: `MW_HOME/jdeveloper`

    ❑ For WebLogic Server: `MW_HOME/wlserver_10.3`

9. You can select the **Discard Changes** option at this point of time to revert back and choose a different directory for your middleware installation.

10. The next screen will allow you to create the following shortcuts for the components:

    ❑ **"All Users" Start Menu folder** will create shortcuts in the **Start** menu, and all users registered on the system can access these shortcuts

    ❑ **Local user's Start Menu** will restrict access to any other user except the current user

11. The next screen will display the installation summary of all the components that will be installed as part of the current installation. The components installed are:

    ❑ JDeveloper Studio

    ❑ Application development framework runtime

    ❑ WebLogic Server

    ❑ Java 6.0 Update 24

> If we had selected the **Custom** installation type, we would have had an option to unselect the **JDK 1.6** installation on the component selection screen. Also remember that JDK has to be installed separately for users who had opted to use a generic installer.

12. Click on the **Next** button to proceed with the installation of the components displayed on the **Installation Summary** screen. During this process, the installation-related artifacts will be displayed along with the progress of the installation. You have an option to exit the installation at any point of time.

13. Once the installation is complete, you will be directed to the **Installation Complete** screen with a message saying **Installation is Complete**. You are provided with an option **Run Quickstart** that will display a wizard to launch installed components, configure the server, and show a way to upgrade the server domains. We can also access the online resources and documentation related to JDeveloper 11*g*R2 using the wizard.

14. Click on the **Done** button to display the **Quickstart** wizard.

15. To verify the components that are installed, you can check the MW_HOME/ registry.xml file.

What just happened?

Congratulations! We just installed JDeveloper 11gR2 Studio Edition on Windows; this means that the initial and most important step for developing this next generation enterprise application is complete.

Starting JDeveloper is the next easy task that follows the installation.

Have a go hero – check the folder structure of JDeveloper

Now it is time for you to have a look at the installation directory of JDeveloper. Perform the following steps to check the folder structure of JDeveloper:

1. List down the folders that you see inside MW_HOME.

2. Familiarize yourself with the directory structure .

3. What can you infer from the folder structure?

Time for action – launching JDeveloper for the first time

By now you will be excited to launch JDeveloper, but since this is your first time, it will be good to know the options available:

1. Launch **Oracle JDeveloper 11g** from the **Quickstart** wizard after the installation is complete. The **Quickstart** wizard is also available from **All Programs | Fusion Middleware 11.1.2.3.0**.

2. The newly installed products are pinned to the **Start** menu for easy access. Click on **JDeveloper Studio 11.1.2.3.0**.

3. You can also click on **All Programs** from the **Start** menu, locate **Oracle Fusion Middleware 11.1.2.3.0**, and click on **JDeveloper Studio 11.1.2.3.0**.

The locations from where you can start JDeveloper apart from the shortcuts are:

♦ MW_HOME/jdeveloper/jdeveloper.exe
♦ MW_HOME/jdeveloper/jdev/bin/jdevw.exe
♦ MW_HOME/jdeveloper/jdev/bin/jdev.exe

The first two options have the same purpose. The last option will open along with a console for diagnostic purposes.

What just happened?

Now you have launched JDeveloper. What do you see? You will see a startup screen called **Oracle JDeveloper 11g** with the Version 11.1.2.3.0.

Have a go hero – have fun with the welcome screen

By now you will have a better idea of the folder structure of JDeveloper. To have some fun, just guess where the welcome screen is coming from.

If you succeed in identifying the location, you can have your own welcome screen every time you start JDeveloper, just by changing it.

Knowing the start-up flags/parameters

There are some flags that you can set to alter the launching behavior of the IDE. These are set as the command-line options for the shortcut that is used to launch the IDE.

JDeveloper is a multiuser-enabled IDE that allows multiple users to share the same workstation. By default, the IDE configuration files are saved in a directory within the user's working directory. The following are the start-up flags/parameters:

◆ `-J-Dide.user.dir=<system_directory>`: Using this property, you can override the default behavior to write the configuration files into the specific directory of choice.

> An alternate way for this is to set the `JDEV_USER_DIR` environment variable that points to the user's current working directory.
>
> `JDEV_USER_HOME` and `JDEV_USER_DIR` are the variables that are listed in the `MW_HOME/jdeveloper/jdev/bin/jdev.boot` file. JDeveloper will look up these variables on startup to set the user's directory. For example:
>
> `set JDEV_USER_HOME=C:\Users\vtkrishn\AppData\Roaming\JDeveloper`
>
> `set JDEV_USER_DIR=C:\JDeveloper\mywork`

◆ `nonag`: This will disable all dialogs or messages displayed while starting the IDE. However, the splash screen will still be displayed to the user. Use `nosplash` to disable the splash screen.

◆ noreopen: This option will not reopen the files that were opened in the previous user session.

 The noreopen option will help JDeveloper to start faster, with there being no open files from the previous user session. All these settings will be displayed in the **Properties** tab of the IDE in **Help | About**. You may find other useful information in this section.

Time for action – setting the start-up options

1. Locate your middleware directory on the **Start** menu.

2. Right-click on **JDeveloper Studio 11.1.2.3.0** and select **Properties**.

3. In the **Target** section, add the following line of code at the end of the line:

```
-J-Dide.user.dir=C:\jdev –nonag –noopen
```

What just happened?

You have selected JDeveloper to have the user directory in the C:\jdev folder and also opted not to open any kind of message or welcome screen while launching the IDE. The IDE will not have the files from your last session open.

Have a go hero – more options

You will find more options listed in the **Help | About** section related to the start-up parameters.

Setting up the user directory (System directory)

The system directory is created when you first start your JDeveloper and it keeps storing the IDE settings thereafter. The default location on Windows for the JDeveloper 11*g*R2 release Version 11.1.2.3 is:

```
C:\Users\%UserName%\AppData\Roaming\JDeveloper\
system11.1.2.3.39.62.76.1
```

To see some information in the system folder, the JDeveloper IDE should be loaded completely and should not be interrupted during startup. The DefaultDomain folder will be created when the integrated server is started for the first time. Other folders in the system folders are also created when the component is accessed for the first time. The following screenshot shows the system folders, their files, and their description:

System Folders	Files	Description
.history		history of the file changes in your workspace
_oracle.ide.rolemgr.11.1.2.2.39.61.83.1	roleprefs.xml	stores the roles for the IDE
o.adf-faces-databinding-dt	preferences.xml	stores data binding settings
o.BC4J	formatinfo.xml	default formats for Date,Currency and Numbers
o.diagram	dt-settings.xml	Co-ordinates of diagram supported files like faces-config.xml, adfc-config.xml and the BC diagram
o.ide	preferences.xml settings.xml windowinglayout.xml	common IDE related settings and layout
o.j2ee	adrs-instances.xml	hold the integrated server setup information within the IDE
o.j2ee.drs		holds the deployed application as part of the domain replication service.
o.jdeveloper	ide.properties	some ide related information like font size, layouts, skin used etc.
o.jdeveloper.rescat2.model	connections.xml rescat-jps-config.xml cwallet.sso rescat-adf-config.xml	
o.jdeveloper.runner.core	hs_breakpoints.xml	breakpoint information for the files

Have a go hero – look for other files in the system folder

Now it's time for you to do some research on the system directory. Perform the following steps:

- List down other configuration files that you can locate in the system directory
- Analyze how and when these files are created as you learn to develop the application
- Change some IDE settings and see which file gets changed

Working with IDE configuration files

There are two files that are used to store the configuration information of JDeveloper IDE. To add memory to the IDE or JDeveloper during startup, we add the following appropriate Virtual Memory options to these files:

- `MW_HOME/jdeveloper/ide/bin/ide.conf`
- `MW_HOME/jdeveloper/jdev/bin/jdev.conf`

To increase the JDeveloper memory, set the following options in the appropriate files specified previously. Some of the JVM options are explained as follows:

- AddVMOption is used to optimize the memory for JDeveloper IDE
- Xms is the initial Java Heap size
- Xmx is the maximum Java Heap size
- XX:MaxPermSize is used to set the maximum Java permanent size

Please note that the following setting depends on the available memory in your system:

Add `AddVMOption -Xms512M AddVMOption -Xmx1024M` in `ide.conf`.

Add `AddVMOption -Xmx512M AddVMOption -XX:MaxPermSize=1024M` in `jdev.conf`.

To configure the boot behavior of the IDE or JDeveloper, we modify the following files:

- `MW_HOME/jdeveloper/ide/bin/ide.boot`
- `MW_HOME/jdeveloper/jdev/bin/jdev.boot`

The settings for the files mostly correspond to the system properties. To configure the JDK-related properties for the IDE, modify `MW_HOME/jdeveloper/ide/bin/jdk.conf`.

For example, you can include options such as the following option for Java2D to allow DirectDraw usage in Windows:

```
AddVMOption  -Dsun.java2d.noddraw=true
```

You can add other VM options to the .conf files as well. The override sequence is jdk.conf, then ide.conf, followed by jdev.conf.

Use `JAVA_HOME/bin/jvisualvm.exe` to monitor and profile `Jdeveloper.exe`. This tool will also help you gather VM options and system properties of the currently running JDeveloper.

Have a go hero – look for other configuration files

Now it's time for you to verify all available configuration files in the middleware directory. Perform the following steps to verify configuration files:

- What are the differences that you see between these files?

- Try changing some properties such as `-Dsun.awt. keepWorkingSetOnMinimize=false` in your `jdev.conf` file and see how it affects the behavior of the IDE. This option becomes more responsive when JDeveloper IDE is restored after minimizing.

Knowing the roles

When you launch the IDE without the `-nonag` startup option, a splash screen followed by a **Select Role** screen is displayed. The **Select Role** screen provides the options to select the role in which you want to start the IDE. This is also referred to as shaping the IDE based on the selection. You have an option to configure this in the **Switch Roles** menu in **Tools**.

- **Studio Developer**: This role will include all the features available for the IDE. You will be allowed to create applications using different technologies. You have the option to choose the features to include in the **Features** menu in **Tools**. This is the commonly used role for ADF development.

- **Customization Developer**: This role is more inclined towards customization for a user to edit the metadata in JDeveloper. This option is used only for ADF customization and is outside the scope of this book.

- **Database Developer**: This role will enable all the features needed for database development using JDeveloper.

- **Java Developer**: This role will enable features that are best suited for Java developers. ADF-related features are not included in this role.

- **J2EE Developer**: Web development using Java EE will be made easy if the user selects this role. All the components related to Java EE development are made available for the user, except ADF technologies.

When JDeveloper IDE is started, the **Tip of the Day** popup will appear that will give some tips on using the IDE effectively.

To add your own tip, go to the following location:

`MW_HOME\jdeveloper\jdev\doc\studio_doc\ohj\tip.jar`

Create an HTML file called `tip_11_0460.html` (just increase the number, for example, `tip_11_0470.html`).

Create an image file called `tip_11_0470.gif` in the images folder if you want to refer to this in your HTML tip.

Have your HTML tip registered in `tip_map.smp` as shown in the following code snippet:

```
<map>
<mapID target="tip_11_0470_
html"url="tip_11_0470.html"/>
</map>
```

Have a go hero – explore the IDE

Now you are at a stage where you can explore the IDE and look for options, as follows:

- What are the new features that you see in JDeveloper IDE? Is the look and feel the same as your earlier development environment?
- Open the entire menu and see the options available in each menu.

Getting familiar with the IDE

JDeveloper is a perfect IDE for designing and delivering high-end web applications. To support complex designing and customization, the IDE provides various tools and menu options to compete with the requirements of the application developer. These compelling tools, which are shown in the following screenshot, are commonly used by developers in their day-to-day application development:

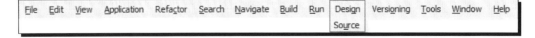

The **Design** and **Source** menus are toggled between the **Design** and **Source** views of the file in the **Editor** window. **History** and **Diagram** menus are also displayed based on the active view of the file.

The toolbar for JDeveloper IDE is displayed just below the **Menu** section, as shown in the following screenshot:

The highlighted tools are added as part of the **External Tools** option in the **Tools** menu. The standout features of JDeveloper are:

- **Drag-and-drop**: You can drag-and-drop the content between windows, panels, and sections.

- **Docking**: Almost all the panels within the IDE are "dockable". You can customize the location of the windows anywhere. Move the panel and drag it to dock the panel or window.

- **Floating**: Panels can be made floating if the `dockable` option is not preferred.

- **Minimize and Maximize**: Panels and windows support minimize and maximize features. Right-click on the panel and select the option as appropriate.

- **Keyboard access**: You can navigate, select, and interact with the IDE using shortcut keys.

- **Searching**: Search for the property in the property inspector, Resource palette, structure window, code editor, and so on.

- **Tabbed view**: All the windows that open in the center of the IDE will have the tabbed view.

- **Splitting**: All code editors support splitting of the documents vertically and horizontally. Drag the horizontal splitter to the bottom-right corner to split the document horizontally and the top-right corner to split it vertically, as shown in the following screenshot:

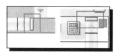

- **Closing**: The **Editor** window supports the **Close**, **Close others**, and **Close all** options.

- **Editing Tools**: Editor tools are available in the **Source** and **Design** view for almost all the files. Some common tools used are **Code highlight**, **Bookmarks**, **Reformat**, **Surround**, **Block coloring**, and so on.

Setting the preferences

There are many configurations, as shown in the following list, related to the IDE that can be configured using the **Preferences** menu in **Tools**:

- ◆ **Environment**: This section will allow the user to change the look and feel and theme of the page, give an option to save the file on exit, check for modified files, and so on. This section has the following options:
  - ❑ **Dockable windows**: This customizes how the docking behaves.
  - ❑ **Local History**: This enables local history for the files stored in the user directory.
  - ❑ **Log**: This enables logging and specifies where to save the logfile. Also, it customizes the size, lines, and color of the log file.

- ◆ **External Editor**: A user can set a preference to open the files in either the external editor or the application. For example, PDF files will be preferred to be opened in an Adobe application.

- ◆ **File Types**: This will let the user decide which extensions can be opened by JDeveloper and which editors are used to open the files within JDeveloper.

 Setting the **Default Editor** option to source view will increase the performance in opening up the files within JDeveloper.

- ◆ **Shortcut Keys**: This is used to configure the shortcut keys for different operations within the IDE.

You can have external applications or tools configured within your IDE using the **External Tools** menu in **Tools**.

Knowing the IDE components

JDeveloper IDE consists of dockable windows and components that will help in developing ADF applications efficiently. Users may take advantage of these windows to keep track of the changes made, switch between windows, identify and modify particular resources that are part of the application.

Let us see some of the panels and components that are very useful for developing any ADF application. Remember that some of these panels are active only when you have an application open in your workspace. When you open the JDeveloper IDE it will look like the following screenshot:

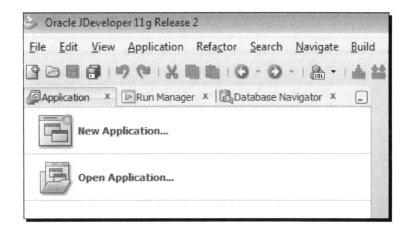

Time for action – opening the sample application

1. Download the sample application from `http://www.packtpub.com` (The `EmpDirectoryApplication` code downloadable with this book).

2. Click on the **Open Application** option and locate the `EmpDirectoryApplication.jws` file.

3. You will now see that the application is listed in the **Application Navigator** window and the projects are listed for `EmpDirectoryApplication`.

What just happened?

We have opened an already existing ADF application to get a feel of how the IDE components work together. Some of the components explained in the following section would need an open application.

Application Navigator

The application-related artifacts are managed in a window called **Application Navigator**. A user can create an application and open existing applications. We will see how to create and open an application in detail in the next chapter.

All open applications are available in the drop-down menu and the user can choose between different applications.

We can select the application, and once the application is selected, we can locate the project and navigate to the related project artifacts. The navigator will display a folder structure of the project that you are currently working on.

The **Application** menu will list out all the options available to configure an application. The options include creating a new project, opening a project, closing the application, securing the application, application properties, and so on, as shown in the following screenshot:

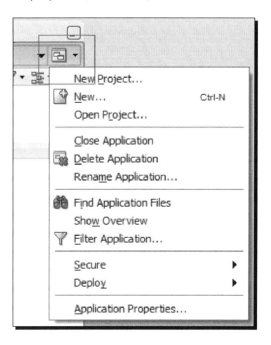

Have a go hero – exploring the Application menu

You are now going to explore the **Application** menu by clicking on each of the options available:

- Try and find what the difference is between the **New Project** and **New** options
- Try to find some application files using the **Menu** option provided
- Identify what **Filter Application** means to you
- Browse through the **Application properties** option and familiarize yourself with the options available

The **Projects** pane will display some options for configuring the projects that are available for the current application, as shown in the following screenshot:

The options on the previous ribbon bar are explained as follows:

◆ **Project properties**: This icon will display the properties that can be configured for the current project.

◆ **Refresh**: This will refresh the current project for any file changes.

◆ **Working sets**: This will help you to filter the current project or files from other open projects. This will be really helpful if you have multiple projects for your application and would like to work on only one project at a time. Having less projects open will load the application faster instead of when all the projects for the application are open.

◆ **Navigator display options**: This will let the user display the structure of the project efficiently.

Have a go hero – exploring the projects pane

Now it's your turn to figure out the options provided for the projects pane:

◆ Open the **Project Properties** pane and check the available settings for the project. We will be using some of these properties in the coming chapters.

◆ Add some files outside JDeveloper in the `Project` folder, and click on the **Refresh** button. Do you see the file in JDeveloper?

◆ Where have you seen the **Manage Working Set** option available in the **Working Sets** menu before?

◆ You are provided with **Navigator Display options** for the projects. Try out different options and look for changes.

Application Resources

The **Application Resources** pane will list out all the common resources available for the application. `Connections` and `Descriptors` are the two folders available in this panel that contain the resources.

◆ `Connections`: This folder displays all the connections available for the application. It can be anything that gives a context of the connection to the server or to the repository available for the applications.

◆ `Descriptors`: This will list all the configuration files and descriptors available for the application. Common descriptors are `adf-config.xml`, `connections.xml`, `cwallet.sso`, `jps-config.xml`, and `Weblogic-application.xml`.

Have a go hero – explore Application Resources

Now you will have to locate the application resource files outside the JDeveloper IDE and then note down the folder structure that you see. Do you see all the files listed under the folder listed in **Application Resources**? The missing files are subsequently created when you add a database connection or when you secure your application.

Data Controls palette

The **Data Controls** pane palette will expose the available **Data controls** options from the model layer to use in the UI layer. You can refresh the data controls or filter out the data controls using the options available.

The **Data controls** palette shown in the following screenshot will not be available in the EmpDirectoryApplication file. This will be created automatically when you have the corresponding component created in the model project. Right now don't worry about that.

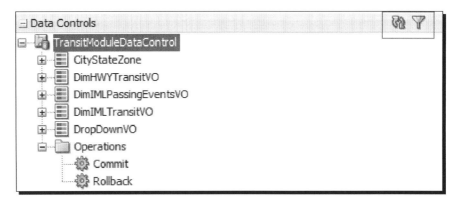

Recently Opened Files

The **Recently Opened Files** pane will list all the files opened recently in the application. This pane should not be confused with the **Reopen** option in the **File** menu. If you have multiple applications in your workspace, this pane will display recent files specific to the application.

Structure window

The **Structure** window, as shown in the following screenshot, will display the structure of the files that the user currently has open. This window is mostly used to insert the components from data control to bind the values. You have an option within the structure window to search for tags.

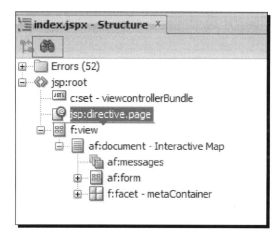

Have a go hero – identify the structure of the file

♦ Double-click on the `web.xml` file available in the `ViewController` project. Do you see any change in the **Recently Opened Files** window?

♦ In the **Structure** window, what do you see?

♦ Click on the **Source** tab of the `web.xml` file and check the changes in the **Structure** window.

♦ Click on the tag displayed in the **Structure** window. What do you see in the **Source** view?

Database Navigator

Database Navigator, as shown in the following screenshot, will display the connection information available for all the applications in the IDE. The **Database Navigator** plugin is a fully functional plugin for a SQL developer. This plugin is not displayed by default, and you can open this from the **Database** submenu in **View**.

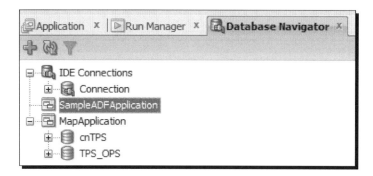

The Resource palette

The **Resource** palette window will allow the user to create IDE resources and assets. Click on the **View** menu to display this palette.

There are two types of resources that can be created from the **Resource** palette. They are **Catalogs** and **Connections**.

- ◆ **Catalogs**: These are user-defined assets from different repositories used for easy access.

- ◆ **Connections**: These are the contexts for the application or IDE added to different repositories or servers.

- ◆ **My Catalogs**: This will list all the user-defined resources added as a catalog. For example, if you have a filesystem connection, the catalog can store the images or contents from the filesystem as a user-defined catalog.

Time for action – creating a catalog

1. Click on the folder icon in the **Resource** palette.

2. Select the **New Catalog** option from the drop-down menu.

3. Provide the name `catalog` in the **Name** box.

4. Click on **OK** to see the new catalog listed in the **My Catalog** section.

5. To add a resource to the catalog, you will have to right-click on the resources that are listed in the **IDE connections** menu. You can add resources from a filesystem connection that is mapped to any of your preferred folders.

6. Select the **Add to Catalog** option from the menu.

7. Select the catalog that you have created from the option.

8. Click on **OK** to add the resource to the catalog.

9. Now the resource will be added to the catalog.

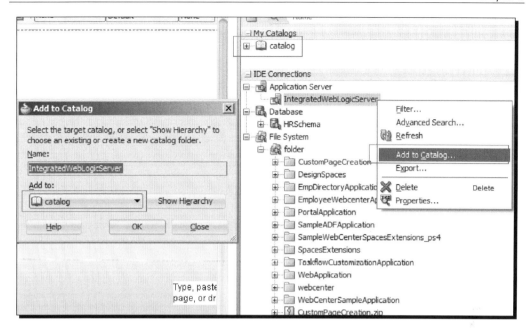

What just happened?

We have now created a catalog for our IDE for the frequent use of resources. Resources added to the catalog are available for the IDE, and we can make use of these resources in different applications and projects.

IDE Connections will have all the connections that are added for the particular IDE. We can use the connections from this window and add them to a particular project by dragging-and-dropping them onto the project displayed in the **Database Navigator** plugin.

The Component palette

The **Component** palette will display all the available components that can be added to the UI page. This palette is categorized with different components based on the technology available for the current project. Within each technology available for the project, components are further classified based on behavior. There is an option to search for the component using the search box available at the top of the palette.

Different components are available for different files. For example, the **ADF Faces** components are displayed if you have the `index.jspx` file as your current open file from a project that supports ADF technology.

Have a go hero – components available for IDE

Now it's time for you to explore different components available for different technologies. Use the `EmpDirectoryApplication` file for your analysis. Perform the following to check for the components available for the IDE:

◆ What are the components listed in the palette for `web.xml`?

◆ Open `trinidad-config.xml` and check if it's listing the same components as in `web.xml`.

Run Manager

Run Manager will display all the current running processes and give an option to terminate whenever needed. This is not shown by default and can be enabled from the **View** menu.

The Log window

The **Log** window will display log messages related to the projects. There are other tabs embedded within the **Log** window to categorize the logs that are generated, as follows:

◆ **IntegratedWeblogicServer**: This displays the log information of the integrated WebLogic server. This **Log** window is helpful in identifying application errors during runtime. It will display the log information while starting and stopping the server.

◆ **Messages**: This tab displays the compilation logs.

◆ **Extensions**: This tab will display logs related to the installed IDE extensions.

◆ **Compiler**: This tab will display the warnings and errors that occurred while the project was being compiled.

Code editor

You will use the code editor section to write the code. The Java code file can be opened in the editor by double-clicking on the **Application Navigator** window. There are different options available within the code editor that will be helpful to run the code efficiently.

Code editor views

◆ **Design**: Files with extension such as `.jsff` or `.jspx` which represent a UI page will have a `Design` mode added to design the pages.

◆ **Source**: The **Source** tab is added for all the files where a user can change the content using the code editor.

- **Bindings**: This section will help the user interact with the data bindings bounded to the UI components. The `page-definition` file will hold the binding information, and it is shown in this view.

- **Preview**: This will help to preview the page designed and imitate the components rendered at runtime.

- **History**: This view is common for all files, and the local history of the file changes is tracked in this view.

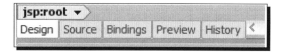

Property Inspector

The **Property Inspector** pane will help to alter the property of the currently selected component or tag in the **Design** or **Source** mode of a page.

All the previously explained windows and panels are available in the **View** menu.

Have a go hero – code editor and Property Inspector

Now it's time for you to check the usage of the code editor and the **Property Inspector** pane as follows:

- Open the `adfc-config.xml` file and check how many views are available. Check the **Overview** tab and see the options to configure the properties declaratively.

- Open the **Source** tab and select any of the tags to see the changes in the **Property Inspector** window.

Pop quiz

Q1. Which role will enable all the features of the IDE?

1. Database developer
2. Java developer
3. Studio developer

Q2. Which IDE component is used to drag the model data and drop it on the UI page?

1. **Application Navigator**
2. The **Data Controls** palette
3. The **Resource** palette

Q3. IDE connections are created only for an application in JDeveloper.

1. True
2. False

Q4. _____ and _____ are the two folders displayed in the **Application Resources** panel of the IDE.

Q5. Which of the following features are supported in JDeveloper?

1. Drag-and-drop
2. Docking
3. Floating
4. Searching
5. All of the above

Summary

Let us recap what we have learned in this chapter. We started our chapter by downloading and installing JDeveloper 11*g*R2. Then we learnt about some important configuration files for JDeveloper IDE. Later we discussed some of the roles to customize the IDE for different users. We also gained some knowledge about the components within the environment.

We got a chance to familiarize ourselves with common tasks, such as docking the panels, searching within the panels, and closing the files and windows. Finally, we learnt where to set preferences and some common user preferences for the IDE.

In the next chapter, we will learn more about the architecture of the ADF framework and how to create and run a sample ADF application.

2
Getting Started with ADF

Application Development Framework (ADF) is a JEE development framework that helps a developer to minimize the effort required for developing robust applications for web, desktop, and mobile devices. With the help of ADF's declarative approach, a developer can visualize the data model and proceed with the development of an application rapidly instead of spending time on writing the code.

The benefits you get from using ADF include a rich user interface, components usage, task flow support, declarative development, drag-and-drop binding, a productive environment, security, and customization.

Application Development Framework (**ADF**) is based on the **Model-View-Controller (MVC)** architecture and exposes its data model as a business service. The ADF model abstracts the business service layer through metadata, thereby providing a consistent set of APIs for developers to work with, independent of the business service implementation technology.

In this chapter, we will cover the following topics:

- Understanding MVC
- The components of ADF
- Creating a simple ADF application in JDeveloper
- Building and running an ADF application

Model-View-Controller

Model-View-Controller is a popular architecture for application development, that separates business logic from client and control flow logic. The core components of this pattern are as follows:

- **Model**: This layer directs the data layer to respond to requests passed from the UI layer. The model layer contains the core business logic of the application.

- **View**: In this layer, the user interacts with the application and requests data to be fetched. The actions performed in the UI layer by the user will command the controller to request data from the model layer.

- **Controller**: This layer controls the UI flow and often gets involved in the navigation from one page to another. The controller is also responsible for directing the requested data from the UI to the model layer.

The following diagram explains the Model-View-Controller architecture:

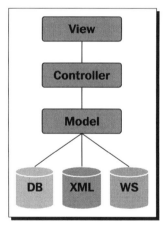

The data service layer can be anything from which the model layer gets the data. This can be obtained using relational data, XML data services, legacy applications, or through web services.

 Enterprise JavaBeans (EJB) serves as the model layer, servlet as the controller, and JSP as the view layer in a typical JEE application.

How ADF implements MVC

Oracle ADF extends the MVC architecture by introducing a generic binding layer as the model. In Oracle ADF, the architecture you use to build Java EE applications is comprised of the view layer (typically represented by ADF Faces), the controller layer (ADF controller), the model layer (represented by ADF data controls and page data bindings), and the business service layer (often ADF Business Components though EJB, web services, POJOs, and more are possible).

Following are the ADF components:

♦ **ADF Business Components**: A business service based on a relational database table schema that, before persisting user data entries, enforces business logic and validation rules.

♦ **ADF Model**: This data binding layer is an abstraction layer that facilitates access to data from underlying business service layers. This layer acts as an interface that exposes the services available from the business service layers to the UI components. This helps the declarative binding of the UI components with the exposed services.

♦ **ADF Task flows**: The ADF controller extends the JSF navigation handler for page navigation and UI component event handling. ADF Task flow is a concept of the ADF controller, that allows you to build reusable navigation units that you can use standalone or chain up to an overall application flow.

♦ **ADF Faces**: This is a JSF-based and Ajax-enabled component set, that provides a rich set of user interface components for building the application's user interface.

The following diagram shows how ADF implements MVC:

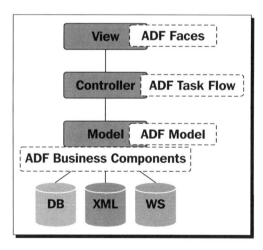

The ADF architecture

ADF is designed to simplify the development of web applications, desktop applications (MS Office), and mobile applications. It is focused on giving a visual and declarative approach to building applications based on the common MVC pattern. This architecture is targeted at providing a service-based, loosely coupled solution with the following five layers:

◆ **Business Service**: This layer is responsible for handling the interactions between the database and the model layer by providing database persistence, object/relational mapping, managing transactions, and so on. Business logic is also taken care of in this layer. ADF Business Components are the first choice to develop the business service layer apart from Java, EJB, and web services.

◆ **Model**: This layer is on top of the business service layer and abstracts the business services exposed to the view layer. The **Data Controls** palette acts as an interface between the view and the business services layers. Data bindings map the exposed services to the UI components. The data control and data binding approaches are collectively represented as ADF Model based on JSR 227 (Java Specification Request).

◆ **Controller**: The navigation from one page to another is handled in this layer using the ADF task flow. Its reusability along with parameter passing, a single point of entry, and allowing re-entry are the highlights of using the ADF task flow. The other technology choice in this layer can be JSF Struts.

◆ **View**: This is the actual presentation layer facing the user directly and passing the inputs to the controller layer for processing. ADF Faces is used for this purpose. ADF Faces uses more than 150 rich components to support the development of competing web user interfaces. ADF Faces is based on JSF, which allows JSF as the second choice for UI development. ADF Desktop Integration will also act as a view layer for standalone applications.

◆ **Metadata services**: Customization and personalization of the application is done using the metadata services framework that uses metadata to store and retain user session information. This is not an architectural layer but an additional service layer on top of the controller and the model layers.

The following diagram shows how ADF layers fit into the Model-View-Controller architecture:

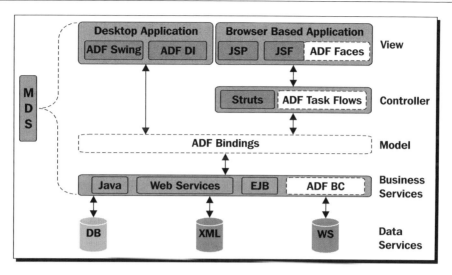

Creating a simple application in ADF

Till now we have been focusing on the architecture; now let us see how ADF development is carried out in a typical web application development environment.

ADF development practice

ADF web application development is classified into two sections—the Business Service development and the UI development. Both these sections can be developed independently, but the development of either of the sections is followed by the development of the other.

The following is a brief description of the two sections:

- **Business Service development**: This section includes the development of objects in the business service layer, which sits on top of the data source. Most of the development is declarative to help the developer concentrate more on the business logic.

- **UI development**: The development of UI pages along with task flow creation for reusability comprises the UI phase. The UI development makes use of rich UI components to create a modern, attractive user interface. The designing of the page involves a drag-and-drop approach for adding and customizing the components using the property inspector.

The development stage is further classified into the following two approaches:

◆ **Top-down**: The development of a UI page is done first, followed by the building of business services. Placeholder data control is used to mock up the business service to simulate enterprise data queries. This approach is mostly used for proof-of-concept studies in which the application's design and flow are more important than the actual business data.

◆ **Bottom-up**: The development of the business service is followed by the designing of UI pages and task flows.

Sample application – employee directory application

It's easy to build a simple application using the HR schema that is shipped with Oracle XE Database. The requirements for building the application are as follows:

◆ **JDeveloper 11.1.2.3.0 Studio Edition**: This is required to develop the ADF web application; we have installed this on Windows as a part of *Chapter 1, Installing and Configuring JDeveloper IDE*.

◆ **Oracle Database Express Edition or any other Oracle DB**: This is required for the HRSchema setup for our sample application.

> Oracle Database 10*g* Express Edition is used at the time of writing the book. It's the user's choice to use either the 10*g* or 11*g* version. You may refer to the following links:
>
> ◆ Download: http://www.oracle.com/technetwork/products/express-edition/downloads/index.html
> ◆ Documentation http://docs.oracle.com/cd/E17781_01/index.htm

The high-level development processes for the employee directory application included in this section are as follows:

1. **Create the application workspace**: Create a new application and set up the workspace for developing with ADF.
2. **Model database objects**: Set up the HRSchema database objects for the application.
3. **Create business components**: Create ADF Business Components corresponding to the DB objects.
4. **Create the UI page**: Use the UI components to represent the data on the page.
5. **Bind the data to the UI components**: Bind the exposed service to the UI components through the data control and bindings.

6.   **Run the application**: Deploy and verify the application.

Time for action – creating the application workspace

We have come to the point where we will start creating the ADF application. We will now get into the step-by-step practice directly, by following these steps:

1.   With JDeveloper open, click on the **New Application** option available in the **Application Navigator** panel. This will open a **New Gallery** window in which you can create a new application.

2.   Select the **Fusion web Application (ADF)** option from **General | Applications Category**. This will open a **Create New Fusion Web Application (ADF)** wizard.

3.   Type in the values for the **Application Name**, **Directory** (location for the application), and **Application Package Prefix** fields. You can browse for the application location. The *package prefix* is the root package that will be applied for the application.

   For example, type the package name as `com.empdirectory.model`. The package structure for the project is visible in the **Application Navigator** panel; this holds all the project artifacts, such as Java classes or ADF metadata files.

4.   In the next screen, you will have to provide the model project name and the directory location for the project. **ADF Business Components** and **Java** are the technology highlights of this project; these are usually defaulted to by JDeveloper.

5.   The default Java settings for the Model project are configured in the next screen. The **Default Package**, **Java Source Path**, and **Output Directory** options are configured in this screen.

6.   The next screen will help you to configure the UI project. This project includes **ADF Faces**, **ADF Page Flow**, **JSF**, and other UI technologies as highlights.

7.   Click **Finish** after configuring the Java settings for the UI project.

What just happened?

You will have the application added to the application navigator with the help of following two projects:

◆   One is the `Model` project that involves the ADF Business Components as the primary technology. This creates the business service for our application.

◆   Another one is the `ViewController` project that involves both the view and the controller layer.

The view layer is developed using the ADF Faces technology. The controller layer is developed using `ADF PageFlow`; this is the logical name in JDeveloper for all libraries required by a project that intend to use the ADF controller and task flow features.

> Application files will have a `.jws` extension whereas project files will have a `.jpr` extension.

The **Application Overview** page will be displayed in the center, and it will guide us with the steps required to create an application. The overview screen will have the following options:

- **Checklist**: This option helps to track the progress of our application development.
- **Java Files**: This option is used to add any Java files to the project. It can be any helper class or utility class that you want to add to your project.
- **Page Flows**: Initially you will have the following two configuration files available:
  - `faces-config.xml`: Any configurations related to JSF go in this file. Some of the ADF-related configurations are also added in this file.
  - `adfc-config.xml`: This file will hold the ADF configurations.
- **Managed Beans**: The Bean class that is added to the `ViewController` project is displayed here. These are JavaBeans that are managed by the ADF controller.
- **Web Tier**: This will list all the files, such as `.javascript`, `.css`, `.jsp`, `.html`, and `.jsf` that are used in the view layer.
- **Business Components**: This option lists all the components, such as **Entity**, **View**, **Associations**, **View Link**, **Application Module**.
- **Binding Files**: The data controls available for the projects are displayed in this section.
- **Offline Database**: If you have any offline database objects created for the project, those files will be listed in this section.

The Model project is empty and the `ViewController` project will have the `WEB-INF` folder populated with the following XML files:

- `adfc-config.xml`
- `faces-config.xml`
- `trinidad-config.xml`
- `web.xml`

Have a go hero – analyze the application directory

Now the sample application in the JDeveloper has been created. It's time for you to analyze all the new changes that you are seeing in the IDE. Look for all the options and just familiarize yourself with the application artifacts. Once you are done with your research, answer the following questions:

1. What is the extension for the sample application that you have created in this section?

2. Which file has the .jpr extension?

3. What is the folder structure of the application from the root folder?

 The overview can be opened by right-clicking on the application from the **Application Navigator** panel and selecting **Show Overview**.

Planning your application

You should always plan the application before opening JDeveloper so you know what you want to build. This, however, requires experience with the concept of ADF.

Proper planning before starting the project is necessary for smooth development of the components and exposing the services to the UI without any hiccups.

Our high-level goal is to achieve the following:

♦ Create business services for the Employee and Department objects.

♦ Expose the components through the data controls.

♦ Manage the Employee and Department information from a page.

Connect to a database

After planning your application, the next step is to connect to the database. The following steps show how to do this:

1. Click on the **Create a Database Connection** button from **Show** Overview in the **Application** menu.

2. The **Create a Database Connection** wizard opens. You have the following two options to create the connection:

   ❑ **Application resources**: This connection will be created only for the current application.

> ❑ **IDE Connections**: This option will make sure that you are creating the connection for the complete IDE, which is shared across multiple applications.

3. Enter the value of **Connection name** as HRSchema, the **username** value as hr, and the **password** value (this will be provided during the installation of Oracle XE 11*g* Express Edition) to connect to the Oracle XE 11*g* Express Edition installed on your machine.

4. Enter the value of **Host name** as localhost as you are running the DB locally; the value of **SID** will be XE, and that of **JDBC port** will be 1521. These are all default settings for the XE database.

5. Click the **Test the connection** button and make sure that you are seeing the **Success!** message.

6. Click the **OK** button to create the connection.

7. Once you have created the connection, you will see the connection added to the **IDE Connections** panel as shown in the following screenshot:

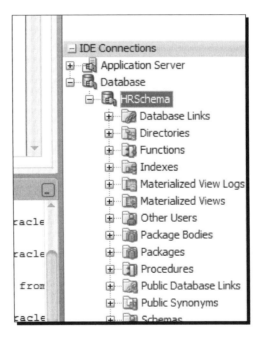

The connection information will be stored in the connections.xml file for the application. For the IDE connection, you will have the information stored in your $USER_DIR/o.jdeveloper.rescat2.model/connections/connections.xml file.

Time for action – setting up the database tables

In order to create the `Employee` and `Department` tables for `HRSchema`, you will have to download the sample script (`Demobld.sql`) from `http://www.oracle-database-tips.com/demobld.html`.

1. In order to run this script, right-click on the **HRSchema** option from the **IDE Connections** panel and select **Open** in **Database Navigator** as shown in the following screenshot:

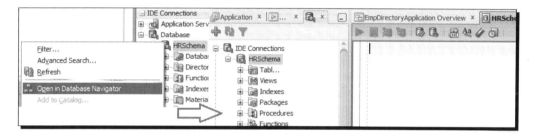

2. This will open the connection in the **Database Navigator** panel, and open an SQL worksheet for you.

3. Copy and paste the SQL statements from `Demobld.sql` to the worksheet.

4. Click on the **Run Script** option available for the worksheet or press *F5*.

What just happened?

The `demobld.sql` script will create the following tables in the `HRSchema` database: `EMP`, `DEPT`, `BONUS`, `SALGRADE`, and `DUMMY`.

These tables can be located from the **Tables** section in `HRSchema`.

 Other tables that you see in `HRSchema` are the tables that get created as part of Oracle XE Express Edition.

Time for action – creating a database connection

To create a connection for the application, you may follow these steps:

1. Create the connection for **Application Resources** as per the previous steps.

2. Click on the **+** (plus) sign to create a new connection.

3. Right-click on **EmpDirectoryApplication** and select **New Connection**.

4. Right-click on **HRSchema** and select **Add to Application**.

5. Drag **HRSchema** from **IDE Connections** and drop it on **EmpDirectoryApplication** in the **Database Navigator** panel.

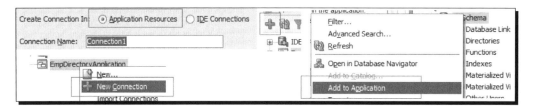

Have a go hero – run some queries

You have all the required tables created in your database. Now it is time to do some practical exercises to fetch the data. You should use the SQL worksheet to write the query and execute it accordingly. The following are some exercises to fetch the data:

1. Display all the records in the EMP and DEPT tables

2. Display the name of department number 10

3. Display all the employees having a salary of less than 1000

4. Display all the employees in the sales department

Build business services

The next step is to create business components.

You will have to click on **Go to Substeps** to list the sub steps involved in creating the business components.

Before starting with the creation of the business components, we will initialize our Model project. The **Project Properties** dialog is accessed by right-clicking on the Model project and selecting the **Project Properties** menu option.

Accessing the project properties

There are two ways to get access to the **Project Properties** dialog; they are as follows:

1. Select the **Model** project and click on the **Project Properties** icon in the **Projects** panel.

2. Right-click on the **Model** project and select the **Project Properties** option from the menu as shown in the following screenshot:

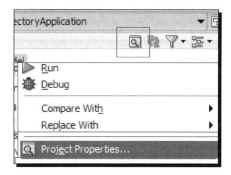

The **Project Properties** dialog will show a list of properties related to the project that you need to configure.

3. Click on **ADF Business Components** and select **Initialize Project for Business Components**. Usually when the business components are created, you will be asked to select the database connection that will initialize the business components. Selecting this option will skip the **Initialize Project for Business Components** dialog.

4. Click on the **OK** button. This will enable the DB connection for the Model project.

 This action will create a .jpx file in the Model project that will have the reference to the connection and other library import references.

Time for action – creating the business components

Let us now create the business components using the following steps:

1. To create a new component, go to **File** | **New**; this can also be done by right-clicking on the Model project, the directory, or the folder, and selecting **New**.

2. In the **Business Tier** section, select **ADF Business Components**.

3. A **Create Business Components from Tables** wizard will open up for you; select the **Entity Objects** option.

 An entity object is a representation of a single row of the table. It is the metadata mapping of a single object in the data source table. We represent the EMP table as an entity object in ADF for the easy mapping of columns and business logic.

4. Enter the package for your entity object as `com.empdirectory.model.entity` and select HRSchema for your data source. You have an option to restrict the filter by table, view, synonym, and others.

5. In the **Name** filter, enter EMP% so that the filter is applied to query the data source. Click on **Query** to search for the filter in the database. Select the **Auto Query** option to query when you type the filter.

6. Shuttle the EMP table to the selected list to create the entity object. Enter the name of the entity object as EmpEO. The entity object will represent the row in the EMP table. We will create the entity object to work with the database objects.

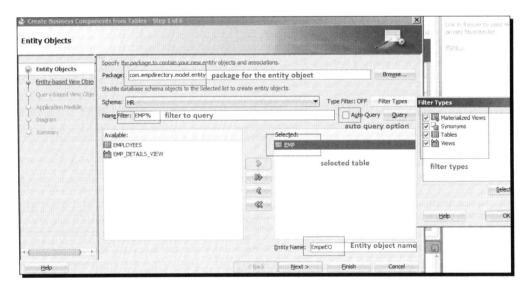

7. Click **Next >** to create a view object based on the entity object.

A view object is the component used to collect data from the data source. It is the mechanism used to retrieve data from the entity object.

We retrieve the `Employee` information using the view object that is based on the entity object, that we have created in the previous section.

8. Name the package as `com.empdirectory.model.view`.

9. Move the available entity object to the **Selected:** list.

10. Enter the name as `EmpVO` as shown in the following screenshot:

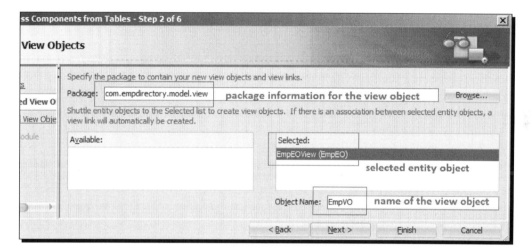

11. The next section will help you to create a query-based view object. The view object can be based on an SQL query that will be used to display the read-only information of the table. View objects without the entity object are read-only and don't update the table. In this example, we don't have any query-based object, so we will skip this section this time.

12. We will create the application module in the next section.

 The application module is the component that corresponds to a particular task, such as updating and creating a record. It manages the data source transaction that is used to accomplish a specific task. The application module uses the `Employee` view object to complete the task of creating, updating, and deleting a record in the `Employee` table.

13. Enter the application module package as `com.empdirectory.model.am` and name it as `EmpDirectoryModule`.

14. The **Add to Application Module** checkbox is checked to add the view object to the application module.

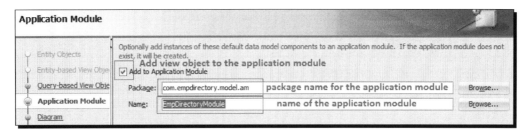

15. Click **Next >** to create a business component diagram for the components that are created. The diagram is helpful in visualizing the relationship between the business components. We can create new entities and view objects from the business component diagram. This is added only for reference and is not used further in the book.

16. Check the **Add to Business Components Diagram** checkbox to add `EmpEO`, `EmpVO`, and `EmpDirectoryModule` to the diagram.

17. Type the package name as `com.empdirectory.model.diagram` and the name of the diagram as `EmployeeDirectoryDiagram`.

18. Select the default selection to include entity objects, view objects, and the application module.

19. Click on the **Next >** button to check for the summary, and click on the **Finish** button to create the components.

What just happened?

Since ADF is a metadata-driven framework, most of the components created will be represented as a `.xml` file.

We have created the basic business components for our sample application. They are as follows:

◆ `EmpEO.xml`: This is an entity object that will represent the `EMP` table in `HRSchema`.

Click on the `EMPEO.xml` file to open the `.xml` file. In the **Attributes** section, you will find all the column information for the `EMP` table.

◆ `EmpVO.xml`: This is a view object based on `EmpEO` that is used to manipulate the `Employee` table through the entity object.

The `EmpVO.xml` file will have the data that was retrieved from the data source using the SQL query. The query section will display the query for the view object as shown in the following screenshot:

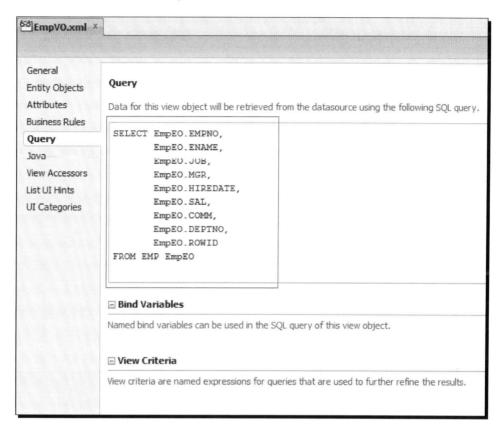

◆ `EmpDirectoryModule.xml`: This is the application module that we have created through the view object to accomplish the create, update, and remove operations for a record in the `Employee` table.

The **Data Model** section of the `EmpDirectoryModule.xml` file will show the usage of the `EmpVO` view object.

 The `bc4j.xcfg` file will have the metadata information about the database connection used by the application module. This file also defines the runtime parameters configured for the application module.

◆ `EmployeeDirectoryDiagram.adfc_diagram`: This is the component diagram that will show the relationship between the components:

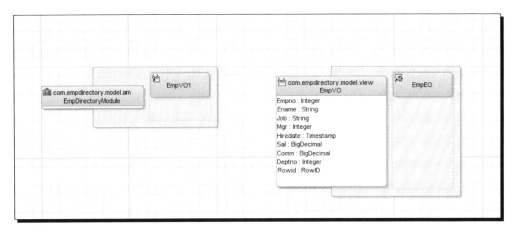

We have seen all the basic components that are used for developing the ADF business components. A detailed description of each and every component will be discussed in the later chapters.

The next step is to run the application module using the AM tester to check if everything is working fine.

 An application module is abbreviated as AM and the BC4j tester is commonly called the AM tester.

Have a go hero – open and analyze the business components

Now that you have your business components created from the previous steps, look closely and try to understand the files generated for the business components.

Answer the following questions to analyze the business components:

◆ What are the common features that you see between the EO and VO XML files?

◆ What options do you see when you open the `Model.jpx` file?

◆ How does the `DeptVO.xml` file refer to the `DeptEO` object in the file?

Running the AM tester

To test the data model created, we have a client application called the AM tester. This application provides a handle to check the business logic quickly without creating the UI pages.

 The AM tester is a client application used to interact with the data model, validate the business logic, and do some of the CRUD (Create- Read- Update- Delete) operations.

Right-clicking on the `EmpDirectoryModule.xml` file and clicking on **Run** will run the AM tester.

The AM tester will open with two panes. The left-hand pane will list the entire view object available for the application module.

When you click on the view object, a form is displayed in the right-hand pane where the user is allowed to interact with the data model. We can use the AM tester to do the following actions:

- **Traverse the record**: Move to the first record, move to the last record, and the next and previous records
- **Add**: Create a new record for the data source, in our case for the EMP table
- **Remove**: Remove the current record from the EMP table
- **Commit**: Commit the changes to the database
- **Rollback**: Revert the changes if the data is not committed to the database
- **Find**: Query a particular record from the table
- **Validate**: Validate the record and check for business logic

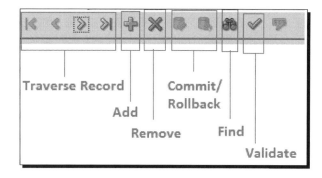

Exposing data to the UI layer

When you create the application module, the data control is automatically exposed in the **Data Controls** panel for the UI component to use the service in a declarative way. The **Data Controls** panel will expose all the available data controls in the IDE, and it will expose the service to the UI layer. This panel is refreshed every time to show the newly created data sources.

Declarative data binding helps to map the UI components to the underlying data.

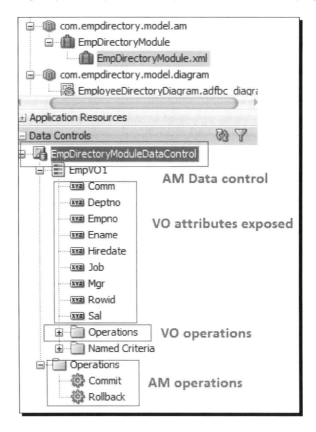

The **Data Controls** panel will expose the following controls:

- The view object
- The view object attributes
- The view object operations

- ◆ The view object criteria
- ◆ The application module operations

Time for action – bind data to the UI components

We will set the third and fourth step in the application overview checklist as *in progress*, as part of this exercise. We will see these steps in detail in *Chapter 3, Understanding the Model Layer* and *Chapter 7, Working with Navigation Flows*.

We will skip section 5.1 from the **Show Overview** page detailing **Design Pages**, and revisit this in the later chapters.

To expose the data to the UI layer, you need to create a page where you will bind the data from the data control that is exposed from the model layer.

1. In the **Create Page** section, click on **Create JSF Page**. This will open a **Select a Project for Action** pop-up window, that will ask you to select the project where you want to create the page. Click on **OK** to proceed.

2. The **Create JSF Page** pop-up window opens up to create the page.

3. Provide the name of the file as index.jspx.

4. The directory is defaulted to the public_html folder in your ViewController project directory—this is the place where you store all the pages. You have an option to select a different directory by clicking the magnifying glass icon.

5. The next step is to select the **Document Type** option as **JSP XML** to create a .jspx file. Facelets will have a .jsf extension.

6. Select the page layout as **Blank Page**. You can select a different page template or create your own template as needed.

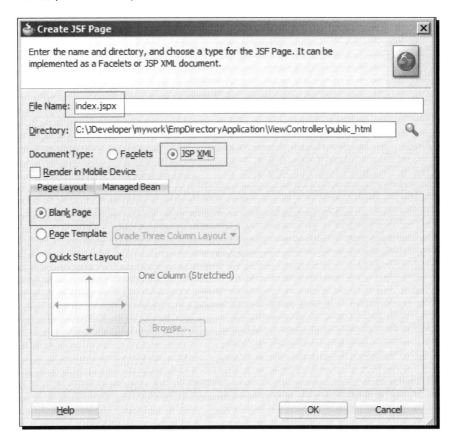

7. Click on the **OK** button to create the `index.jspx` page. This creates a page for our UI layer. This will be of the `.jspx` extension, with only the root tag.

This page will contain the basic tags and elements that are used to display a blank page on the website. We will include these components in this page to add more dynamic content to the page.

8. Refresh the data controls using the **Refresh** button in the **Data Controls** panel. Filter out `EmpDirectoryModuleDataControl` using the filter option from the **Data Controls** panel and open the data controls.

9. You will have a view object listed; drag this view object and drop it onto the **Design** view of the page.

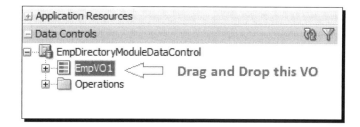

10. Select **Table** and then select **ADF Table** as shown in the following screenshot:

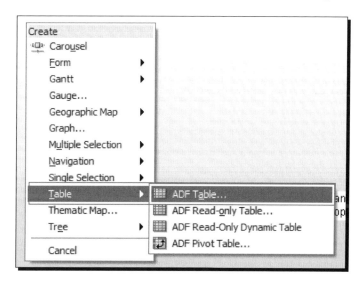

11. A pop-up window will be displayed to select the display behavior of the content. You can choose it to be displayed in **ADF Table** in a grid-like layout with rows and columns, and the user can edit the data in it.

The **ADF Read-only Table** option will have a read-only table displayed and will not allow the user to edit the content. The other two options displayed will be explained later.

12. The **Edit Table Columns** page will let you choose from the options available to customize the table displayed in the UI page as follows:

- ❏ The row selection can be single or multiple rows
- ❏ The sorting and filtering in the table can be selected
- ❏ You can add and delete columns, and customize the components to display the desired column data

❑ The **Value Binding** section will display the binding of the data layer to the UI components

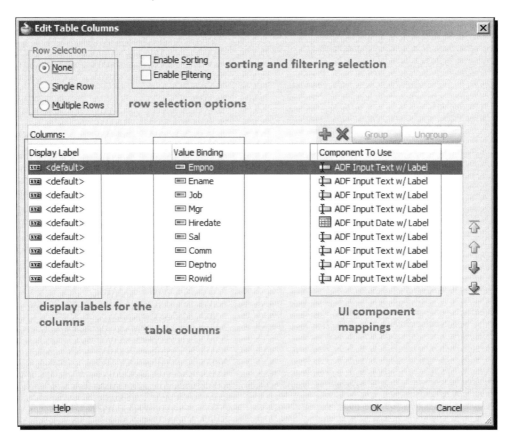

13. Click on the **OK** button to accept the settings and to create the table for your page, which will bind the UI component to the underlying model data.

What just happened?

You will have the following setup in the **Design View** pane of the index.jspx page. In the source view, you will have some of the tags that correspond to the table view and the components will have the value bindings for the attributes representing the underlying data, as shown in the following screenshot:

Each page will have a corresponding page definition file that will hold the bindings mentioned in your page. In this case, we will have the `indexPageDef.xml` file created for the `index.jspx` file. This is because we have an ADF binding for the UI components defined in our `index.jspx` page as shown in the following screenshot:

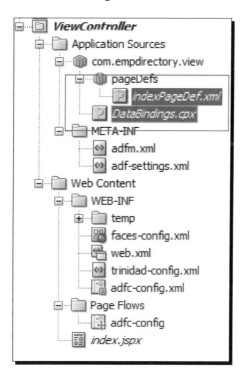

When we use the **Data Control** panel for the first time, a control palette XML file named `DataBindings.cpx` is created to define the binding context for the entire application. This file will have the following references:

♦ Reference to the page definition file used for each page in the entire application

◆ Reference to the data control from which the binding objects are created at runtime

 The `adfm.xml` file will hold the reference to the `DataBindings.cpx` file. Apart from this, the file will also hold a reference to the `.dcx`, `.xcfg`, and `.jpx` files. This file is located in the `adfmsrc/META-INF` folder of your project.

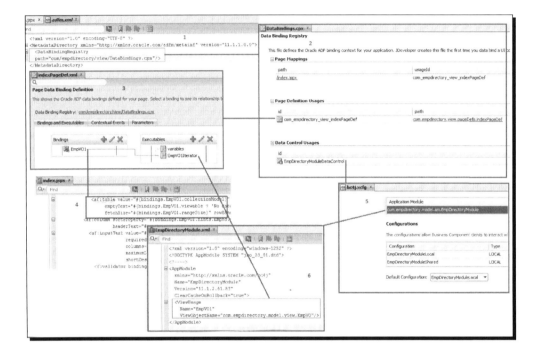

Have a go hero – analyze the artifacts

Since you have your UI-related artifacts, it is time for you to do some exercises based on the previous action.

1. List down all the artifacts created as part of the action.

2. Learn how the `index.jspx` page and the corresponding page definition file are mapped to render the data

3. Try to understand the components and the properties that were added to the `index.jspx` file.

Time for action – running the application

Let us see how to run the ADF application using the following steps:

1. To run the page, we will have to right-click on the `index.jspx` page and select the **Run** option.

2. The page that we have created will be displayed in the default browser as shown here in the following URL:

   ```
   http://127.0.0.1:7101/EmpDirectoryApplication-ViewController-
   context-root/faces/index.jspx
   ```

    `EmpDirectoryApplicaion-viewcontroller-context-root` is the context root for the application. This can be changed from **Project Properties** and **Java EE application** of the `ViewController` project. Java EE web context root will hold the context root for the project.

3. Verify the contents of the page. It will display the content of the EMP table in a grid layout with all the information bound to the UI components. The layout of the page will be ugly with a lot of spaces and will have a horizontal scroll bar. This will be fixed in the *Chapter 6, Displaying the Data*.

What just happened?

The integrated WebLogic server will be started when you run the `index.jspx` page. If it is the first time a user starts WebLogic, the user will be asked to provide an administrator username-password pair. You can also set the server to listen to a single host such as localhost. You will see the console log of the server in the log window. You will see the highlighted statement in the console when the server is started.

The deployment of the application follows immediately after the server is started. The application is deployed as a WAR file, and the user is provided with a target URL to access the page.

 The web application module and enterprise application module are written to the `$USER_DIR/o.j2ee/drs` folder. In Windows, `$USER_DIR` will be in `C:\Users\{username}\ AppData\ Roaming\Jdeveloper\ system11.1.2.3.39.62.76.1`.

Now let us see what happens behind the browser when the URL is accessed:

♦ When the first request for the ADF page occurs, the application invokes both the ADF life cycles; they are a superset of the JSF life cycle. The JSF lifecycle will be responsible for request processing using the `FacesServlet` servlet. This servlet will filter the request that comes after the `/faces/` section of the URL.

♦ This servlet is responsible for registering `ADFBindingFilter` defined in the `web.xml` file. The filter will first look for the binding context in the HTTP session. If it's not available, the binding context is created in the session.

♦ The binding context will then look for the `indexPageDef.xml` file that is associated with the `index.jspx` page. This page definition file can be found in the `DataBindings.cpx` file, which has already been loaded by `adfm.xml`.

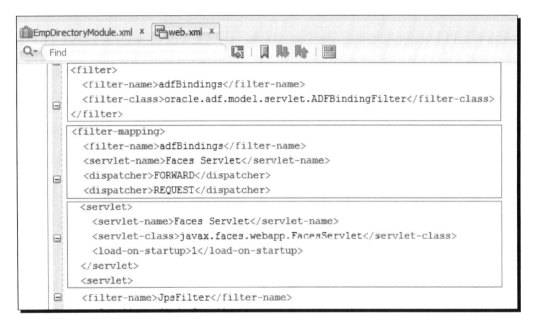

♦ The binding container is created for the page definition file and the `#{bindings}` EL expression is also resolved to access the created binding container.

♦ The page then gets the data available in the binding container using the bindings.

Have a go hero – find out where the application is running from

Now that we have our application running, it is fun to see the underlying data displayed in a browser. However, have you ever wondered how and from where these files are being displayed? Find the answers to the following questions to determine where the application is running from:

1. Can you find the location from where the application is running?

2. Which are the components that get deployed along with the `index.jspx` page?

3. What difference do you see between the `adfc-config.xml`, `faces-config.xml`, and `web.xml` files?

Pop quiz

Q1. Which of the following layers is not included in the MVC architecture?

1. Model

2. Controller

3. Business

4. View

Q2. _____ and _____ are the two ADF development stages that can be performed independently of each other.

Q3. To work with the database in JDeveloper, you will first have to create a...

1. Catalog

2. Resource

3. Connection

4. File

Q4. An entity object is a representation of a row in a table.

1. True

2. False

Q5. The business services from the model layer are exposed to the UI layer with the help of _____.

1. Application Module
2. View Object
3. Data control
4. Binding

Summary

Let us recap what we have learned in this chapter. We started by learning about the Model-View-Controller architecture and understood how ADF implements this architecture. We understood the building blocks of the ADF architecture: ADF Model, ADF Controller, and ADF Faces.

We started by creating a simple ADF application with an entity object, view object, and application module in the Model project. We verified the application module using the BC4j tester.

After that, we started creating the UI page in the `ViewController` project. We bound the data to the UI components and displayed the information in a table. Finally, we ran and verified the application.

In the next chapter, we will learn more about the business components involved with developing the sample application.

3
Understanding the Model Layer

In the previous chapter, we had an overview of the framework in action. We created a sample application using the ADF components and ran it successfully. Isn't it easy to develop a complete application in this way? The answer is most probably yes, because we hardly wrote any code and yet we had a complete, working web application.

So what's next? We will dig deeper into the ADF business components to know more about the capabilities of the framework in the real world. ADF business components will help the developers to reduce the time taken to build objects for communicating with the database and manipulating the records. These components are also responsible for maintaining and managing the transactions efficiently.

In this chapter, we will learn the following:

- About different business components
- How these components are interrelated
- How the components work
- Options available in each of the components

ADF business components

In the previous chapter, we created a set of components in the model layer to expose the business service to the UI Layer. The business components are used to simplify the developer's interaction with the database layer in a typical JEE application.

The common uses of the business components are as follows:

◆ Performing Create, Retrieve, Update, Delete (CRUD) operations

◆ Apply business logic and validations to the database objects

◆ Transaction management

Some of the highlights of using ADF business components are as follows:

◆ Simplified data access

◆ It is based on XML and Java

◆ Works with different application servers and databases

◆ Uses some of the design patterns that are widely accepted

◆ Components are metadata-driven, with optional Java coding

The following are the core components of ADF business components:

◆ Entity objects

◆ Associations

◆ View objects

◆ View links

◆ Application module

Let us consider the `EmpDirectoryApplication` module, which we created in the previous chapter. The `DeptEO` and `DeptVO` objects will be created in this chapter, which is why it is not shown with the icons in the following diagram:

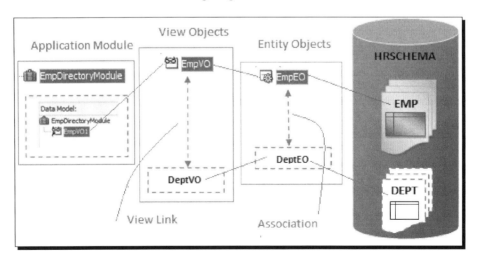

What is an entity object?

Remember that the EmpEO.xml file is mapped to the EMP table in HRSchema. What does this really mean? We are representing the database table as an XML file that has a configuration based on the table column and constraint definitions in our application. This is so that we can interact with this particular table using the metadata defined in the XML file. The location of the EmpEO.xml file is shown in the following screenshot:

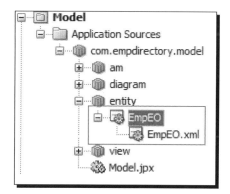

The database columns for the EMP table are represented as attributes in the EmpEO.xml file. The data types in the database column are mapped to a corresponding Java data type; the following diagram is an example of this statement:

The EMPNO column in the EMP table is mapped to the Empno attribute of the EmpEO.xml file. Here, the data type of Number (4,0) is mapped to the java.lang.Integer Java data type. Similarly, all the columns and data types from the table are mapped to the entity objects.

The data type mapping is set when a business component is initialized, as shown in the following screenshot:

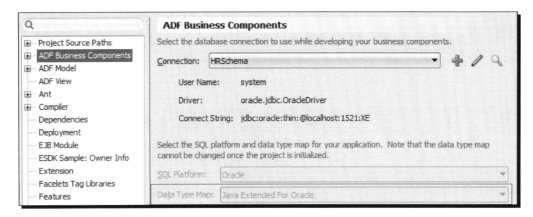

The available options are Oracle Domain and Java Extended for Oracle and Java, respectively.

Integer and BigDecimal, which was oracle.jbo.domain.Number in the previous versions, are the types used by default in 11*g*R2.

The options for this can be changed by editing the Model.jpx file. The options are OracleApps, OracleDomains, and Java. For example, <Attr Name="_jbo.TypeMapEntries" Value="OracleApps"/>.

Time for action – checking the attributes of an entity object

Carry out the following steps to check the attributes of an entity object:

1. Select the EmpEO.xml file from the Model project in the **Application Navigator** panel.

2. You will see the the structure of the entity object in the structure window.

3. Double-click the EmpEO.xml file to open the file in the **General** tab.

4. Click on the **Attribute** section to see all the attributes listed for the entity object.

5. Now, when you click on the Empno attribute, you will see that the structure window listing gets updated, thereby corresponding to the attribute section in the entity object.

6. At the same time, you will see a section shown below the attribute listing with all the information related to the selected attribute.

7. The attribute details will list down all the information related to the attribute. The information is grouped under different tabs.

8. Select the `Ename` attribute from the structure window. The attribute and its corresponding information will be displayed, as shown in the following screenshot:

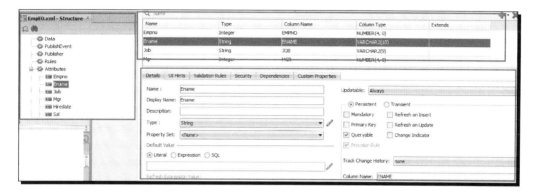

What just happened?

In the preceding section, we have individually checked the attributes available for the entity objects. There are two ways to check the attributes—one way is to look for the attributes from the structure window, where an outline of the entity object is listed. Once the attribute is selected in the structure window, we will see the property inspector listing the related properties for the selected attributes. An alternate way is to select the attribute from the **Overview** tab.

Have a go hero – check the column mappings

At this point, let us try to analyze how all the database columns of the EMP table are mapped to the EmpEO.xml file; see the following screenshot for reference:

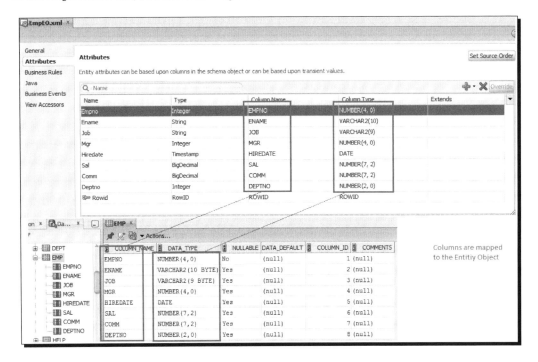

Go through the following exercise:

1. List down the columns and the corresponding attribute mappings.

2. Find how the entity objects attribute differs from the column attribute. The column information and the table structure is viewed by using the **Database Navigator** panel from the **View | Database** menu, as explained in *Chapter 2, Getting Started with ADF*.

Time for action – creating an entity object for DEPT table

In this section, we will create another entity object for the DEPT table from HRSchema. There are two ways of creating an entity object—the first way of creating an entity object was explained in *Chapter 2, Getting started with ADF*. Now, we will see how to create an entity object using another way.

1. Right-click on the `com.empdirectory.model` package from the Model project in the **Application Navigator** panel where the `EmpEO.xml` is located and select the **New Entity Object** option from the menu.

2. This will open the **Create Entity Object** wizard for you to create the entity object.

3. Enter `com.empdirectory.model.entity` as the package information for the entity object and `DeptEO` as its **Name**, as shown in the following screenshot:

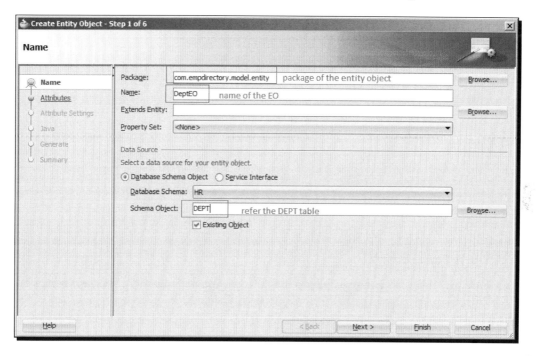

4. Select the **HR** schema from the drop-down menu and the **DEPT** table using the **Browse** button. Alternatively, we can directly enter **DEPT** in the **Schema Object:** box, if we know the table name correctly.

5. Move to the next screen to accept the listed attributes and then click on the **Next >** button.

6. In the next screen, the `Deptno` attribute settings and information related to the attribute can be selected.

7. When you attempt to move to the next screen, a message, which warns the user that there was no primary key attribute selected for the entity object, will be displayed.

The message is displayed only when there is no primary key defined in the database table. ADF will ask if you want to create a primary key named ROWID.

 The demobld.sql file, which we have used to create the database table, does not include constraint definition.

8. You can cancel the message and go back to select the **Primary Key** option for the Deptno attribute. This option was not checked for EmpEO.xml, hence we could see a column called Rowid added to the entity object.

   Once the primary key option is checked, we can remove the Rowid attribute from the EmpEO.xml file. In reality, the database table will surely have a primary key defined and most of the time, Rowid will not be generated.

9. The next screen will provide you with an option to create a Java class for the entity object. We will not do any coding in Java right now, so we will skip this section and move forward.

10. The next option will allow you to create a view object and add the view object to the application module. Select the **Generate Default View Object** checkbox and modify the package name from com.empdirectory.model.entity to com.empdirectory.model.view. Enter DeptVO in the name box.

11. Check the **Add to Application Module** option to add the view object to the already existing EmpDirectoryModule module.

   You may skip this option to create the view object from scratch by selecting DeptEO after completing all the steps.

12. Click **Next >** to accept the summary and click on the **Finish** button to create the DeptEO entity object.

What just happened?

We have now created an entity object which maps to the DEPT table. So, we have the entity object in the same package in which we had created our entity object for the EMP table. The DeptEO.xml file will have all the columns mapped to the corresponding attributes.

You can verify the creation of the attributes in the `DeptEO.xml` file and compare the columns in the `DEPT` table.

Have a go hero – set the primary key for the EmpEO.xml file

Now we have two entity objects in our `com.empdirectory.model.entity` package—one is `EmpEO.xml` and the other is `DeptEO.xml` file. We have set the `Deptno` attribute as the primary key for `DeptEO.xml`.

We have not created a separate `Rowid` attribute to represent a primary key for the entity object. So, now it's your job to set the `Empno` as a primary key for the `EmpEO.xml` file.

Bravo! You have set the `Empno` as the primary key. Now we have two attributes as the primary key. Don't worry about that right now; we will take care of this later as we proceed.

Why association?

As the name suggests, *association* is used to associate entity objects. When you look closely at the `EMP` table, you will find a `DEPTNO` column. In database terms, it is called a foreign key because `DEPTNO` is the primary key for the `DEPT` table. The foreign key association for entity objects is done using associations.

The usage of association is exactly as that of a foreign key in a relational database for maintaining referential integrity. When the database has a foreign key constraint, the association is created automatically by ADF. The following screenshot explains the relationship between the `EMP` and `DEPT` table through `Deptno`:

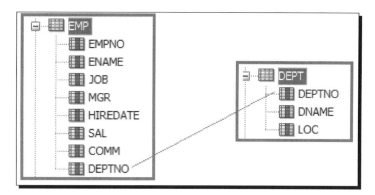

Time for action – creating an association between EmpEO and DeptEO objects

Carry out the following steps to create an association between EmpEO and DeptEO objects:

1. Select the **New** option from the **File** menu and select **ADF Business Component** from the Business Tier.

2. Enter the package name as com.empdirectory.model.association and the name as EmpEOToDeptEOAssoc in the **Create Association** wizard. The package structure for all these business objects can be predefined from the **Tools | Preferences | ADF Business Components | Packages** section.

3. Click on the **Next >** button to create an association between the entity objects. Select the value of **Cardinality** as * to 1 from the drop-down menu to represent the many-to-one relationship between EmpEO and DeptEO.

> The reason for setting the relations as many-to-one is to represent that many Employee entities are available in a single Department entity. Department is a single entity that represents the collection of employees in it.

4. Locate the Deptno attribute from EmpEO listed in the **Source Attribute** section and map it to the Deptno attribute of DeptEO in the **Destination Attribute** list.

5. After the selection, click on the **Add** button to add the association entry for the attributes.

6. Click on the **Next >** button to select properties for the association. Right now, you can accept the default settings in the *Options for the Business Components* section in this chapter.

7. Click on the **Finish** button in the **Summary** section to complete the creation of the association.

What just happened?

We have now created an association between the EmpEO and DeptEO.xml files. The *accessor* attribute for DeptEO is created in EmpEO, and for EmpEO one accessor is created in DeptEO. This can be configured in the **Accessor** section of the association object. The association relationship is referenced in the following diagram:

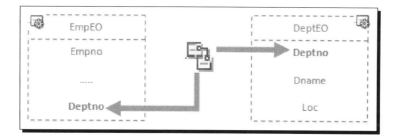

Have a go hero – drag-and-drop components

So now, let us try to drag-and-drop the EmpEO and DeptEO entity objects and the newly created association together onto the EmployeeDirectoryDiagram diagram created in *Chapter 2, Getting Started with ADF*.

About the view object

In the previous chapter, we created the EmpVO.xml file, which is the view object used to collect, retrieve, and manipulate data from the data source. EmpVO will have a reference to EmpEO as the entity object that will be used to refer to the EMP table.

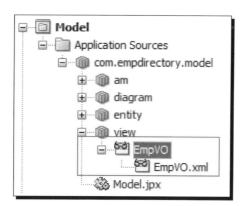

The use of having a view object is as follows:

- ◆ To fetch information from the data source using SQL query
- ◆ To sort, filter, project, and join data
- ◆ To isolate the view data from other parts of the application

Types of view object

We can create a view object from four different data sources; they are *entity object*, *SQL query*, *programmatic query*, and *static list*.

◆ **View object based on an entity object**: A view object will be based on an entity object for any interaction with the database. The entity object data source is responsible for updating the data, validating the business logic, and synchronizing data with the database.

The advantage of using an entity data source is that it will take care of maintaining consistency in the data that is being fetched from the database, by providing an entity cache. The EmpVO.xml view object is an entity-based view object, which is based on the EmpEO entity object.

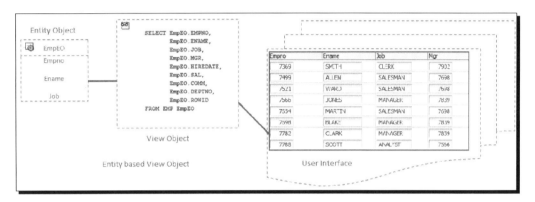

◆ **View object based on SQL query**: The view object based on SQL query is read-only and is not meant for updating the database table. The query will hold all the information that has to be retrieved from the database, as shown in the following screenshot:

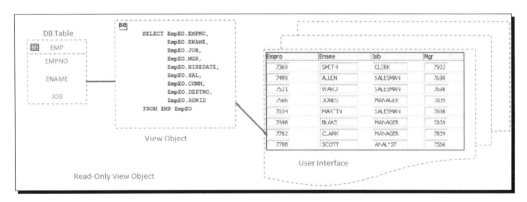

◆ **Programmatic query**: The view object can be created programmatically using Java code. In some special cases, we can create a view object customized for our business needs. The options available in a normal view object will be created programmatically using the API provided for the creation of a view object.

◆ **Static list**: Sometimes, we would like to have a list of values displayed in the user interface for the purpose of selecting a value. The static list can be provided by the user during the design phase and the list will be displayed in the same order it was entered as a list at runtime to the user. A static list will not contain any SQL query, it will contain only the attributes that have to be listed in the UI.

Time for action – creating an entity-based view object

We have the entity object for DEPT table created as DeptEO. Now it's time for us to create a view object based on this entity object. The view object can be created at the time of creating the entity object, by checking the option to create the view object in the create entity wizard. We had skipped that step so that we can create the view object now, using the following steps:

1. Right-click on the com.empdirectory.model.view package and select the **New View Object...** option. The creation of the view object can also be done from **File | New** and selecting **View Object** under the **ADF Business Components** section.

2. Enter the object's name as DeptVO in the **Name** box and select an entity object as the data source in the next screen.

3. In the next screen, you will have to select the `DeptEO` as the entity object for the view object. Select the **Updateable** option to make the entity object updateable from the view object, as shown in the following screenshot:

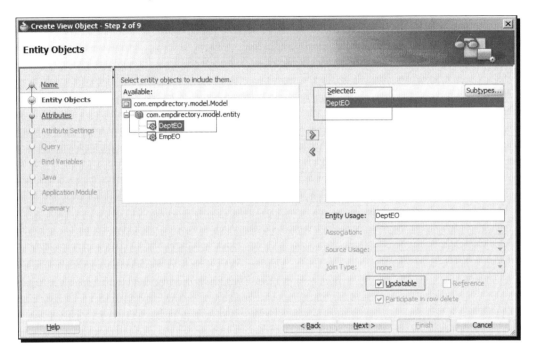

4. In the next screen, select the Attributes from the entity object to be displayed in the view object. You can select all the attributes from the **Available** list and shuttle it to the **Selected** list

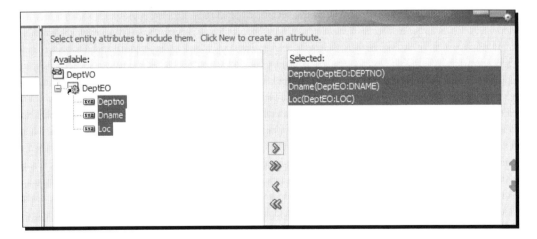

5. Click on the **Next >** button to change the **Attributes** settings for the view object. Currently, we do not have to make any changes, so we can move forward.

6. The next screen will display the SQL query that will be used to retrieve information from the DEPT table through the DeptEO object. You cannot change the query if the data source for the view object is an entity object. You have an option to update the **Where:** and the **Order By:** clause.

   The **Binding:** option will help you to choose the type of binding to be used for the view object. The **Order By:** option is provided in order to see the data sorted column-wise:

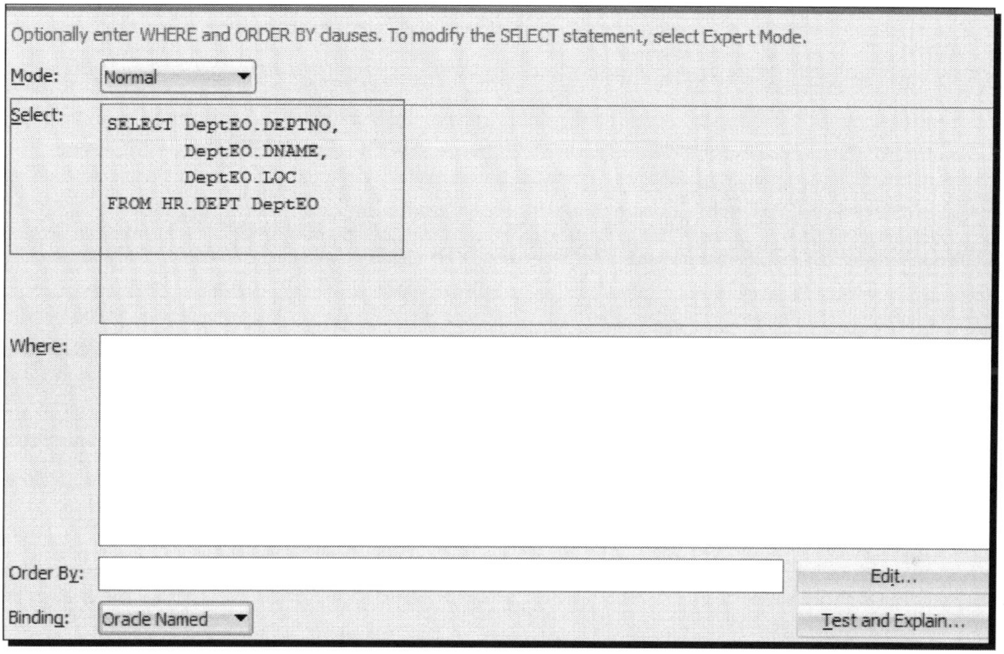

7. In the next screen, you can choose to create a *bind variable* to pass to the view object query. The bind variable is helpful in retrieving the values from the data source at runtime. It is used as placeholders in a WHERE clause of a query or in combination with view criteria.

   A *view* criterion is a named WHERE clause added to the view object which is applied at runtime based on our business needs.

8. The next screen can be used to generate Java classes for the view object. The Java classes are used to override the framework code and do some advanced operations for the view object—this will be explained in *Chapter 11, Advanced Features of ADF*.

9. In the next screen, you can check the **Add to Application Module** to add the view object to the application module. Move to the next screen after entering the application module as `EmpDirectoryModule` in the **Name:** box:

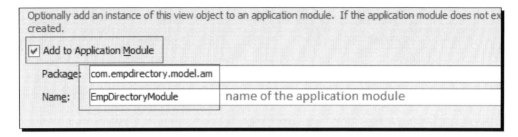

10. At the end, a summary screen will be displayed with all the options selected in the wizard. Once the **Finish** button is clicked, the view object will be created.

What just happened?

So now we have the view object created for the `DeptEO` as well:

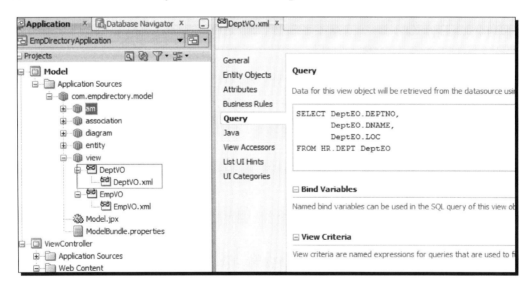

Importance of a view link

View links are the components to link two view objects. The relationship between view objects can be one-to-one, one-to-many, many-to-one, or many-to-many. This is similar to the association component that we have for the entity object. The only difference is that the view link is used in the presentation layer to fetch data if the child and the master view object are connected through related attributes.

If we have two view objects that have an entity object as a data source, then we can map our view link based on the association between the entity objects. View links based on associations are used to traverse master-detail behavior at the entity level.

A view link can also exist without association by relating two attributes from the view object. The following diagram will explain the view link relationship between EmpVO and DeptVO:

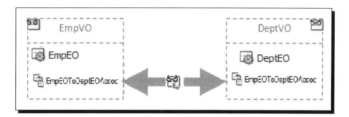

Time for action – creating a view link between EmpVO and DeptVO

Now in the following steps, we will see how to create a view link between EmpVO and DeptVO:

1. Since both the view objects are based on entity objects, we can map the view link based on the association between EmpEO and DeptEO.

2. Right-click on the com.empdirectory.model.view package and select **New View Link**.

3. In the **Create View Link** wizard, enter `com.empdirectory.model.viewlink` as the **Package** name and `EmpVOToDeptVOLink` as the **Name** value:

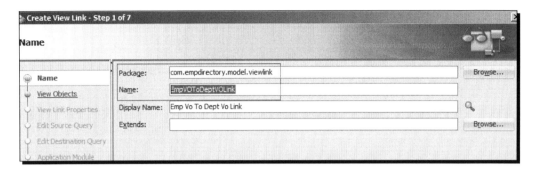

4. In the next screen, we will select the cardinality as *** to 1** which represents a many-to-one relationship and map the association `EmpEOToDeptEOAssoc` between `EmpVO` and `DeptVO`.

5. Click on the **Add** button to add the view link:

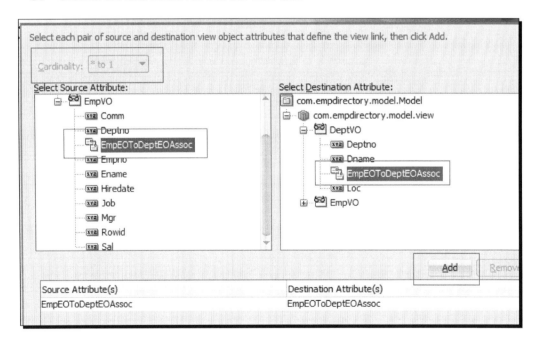

6. Click on the **Next >** button to select the view link accessor attribute for the source view object and the destination view object.

7. Check the **In View Object: DeptVO** option to have this accessor attribute created in EmpVO. This accessor is used to retrieve the related information from the DeptVO:

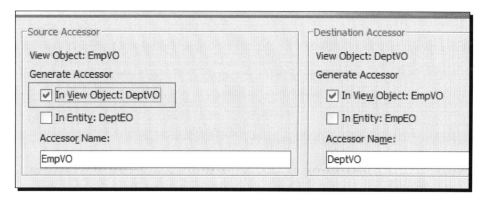

8. The next two screens will display the source and destination WHERE clause to fetch the relevant data from the view object, as a result of the view link

9. As usual, the next screen will ask you to add the view link to the application module, which we will skip this time and discuss in the next section.

10. The last screen will list out a summary of the options selected, and clicking on the **Finish** button will create the view link.

What just happened?

We have created a view link between the EmpVO and DeptVO objects. The accessors will be listed in both the view objects.

Have a go hero – drag-and-drop remaining components

Once again, let us try to drag-and-drop the EmpVO and DeptVO view objects and the newly created view link together onto EmployeeDirectoryDiagram.

What is an application module?

We had our transaction managed by the `EmpDirectoryModule.xml` file. The commit and rollback operations are a part of the transaction management of the application module. The following screenshot will show the `EmpDirectoryModule` application module, which we had created in the previous chapter:

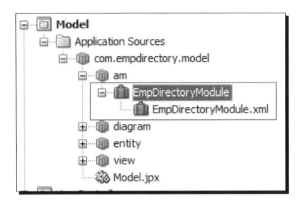

In the previous chapter, we created an application module using the **Create Entity Wizard** for `EmpDirectoryApplication`. We will now create another application module directly from the **File | New** option. There is no harm in creating an extra application module; we may use this to separate the logical unit and the transaction later as we proceed.

Time for action – creating an application module

Now we will see how to create an application module using the following steps:

1. With JDeveloper open, locate the Model project and look for the `com.empdirectory.model.am` folder. Right-click on this directory and select the **New Application Module** option.

2. The package name and the name of the application module can be kept as it is.

3. In the **Data Model** section, you can select the view object and shuttle to the other side. We are not doing this also. Click on the **Next** button.

4. In the next screen, we will move any available application module to the current one as a child application module. In this case, the root application module will be maintaining the transaction for the child application module—skip this section also.

5. The next screen can be used to create a Java class for the application module, which we do not need right now.

6. At the end is the summary page, and clicking on the **Finish** button will create the application module for you.

What just happened?

We have now learnt to create an application module without using the wizard. The application module is essential for the project, in order to maintain the transaction in a secured way.

The application module that is created can be nested within another application module to share the transactional information with the parent application module. Application modules can have Java classes that can override the framework code to bypass the business logic on commit() and rollback() operations.

Time for action – adding the view link to the application module

Now we are going to add EmpVOToDeptVOLink to the application module to display the master-detail relationship between the EmpVO and DeptVO objects. Adding the view link to the application module will help in retrieving the employees within a particular department.

The following steps show how to add a view link to the application module:

1. Double-click on the EmpDirectoryModule.xml file from com.empdirectory. model.am.

2. Open the **Data Model** section to select the view object instances.

3. Select the view link accessor for the DeptVO in the **Available View Objects:** section. In the **Data Model** section, select DeptVO1 (which is the view object instance name in EmpDirectoryModule).

4. Shuttle the view object to the **Data Model** section. Now the EmoVO2 object will be added as a child to DeptVO1. This represents the view link association between DeptVO and EmpVO.

5. The instance name for the view link is EmpVO3, in my case.

6. Save the `EmpDirectoryModule.xml` file:

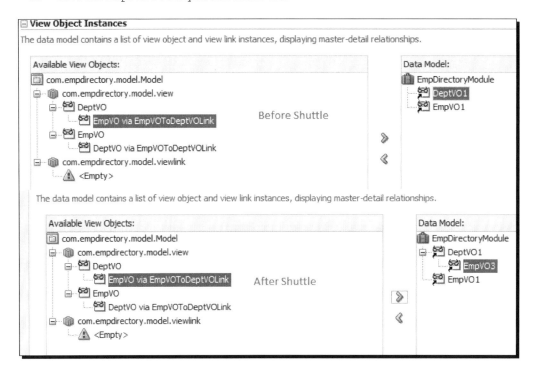

What just happened?

We have now added a view link to the application module. The view link instance represented in the `EmpDirectoryModule` application module can now be used.

In the previous screenshot, the `EmpVO1` instance is added directly to the application module that will display all the employee information. The `EmpVO3` instance that was added under `DeptVO1` will display only the employee records that match with the `Deptno` attribute.

For example, if the user is interested in department number 10, then the employees whose `deptno` value is `10` is filtered and shown to the user. The view link is essential to filter out the information from the child module and display only the relevant data from the master data.

Business components in action

In this section, we will see how the business components are working at runtime. When we run the application module, the view object instances that are added to the application module will be loaded at runtime and the data will be shown to the user, as per the user interaction.

Time for action – running the application module

We will run the AM tester using the following steps and see how the components work in action:

1. Right-click on `EmpDirectoryModule` and select the **Run** option from the menu.

2. When the AM tester is ready, click on the view link created. In this case, it will be `EmpVOToDeptVOLink2`.

3. This will open records of the `ACOUNTING` department. You will see that there are only three employees in this department, from the `HRSchema` database we created in *Chapter 2, Getting Started with ADF*.

 The records were created using the `demobld.sql` file.

4. Click on the **Forward** button to see that the data changes as per the action. Now you will see that the `RESEARCH` department has five employees within it.

5. Traverse to the `OPERATIONS` department; you will not see any employees within this department.

6. Now we are going to create a new department named `HR`.

7. Click on the + (add) icon for the department table—you will see a new record created for you.

8. Now enter in the following details:

Deptno 50

Dname HR

Loc NEW YORK

9. Click on the **Commit** button to save this department in the database.

10. We will create one employee for this department. Click on the + (add) button for the employee and then enter the following data:

- ❑ **Empno** 1234
- ❑ **Ename** JACK
- ❑ **Job** MANAGER
- ❑ **Mgr** 7499—this number refers to an employee named ALLEN in the SALES department (this is just a random number now. In real life, HR will never report to a salesman)
- ❑ **Hiredate** 1981-02-20 00:00:00.0
- ❑ **Sal** 2000
- ❑ **Comm** 200
- ❑ **Deptno**—this will be 50, which is automatically populated as we are creating the employee for the department that has this value set as 50
- ❑ **Rowid**—this will get generated when you save the record

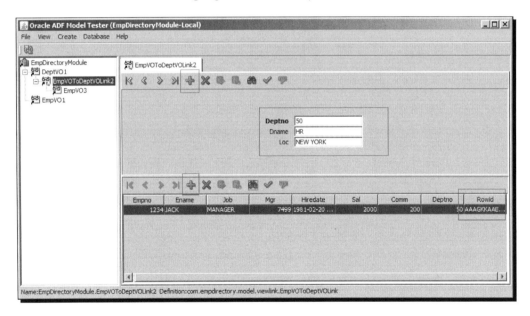

What just happened?

We created a department in the DEPT table with the department number as 50. We also created an employee named JACK in the HR department.

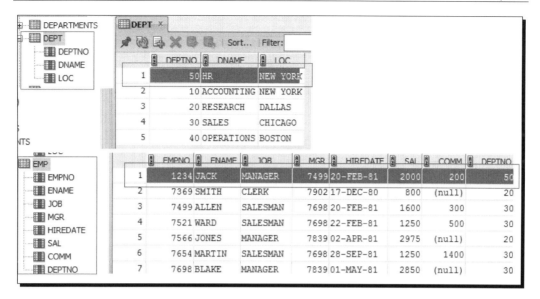

Have a go hero – play with the AM tester for a while

This exercise is more fun as you are going to work with the data. You are going to perform some basic CRUD operations by yourself, using the following exercise:

- Create an employee for the operations department
- Delete the employee named MARTIN in the sales team
- Update the RESEARCH team location from DALLAS to HOUSTON

After all these operations, commit the record and verify in the database if the values have been saved correctly.

Options for the business components

Now that we understand how to create the business components, let's dive deeper into each and every component and look for the options available for each of these components. Some of the options explained in this section are a part of the advanced topics and will be explained in detail in *Chapter 11, Advanced Features of ADF*.

Let us analyze the business components options briefly.

Entity object

The options for an entity object are changed in the **Overview** tab. Some settings related to attributes can be changed using the **Property Inspector** window. Let us explore the options under the entity object.

General

Some general settings for the entity object are as follows:

◆ **Name**: This section displays the name of the entity object. This section is editable, and changing the name will affect all the artifacts related to the entity object.

◆ **Package**: This section displays the package for the entity object. The *pencil* icon next to the option will help to change or refactor the value.

◆ **Extends**: This option is used to extend another entity object. The extended entity will become the parent of the current entity. A window will be shown to the user to select the parent entity.

   For example, if you have `SalesAccountEO` and `CustomerAccountEO`, then these two entity objects can extend the `AccoutEO` to inherit the common features.

◆ **Property Set**: We can have properties and messages defined as a named-value pair in property sets. Property sets are created from the **New Gallery** wizard under the **ADF Business Components** section.

◆ **Schema Object**: This is the actual name of the table. The pencil icon will help the user to select the schema object from the database if the user decides to change the table associated with the entity object.

Alternate key

We can create an alternate key, other than a primary key, to uniquely identify a row. The alternate key will usually be defined on an attribute other than the primary key. For example, alternate keys can be defined on a `Name` attribute for uniqueness.

Tuning

The tuning settings are as follows:

◆ **Use Update Batching**: This setting is used to update the entities in a batch when the number exceeds the number provided in the space available. For example, if the entity is getting updated from multiple sources, then this option will enable us to issue a single collective DML statement for bulk CRUD operation. Using this property will reduce the number of statements getting generated.

◆ **Retain Association Accessor Rowset**: This setting is used to tell the instance of an entity object to retain the accessor rowset, when accessing the object using an association. The rowset is created every time an access is made through association. Setting this property will retain the source accessor rowset for performance instead of creating it every time.

◆ **Custom Properties**: You can add some properties here, defined as named-value pair, to be assessed at runtime.

Security

You can set the security for the entity object using the **Read, Update, removeCurrentRow** option. You need permissions to be added to the `jazn-data.xml` file to read data through an entity if the options were selected.

Business Logic Group

This is helpful if you want to store properties, control hints, validations, localizations, and messages based on a group. The logical group needs a business logical unit, which will be loaded at runtime based on the value of the discriminator.

Attributes

The options listed in this section are specific for the entity object attributes, which is updated using the **Property Inspector** window. You can select the attribute from either the structure window or the **Overview** tab.

Details

◆ **Name**: This setting displays the actual name of the attribute. The column name of the table is represented in a *CamelCase* for the entity object.

◆ **Display Name**: This is the display name for the attribute that will be shown in the business component diagram.

◆ **Description**: A description for the attribute is added in this section.

◆ **Type**: This setting displays the data type of the attribute. Some of the common types are `java.lang`, `Integer`, `java.lang.String`, `oracle.jbo.domain.Timestamp`, and so on. These are the types that correspond to the database column type `VARCHAR2`, `NUMBER`, and `DATE`, respectively.

◆ **Property Set**: This is the property set that has to be applied to the attribute.

◆ **Default Value**: You can provide a default value for the attribute using this setting.

◆ **Literal**: The default value will be a literal value.

◆ **Expression**: This setting lets you default the attribute to an expression. Groovy expression language is used to define the expression. Groovy is a Java-like language used for scripting.

◆ **Refresh Expression Value**: This is the condition provided to recalculate the expression value.

◆ **SQL**: This setting lets you default to the output of an SQL query.

◆ **Polymorphic Discriminator**: Checking this option makes the attribute the discriminator column, which is used to identify the type of the entity object we already knew we are working with and it also identifies the entity object that is extended from a parent entity object.

◆ **Effective Date**: This is related to the *Effective Date* functionality to get the information at a particular time. Sometimes information may change during a single day, so to keep track of the change in information, we use this option.

For an effective date, you would need a column representing a start date, an end date, a sequence, and a sequence flag. These attributes are mapped to the corresponding available options.

  ❏ **Start Date**: This is the attribute with a start date

  ❏ **End Date**: This is the attribute with an end date

  ❏ **Sequence Flag**: This is the attribute mapped for a sequence flag

  ❏ **Sequence**: This is the attribute mapped for the sequence

◆ **Updateable**: This sets the attribute as updateable. If this is not checked, then the attribute value cannot be updated and trying to update it will result in an exception. The following options will define when the attribute should be updateable:

  ❏ **Always**: This option defines that the attribute is always updateable.

  ❏ **While New**: This option defines that the attribute is updateable only when the attribute is newly created or initialized.

  ❏ **Never**: This option defines that the attribute can never be updated. The attribute will be displayed as read-only in the UI.

◆ **Persistent**: This option defines if the attribute value should be stored in the database.

◆ **Transient**: This option defines that the attribute value is not persisted to the database and is used to calculate the values in the middleware layer.

◆ **Mandatory**: This option sets the attribute as required. If the attribute is not given a value, then ADF will prompt to provide a value for this attribute.

- **Primary Key**: This option sets the current attribute as a primary key.

- **Queriable**: This option sets the attribute to take part in a query. If this option is not set, then the attribute will not be displayed in the UI as a queriable attribute.

- **Refresh on Insert**: This is a trigger which causes the attribute to refresh from the database when a new row is inserted.

- **Refresh on Update**: This option causes the attribute to be refreshed when the row is updated.

- **Change Indicator**: This option sets the attribute as the change-indicator value, which will help in versioning the row.

- **Precision Rule**: This option is used to set a strict precision rule.

- **Track Change History**: This option is used to have a version number for history columns **created on**, **created by**, **modified on**, **modified by**, and **version number**.

- **Column Name**: This option defines a column name in the database.

- **Column Type**: This option defines the data type of the column.

UI Hints

- **Display Hints**: This option defines whether to display the attribute or hide it in the UI.

- **Label**: This option defines the label to be displayed for the attribute in the UI.

- **ToolTip**: This option defines if you want to show any tip.

- **Format Type**: This option defines the format for date field; for example, Simple Date.

- **Format**: This option defines the format pattern for the date.

- **Control Type**: This option defines the display control hints such as checkbox, date, image, and others.

- **Display Width**: This option defines the display width for the attribute when displayed in the UI.

- **Display Height**: This option defines the height of the field in the UI.

- **Form Type**: This option causes the attribute to be displayed in summary when it is shown in a form.

- **Auto submit**: This option can be set to `true` or `false` in order to refresh the dependent component based on this attribute.

Validation Rule

You can set validation for the attribute. The business logic can be set declaratively in this section. Some of the validations are **Compare**, **Range**, **regular expression**, **Script**, and so on.

Security

This setting defines restrictions for updating the attribute.

Dependencies

This setting is used to select the attribute on which the current attribute is dependent on for recalculation or database refetch.

Custom Properties

You can add custom properties to access at runtime.

Business Rules

You can set the business validation and rules here, same as the validation rule section in the attribute. Here, you can set the business rule for the complete entity. The two extra validations available here are **Collection** and **UniqueKey**.

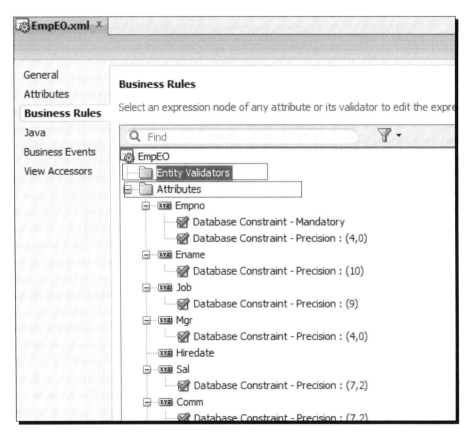

Java

If you want to add a Java class for your entity object, you can add it here. There are three types of Java classes that you can add. They are as follows:

- **Entity object class**: This class contains the accessor information
- **Entity collection class**: This class maintains the entity collection
- **Entity definition class**: This class will refer to the definition of an entity

Business Events

This section is used to raise events based on some business operation. For example, we have to notify some other application or service if a row is inserted into the database. We can publish an event from this section using the payload.

View Accessor

This section is used to provide a list source for the attribute. For example, you would want to show the department names as a list option instead of showing the department ID.

Association

Some important settings for the association are explained in this section.

Relationship

The **Behavior** section is used to specify the behavioral aspect of the association. Some of the behavior's settings are:

- **Use Database Key constraints**: Selecting this property will make sure that the database constraint is added to the `source` and `target` entity objects.
- **Composition Association**: The composition association is enabled between the entity objects. This option is helpful for master-detail mapping with one-to-many relationships. This setting will make sure that the parent-child relation remains intact and works properly.

  The following options will be enabled only for **Composition Association**.

  - **Optimize for Database Cascade Delete**: This setting will make sure that the **Cascade Delete** option works fine for parent-child relationships and optimizes the deletion of the child objects row when the parent entity objects are deleted.

- **Implement Cascade Delete**: This option will be enabled only if the previous option is not chosen. This will make sure that all the child entity object records are deleted before deleting the parent entity.

- **Cascade Update Key Attributes**: This setting will update the foreign key attribute in cascade when the parent key changes.

- **Update Top-level History Columns**: This setting will update the parent's history columns before updating the child's records.

- **Lock Level**: This option will determine at which level the lock has to be applied during the UPDATE operations.

- **Lock Container**: This will lock the container of the entity for which the framework acquires the lock.

- **Lock Top-level Container**: The framework will lock the top-most entity in the composition hierarchy when the child entity object is locked for the UPDATE operation.

View Object

We went through some of the common options in the entity object section. Let us discuss a few more important options for the view object in this section.

General

This section will explain some of the options available for the view object in the **Overview** tab and other options available from the **Property Inspector** window.

Tuning

This section has some of the tuning properties that can be set for the view object. The tuning options used for the performance of the view object are as follows:

- **All Rows**: This option is used to retrieve all the rows from the database.

- **Only up to row number**: Using this option, you can set the row number up to which you want to retrieve the rows.

- **In Batches of**: This option can be used to say how many batches you want to retrieve from the database.

- **As needed**: Using this option, you can have rows fetched as needed from the database.

- **All at once**: This option can be used to get the rows all at once at first retrieval upon executing the query.

- **At most one Row**: This option can be used to get at the most one row when the view object query is executed.

- **No rows**: This option can be used retrieve a no rows event after querying the database using the view object.

- **Query Optimizer hints**: This option provides an optimizer hint to make the view object performant in retrieving the data.

- **Fill last page of rows**: This option will display the result of the query when working with pagination in the UI. Pagination is displaying the result of the query in pages, with a range of data.

- **Passivate State**: This option is used to maintain the state of the object on failover by passivating the view object collection data. This option is used in a clustered environment, where the activation and passivation of query results is mandatory for the highly available application.

- **Access Mode**: This setting provides options to support pagination in the UI.

- **Range size**: This option defines the range size of the rows in each paging view.

Entity Objects

The view object is created based on the entity that you will select. The view object can be based on multiple entity objects, using joins.

Attributes

The **Attributes** section defines the following properties:

- **SDO Property**: Sometimes, a view object is used as a service. Check if this is acting as a service definition object.

- **XSD Type**: This option defines the **XML Schema Definition (XSD)** type to be used for a service definition.

List of Values

You can use this setting to provide a list to be shown for the attribute in the UI.

Query

The SQL query defined for the view object is shown in this section. We can change the **Where:** and the **Order by:** clause in this section, if the view object is based on an entity object.

Bind Variable

This section defines the bind variable for the view object query. This is used to fetch the desired result set by passing the value to the bind variable.

View Criteria

This section provides support for creating custom criteria which is more flexible for use in fetching data efficiently.

Pop quiz

Q1. _____ component is used as a foreign key reference between two entity objects.

1. View link
2. View object
3. Association

Q2. Which of the following cannot be used as a data source to create the view objects?

1. Entity object
2. Programmatic
3. View object
4. SQL query

Q3. If a view object is based on an entity object, then we would create a view link based on the association.

1. True
2. False

Q4. _____ component is responsible for transaction management.

Q5. Which of the following options are used to make the attribute as required in the entity object?

1. Required
2. Primary Key
3. Mandatory
4. Queriable
5. None of the above

Summary

Let us recap what we have learned in this chapter. We saw several ADF business components; they are entity object, association, view object, view link, and application module. The interactions between these objects are also discussed. The runtime behavior of the components is explained and the CRUD operations are performed using these business components. Various options available for the components are also examined.

In the next chapter, we will see how to do the validation for the ADF model layer. We will learn more about the declarative validations and the APIs available for the business components.

4
Validating and Using the Model Data

Validating data is important as business depends on the data that gets stored in the database. So how do we validate the data? Validation is something that makes sure that valid data is getting stored in the database. Validation could be anything from comparing two fields in a table to multiple validations on a single field involving different columns from a different table.

In any other framework, we would end up writing a lot of code even for a small validation. But in ADF, we do little or no coding at all, and most of the validations are achieved declaratively.

In this chapter, we will learn the following topics:

- ◆ Declarative validation
- ◆ Groovy expressions
- ◆ Learning about APIs
- ◆ Managing transactions
- ◆ Exposing data

Declarative validation

It's easy to set up declarative validation for an entity object to validate the data that is passed through the metadata file. *Declarative validation* is the validation added for an attribute or an entity object to fulfill a particular business validation. It is called declarative validation because we don't write any code to achieve the validation as all the business validations are achieved declaratively. The entity object holds the business rules that are defined to fulfill specific business needs such as a range check for an attribute value or to check if the attribute value provided by the user is a valid value from the list defined. The rules are incorporated to maintain a standard way to validate the data.

Knowing the lifecycle of an entity object

It is important to know the lifecycle of an entity object before knowing the validation that is applied to an entity object. The following diagram depicts the lifecycle of an entity:

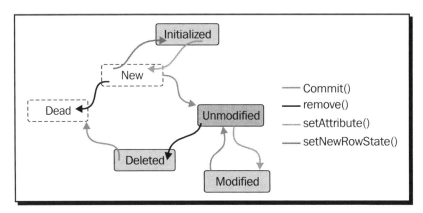

When a new row is created using an entity object, the status of the entity is set to NEW. When an entity is initialized with some values, the status is changed from NEW to INITIALIZED. At this time, the entity is marked invalid or dirty; this means that the state of the entity is changed from the value that was previously checked with the database value.

The status of an entity is changed to UNMODIFIED, and the entity is marked valid after applying validation rules and committing to the database. When the value of an unmodified entity is changed, the status is changed to MODIFIED and the entity is marked dirty again. The modified entity again goes to an UNMODIFIED state when it is saved to the database. When an entity is removed from the database, the status is changed to DELETED. When the value is committed, the status changes to DEAD.

Types of validation

Validation rules are applied to an entity to make sure that only valid values are committed to the database and to prevent any invalid data from getting saved to the database. In ADF, we use validation rules for the entity object to make sure the row is valid all the time.

There are three types of validation rules that can be set for the entity objects; they are as follows:

- Entity-level validation
- Attribute-level validation
- Transaction-level validation

Entity-level validation

As we know, an entity represents a row in the database table. *Entity-level validation* is the business rule that is added to the database row. For example, the validation rule that has to be applied to a row is termed as entity-level validation.

There are two unique declarative validators that will be available only for entity-level validation—*Collection* and *UniqueKey*. The following diagram explains that entity-level validations are applied on a single row in the EMP table. The validated row is highlighted in bold.

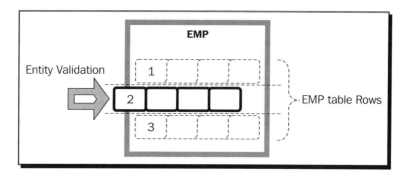

Attribute-level validation

Attribute-level validations are applied to attributes. Business logic mostly involves specific validations to compare different attribute values or to restrict the attributes to a specific range. These kinds of validations are done in attribute-level validation. Some of the declarative validators available in ADF are *Compare*, *Length*, and *Range*.

The *Precision* and *Mandatory* attribute validations are added, by default, to the attributes from the column definition in the underlying database table. We can only set the display message for the validation.

The following diagram explains that the validation is happening on the attributes in the second row:

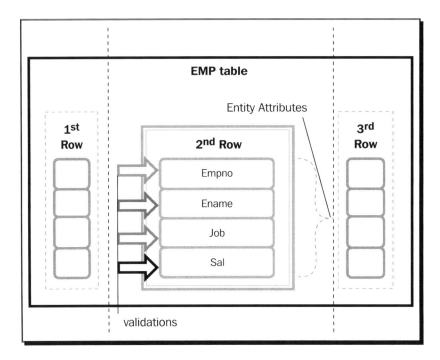

There can be any number of validations defined on a single attribute or on multiple attributes in an entity. In the diagram, Empno has a validation that is different from the validation defined for Ename. Validation for the Job attribute is different from that for the Sal attribute. Similarly, we can define validations for attributes in the entity object.

Transaction-level validation

Transaction-level validations are done after all entity-level validations are completed. If you want to add any kind of validation at the end of the process, you can defer the validation to the transaction level to ensure that the validation is performed only once.

Built-in declarative validators

ADF Business Components includes some built-in validators to support and apply validations for entity objects. The following screenshot explains how a declarative validation will show up in the **Overview** tab:

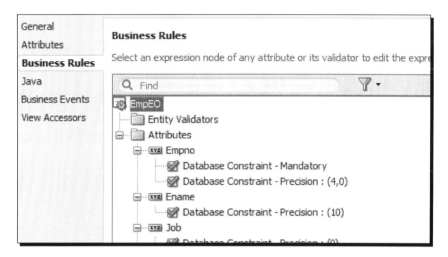

The **Business Rules** section for the `EmpEO.xml` file will list all the validations for the `EmpEO` entity. In the previous screenshot, we will see that the there are no entity-level validators defined and some of the attribute-level validations are listed in the **Attributes** folder.

Collection validator

A Collection validator is available only for entity-level validation. To perform operations such as `average`, `min`, `max`, `count`, and `sum` for the collection of rows, we use the collection validator.

Collection validators are compared to the `GROUP BY` operation in an SQL query with a validation. The aggregate functions, such as `count`, `sum`, `min`, and `max` are added to validate the entity row. The validator is operated against the literal value, expression, query result, and so on. You must have the association accessor to add a collection validation.

Time for action – adding a collection validator for the DeptEO file

Now, we will add a Collection validator to `DeptEO.xml` for adding a count validation rule. Imagine a business rule that says that the number of employees added to department number `10` should be more than five. In this case, you will have a `count` operation for the employees added to department number `10` and show a message if the count is less than `5` for a particular department.

We will break this action into the following three parts:

◆ **Adding a declarative validation**: In this case, the number of employees added to the department should be greater than five

◆ **Specifying the execution rule**: In our case, the execution of this validation should be fired only for department number 10

◆ **Displaying the error message**: We have to show an error message to the user stating that the number of employees added to the department is less than five

Adding the validation

Following are the steps to add the validation:

1. Go to the **Business Rules** section of DeptEO.xml. You will find the **Business Rules** section in the **Overview** tab.

2. Select **Entity Validators** and click on the **+** button. You may right-click on the **Entity Validators** folder and then select **New Validator** to add a validator.

3. Select Collection as **Rule Type** and move on to the **Rule Definition** tab.

4. In this section, select Count for the **Operation** field; Accessor is the association accessor that gets added through a *composition association* relationship. Only the composition association accessor will be listed in the **Accessor** drop-down menu. Select the accessor for EmpEO listed in the dropdown, with Empno as the value for **Attribute**.

> In order to create a composition association accessor, you will have to create an association between DeptEO.xml and EmpEO.xml based on the Deptno attribute with cardinality of 1 to *. The Composition Association option has to be selected to enable a composition relationship between the two entities.

5. The value of the **Operator** option should be selected as Greater Than. **Compare with** will be a literal value, which is 5 that can be entered in the **Enter Literal Value** section below.

Specifying the execution rule

Following are the steps to specify the execution:

1. Now to set the execution rule, we will move to the **Validation Execution** tab.

2. In the **Conditional Execution** section, add Deptno = '10' as the value for **Conditional Execution Expression**.

3. In the **Triggering Attribute** section, select the **Execute only if one of the Selected Attributes has been changed** checkbox.

4. Move the Empno attribute to the **Selected Attributes** list. This will make sure that the validation is fired only if the Empno attribute is changed:

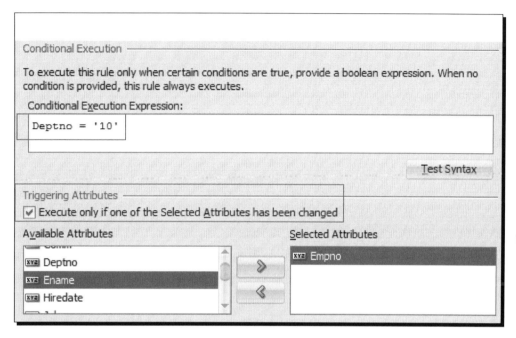

Displaying the error message

Following are the steps to display the error message:

1. Go to the **Failure Handling** section and select the **Error** option for **Validation Failure Severity**.

2. In the **Failure Message** section, enter the following text:

```
Please enter more than 5 Employees.
```

3. You can add the message stored in a resource bundle to **Failure Message** by clicking on the magnifying glass icon.

What just happened?

We have added a collection validation for our `EmpEO.xml` object. Every time a new employee is added to the department, the validation rule fires as we have selected `Empno` as our triggering attribute. The rule is also validated against the condition that we have provided to check if the department number is 10. If the department number is 10, the count for that department is calculated. When the user is ready to commit the data to the database, the rule is validated to check if the count is greater than 5. If the number of employees added is less than 5, the error message is displayed to the user.

When we add a collection validator, the `EmpEO.xml` file gets updated with appropriate entries. The following entries get added for the aforementioned validation in the `EmpEO.xml` file:

```
<validation:CollectionValidationBean
    Name="EmpEO_Rule_0"
    ResId=
      "com.empdirectory.model.entity.EmpEO_Rule_0"
    OnAttribute="Empno"
    OperandType="LITERAL"
    Inverse="false"
    CompareType="GREATERTHAN"
    CompareValue="5"
    Operation="count">
    <validation:OnCondition>
      <![CDATA[Deptno = '10']]>
    </validation:OnCondition>
</validation:CollectionValidationBean>
<ResourceBundle>
    <PropertiesBundle
      PropertiesFile=
        "com.empdirectory.model.ModelBundle"/>
</ResourceBundle>
```

 The error message that is added in the **Failure Handling** section is automatically added to the resource bundle.

The Compare validator

The `Compare` validator is used to compare the current attribute value with other values. The attribute value can be compared against the literal value, query result, expression, view object attribute, and so on. The operators supported are equal, not-equal, less-than, greater-than, less-than or equal to, and greater-than or equal to.

The Key Exists validator

This validator is used to check if the key value exists for an entity object. The key value can be a primary key, foreign key, or an alternate key. The `Key Exists` validator is used to find the key from the entity cache, and if the key is not found, the value is determined from the database. Because of this reason, the `Key Exists` validator is considered to give better performance. For example, when an employee is assigned to a department `deptNo 50` and you want to make sure that `deptNo 50` already exists in the `DEPT` table.

The Length validator

This validator is used to check the string length of an attribute value. The comparison is based on the *character* or *byte* length.

The List validator

This validator is used to create a validation for the attribute In a list. The operators included in this validation are `In` and `NotIn`. These two operators help the validation rule check if an attribute value is in a list.

The Method validator

Sometimes, we would like to add our own validation with some extra logic coded in our Java class file. For this purpose, ADF provides a declarative validator to map the validation rule against a method in the entity-implementation class. The implementation class is generated in the Java section of the entity object. We need to create and select a method to handle method validation. The method is named as `validateXXX()`, and the returned value will be of the `Boolean` type.

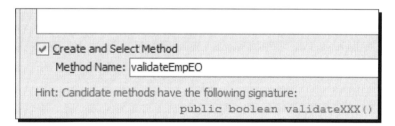

The Range validator

This validator is used to add a rule to validate a range for the attribute value. The operators included are `Between` and `NotBetween`. The range will have a *minimum* and *maximum* value that can be entered for the attribute.

The Regular Expression validator

For example, let us consider that we have a validation rule to check if the e-mail ID provided by the user is in the correct format. For the e-mail validation, we have some common rules such as the following:

- The e-mail ID should start with a string and end with the @ character
- The e-mail ID's last character cannot be the dot (.) character
- Two @ characters are not allowed within an e-mail ID

For this purpose, ADF provides a declarative *Regular Expression* validator. We can use the `regex` pattern to check the value of the attribute. The e-mail address and the US phone number pattern is provided by default:

- **Email**: `[A-Z0-9._%+-]+@[A-Z0-,9.-]+\.[A-Z]{2,4}`
- **Phone Number (US)**: `[0-9]{3}-?[0-9]{3}-?[0-9]{4}`

    You should select the required pattern and then click on the **Use Pattern** button to use it. `Matches` and `NotMatches` are the two operators that are included with this validator.

The Script validator

If we want to include an expression and validate the business rule, the `Script` validator is the best choice. ADF supports Groovy expressions to provide `Script` validation for an attribute.

The UniqueKey validator

This validator is available for use only for entity-level validation. To check for uniqueness in the record, we would be using this validator. If we have a primary key defined for the entity object, the **Uniqueness Check Definition** section will list the primary keys defined to check for uniqueness, as shown in the following screenshot:

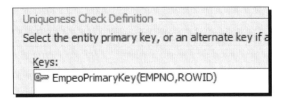

If we have to perform a uniqueness check against any attribute other than the primary key attributes, we will have to create an alternate key for the entity object.

Time for action – creating an alternate key for DeptEO

Currently, the `DeptEO.xml` file has `Deptno` as the primary key. We would add business validation that states that there should not be a way to create a duplicate of the department name that is already available. The following steps show how to create an alternate key:

1. Go to the **General** section of the `DeptEO.xml` file and expand the **Alternate Keys** section. Alternate keys are keys that are not part of the primary key.

2. Click on the little **+** icon to add a new alternate key.

3. Move the `Dname` attribute from the **Available** list to the **Selected** list and click on the **OK** button.

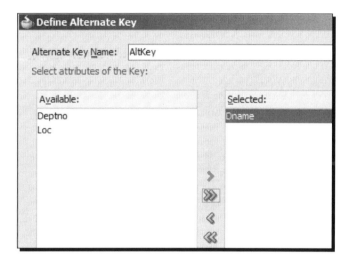

What just happened?

We have created an alternate key against the `Dname` attribute to prepare for a unique check validation for the department name. When the alternate key is added to an entity object, we will see the `AltKey` attribute listed in the **Alternate Key** section of the **General** tab.

In the `DeptEO.xml` file, you will find the following code that gets added for the alternate key definition:

```
<Key
    Name="AltKey"
    AltKey="true">
    <DesignTime>
      <Attr Name="_isUnique" Value="true"/>
```

```
        <Attr Name="_DBObjectName" Value="HR.DEPT"/>
    </DesignTime>
    <AttrArray Name="Attributes">
      <Item Value=
        "com.empdirectory.model.entity.DeptEO.Dname"/>
    </AttrArray>
</Key>
```

Have a go hero – compare the attributes

For the first time, we have learned about the validations in ADF. So it's time for you to create your own validation for the `EmpEO` and `DeptEO` entity objects. Add validations for the following business scenarios:

1. Continue with the creation of the uniqueness check for the department name in the `DeptEO.xml` file.

2. The salary of the employees should not be greater than 1000. Display the following message if otherwise:

   Please enter Salary less than 1000.

3. Display the message **invalid date** if the employee's hire date is after 10-10-2001.

4. The length of the characters entered for `Dname` of `DeptEO.xml` should not be greater than 10.

5. The location of a department can only be `NEWYORK`, `CALIFORNIA`, or `CHICAGO`.

6. The department name should always be entered in uppercase. If the user enters a value in lowercase, display a message.

7. The salary of an employee with the `MANAGER` job role should be between 800 and 1000. Display an error message if the value is not in this range.

8. The employee name should always start with an uppercase letter and should end with any character other than special characters such as `:`, `;`, and `_`.

9. After creating all the validations, check the code and tags generated in the entity's XML file for each of the aforementioned validations.

Groovy expression

ADF Business Components utilize Groovy expressions to support scripting. Groovy is an open source, Java-like scripting language that can be stored in an XML definition file. For instance, the attribute name for the employee name `Ename` can directly be used in a Groovy expression to represent the value of the `Ename` attribute.

Groovy follows the same JavaBeans way of accessing the methods of an entity object that is defined in the Java class. Following are some of the ways to call the method of entity objects in a Groovy expression:

Java method	Groovy expression
isEmployee()	employee
getEmployee()	employee
getEmpNo(int n)	source.emp(5)
checkEmployeeName()	source.checkEmployeeName()
checkEmployeeNo(int n)	source.checkEmployeeNo(5)

Setting a default value

We can set a default value for an attribute in the entity or view object by using the Groovy expression. The **Default Value** section for the attribute is provided with three options—**Literal**, **Expression**, and **SQL**. For the **Literal** value, we can provide a literal value. The Expression option is used to provide a value that is evaluated at runtime and to dynamically assign a default value to the attribute.

Time for action – setting a default salary for employees

For example, consider a case wherein we want to set a default value for the salary attribute in the EmpEO.xml file based on the Deptno attribute. In this case, we have to provide an expression that will be evaluated at runtime to provide the default value. The following steps show us how to do this:

1. Click on the Sal attribute from the list of attributes displayed in the **Attributes** section of EmpEO.xml.

2. In the **Default Value** section, select the **Expression** option. Now the *pencil* icon will be enabled for the textbox below the **Expression** option.

3. Click on the pencil icon to open an **Edit Expression Editor** window, and add the following code in the **Expression** editor box:

```
if(Job == 'MANAGER'){
  Sal = 1000;
}
else{
  Sal = 2000;
}
```

4. Select the `Job` attribute as the calculation is dependent on it.

5. Now click on the **OK** button to add the expression for setting a default value for the `Sal` attribute.

What just happened?

We have created the default value for the attribute whose value is determined at runtime, using Groovy expression. This means that whenever we create a new record for the EMP table through EmpEO, If job is MANAGER, the `Sal` attribute is defaulted to `1000`; otherwise the `Sal` attribute is defaulted to `2000`. We will have a dependency set for the `Sal` attribute on `job`; this means whenever the value of `job` changes, the value of the `Sal` attribute is recalculated.

Have a go hero – set some default values for other attributes

We have now learned to set the default attribute using Groovy expressions. We will perform the following exercises to get familiar with the language:

1. Set the default value for Job to CONTRACTOR when the value of Empno is greater than 100 in EmpEO.

2. The Loc attribute for the DeptEO object will default to CHICAGO every time.

Validation execution

Validation execution is a section in attribute validation to set the execution rule. This is similar to the execution rule that we had set for entity-level validation. The validation for the attribute is executed only if the condition added to the expression editor is satisfied.

For example, we can have a compare validation set on the Sal attribute against 1000, say 9, and set the validation execution condition as Job == 'MANAGER'. This means the compare validation is executed only if the Job attribute is equal to MANAGER.

 The validation execution section for entity-level validation will include a triggering attribute section that is not available in attribute validation.

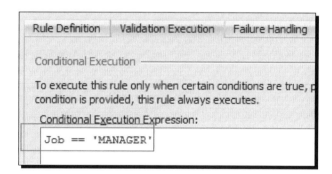

Some commonly used expressions

Groovy expressions are used in ADF Business Components to evaluate and validate business logic. Groovy expression is preferred declarative expression language for the entity and view objects.

 Sometimes, we will add an attribute for the entity or the view object with the values defaulted using Groovy expression as a calculated attribute known as *transient attribute*.

The following table gives the expressions and their functionalities:

Expression	Functionality
`getAttribute("Sal")`	This expression will fetch the `Sal` attribute.
`(Date)getAttribute("HireDate")`	This expression will cast the `HireDate` attribute value to `Date`.
`new TimeStamp(System.currentTimeMillis())`	This expression will create a new `Timestamp` object from the current system time in `long`.
`newValue`	This expression will get the new value for the attribute in the attribute-level validator.
`oldValue`	This expression will get the old value for the attribute in the attribute-level validator.
`source`	This expression will refer to the current entity object.
`adf.context`	This expression will refer to the `ADFContext` object.
`adf.object`	This expression will refer to the current object to which the expression is applied.
`adf.error`	This expression will give the reference for the current error handler object.
`adf.error.raise`	This expression will raise an exception.
`adf.error.warn`	This expression will raise a warning.
`adf.currentDate`	This expression will refer to the `current date` with no time.
`adf.currentDateTime`	This expression will refer to the current date and time.
`rowSetAttr.sum(),rowSetAttr.count(), rowSetAttr.min(), rowSetAttr.max(), rowSetAttr.avg()`	You can call the aggregate function on the ADF RowSet object. `RowSet` is a collection of rows returned through an association accessor.

Most of the Java methods such as `subString()`, `compareTo()`, and `equals()` can also be used in Groovy expressions along with some specific methods from `EntityImpl`.

Time for action – adding a script expression

Let us work on the *Script expression* validator for the `Job` attribute to understand the full advantages of Groovy expressions. Follow these steps:

1. Select the `Job` attribute in the `EmpEO` entity object from the `Attributes` list.

2. Click on the **+** icon to add a new validator.

3. Select the **Script Expression** validator for the **Rule Type** option. This will open an **Expression** editor section to write the script.

4. Enter the following code in this editor section:

```
String value = newValue;
String trim = value.trim();
if(trim.equals('MANAGER')){
adf.error.warn('NO_VACANCY');
return false;
}
return true;
```

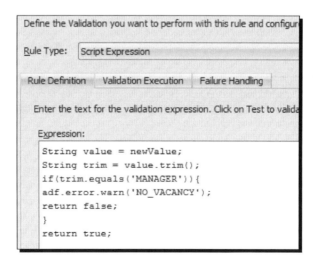

5. You can click on the **Text Syntax** button to check if the syntax is correct.

6. Click on the **OK** button to add the script expression.

What just happened?

We have added a script validation for the `Job` attribute. The script is written to do the following:

1. Assign the current value to the variable called `value`.

2. The trimmed value is saved in a variable called `trim`.

3. We are checking if the value of `trim` is equal to `MANAGER`.

4. If the trimmed value is equal to `MANAGER`, then raise a warning from the property file for the resource bundle that says "**No Position available to add more Managers**".

   To add the warning message, you will have to select the **Failure Handling** tab and click on the magnifying glass icon.

5. The ADF warning is displayed from the resource bundle, and in this case, there is no need to add a failure-handling message as we are already displaying a warning to the user.

6. The return statement `true` or `false` signifies whether the result for the expression has passed or failed.

Have a go hero – try more features of Groovy expressions

You should try out more features of Groovy expressions to increase your proficiency in writing efficient scripting code and add declarative validation without having a separate class for the Java API.

You may try the following exercise:

1. Try adding an attribute called `DeptName` to the `EmpEO` entity object and provide the default value as `DepName-` along with the `Deptno` entity added at the end.

   For example, if an employee belongs to department number 50, the `DeptName` attribute should default to `DepName-50`.

2. List down all the common methods between Java and Groovy expressions, and note down how these methods differ.

Learning about APIs

Until now, we have seen the declarative power of ADF business components. Now we will see its programming capabilities and how ADF can leverage complex business scenarios using the Java API.

From all of the ADF components available, only the entity object, view object, and application module will allow the user to generate and extend the Java API. Every class created for the business components will extend the parent class, which will take care of the logic of an entire complex framework.

Generating an entity implementation class

Generating a Java API for a business component is a straightforward task. Most of the time, the user is given an option to generate the Java API while creating the entity object, view object, or an application module. If the user skips this step, we can add the API for the business components from the **Java** tab.

Java classes in entity objects

An entity object will allow you to generate three types of Java classes. Each of these APIs is separated to handle and maintain different sections of the entity object within the framework. The three classes are as follows:

- **Entity object**: This class will have all the methods that represent the database rows. The attributes in this class represent columns in the database table.

- **Entity collection**: This class will be used to cache the queried rows for the EntityImpl class.

- **Entity definition**: This class will have the metadata definition of an entity object class.

Time for action – generating a Java API for DeptEO

In our previous exercise, we did not select the options to generate the Java API in **Create Component Wizard**. The following steps will show how to generate a Java API for the EmpEO.xml file:

1. Select the EmpEO.xml file from the Model project in the **Projects** pane.

2. Click on the **Java** tab and then click on the pencil icon. This will open the option to select the Java class files:

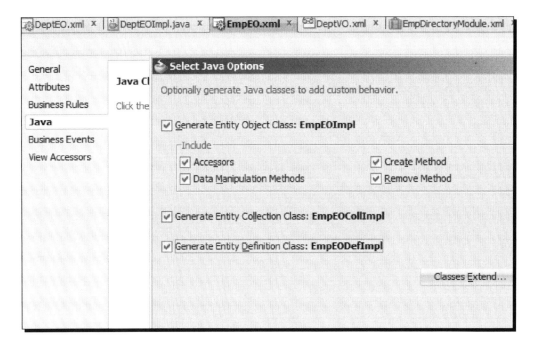

3. Check the **Generate Entity Object Class EmpEOImpl** checkbox. This will create the `EmpEOImpl` class that will extend the `EntityImpl` class.

4. Select the **Accessors** option to generate the attribute's `getter` and `setter` methods; **Create Method** will generate the `create()` method; **Data Manipulation Methods** will create the `lock()` and `doDML()` methods and **Remove Method** will create the `remove()` method.

5. Checking the **Generate Entity Collection Class EmpEOCollImpl** checkbox will create the `EmpEOCollImpl` class that will cache the queried entity row. This class will extend the `EntityCache` class to store the rows queried in the cache.

6. Checking the **Generate Entity Definition Class EmpEODefImpl** option will create the `EmpEODefImpl` class where you can store the metadata information for the entity object class.

7. Click on the **OK** button to create the classes. The `getDefinitionObject()` method in the `EntityImpl` class will help in retrieving the definition object for the entity. The definition object is used to retrieve the definitions of the entity attributes, display name, UI hints, and so on.

You can choose *base* classes from **Tools | Preferences | ADF Business Components | Base Classes**. The **Class Naming** section will display the naming format for the Java classes.

What just happened?

We have created three classes for `EmpEO`. Most of the time, we will be working on the `EntityImpl` class for doing any business operations.

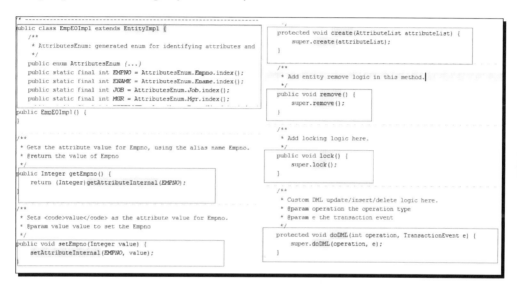

Let us see some of the useful entity methods that can be overridden from the base class to perform various operations on entity objects:

Operation	Explanation
`setAttribute()`: For example, if the attribute is Empno, the setter will be `setEmpno()`.	This method is used to set the attribute information for an entity object.
`getAttribute()`: For example, if the attribute is Empno, the setter will be `getEmpno()`.	This method is used to get the attribute value of an entity object.
`create()`	This is used to create a new entity object.
`initDefaults()`	The defaulting logic for an entity object can be added to this method.
`validateEntity()`	This method is used to validate an entity.

beforeCommit()	Logic that has to be applied before committing the record is added in this method.
afterCommit()	Logic that has to be applied after committing the record is added in this method.
remove()	This method is used to remove an entity object.
doDML()	This method is used to perform operations based on the DML operations INSERT, UPDATE, and DELETE.

Classes for view objects

A view object also has three classes that are used to represent the view object and its metadata information. A view object's classes are also generated in the same way as that of an entity object. The three classes are as follows:

♦ **View object**: This class will represent the view object itself. All operations related to the view object can be performed using this class.

♦ **View row**: This class will represent and provide access to the row of a view object. This class is similar to the entity object class.

♦ **View definition**: This class will hold references to the metadata information of the view object. We can usually access the definition object by using the getDef() method from the ViewObjectImpl class.

Most of the time, we will be working with the view object class to perform tasks programmatically. There are some operations that are used quite often in a view object implementation class; they are described in the following table:

Operation	Explanation
setWhereClause()	This method is used to set the **Where** clause for a view object.
createViewCriteria()	This method is used to create view criteria programmatically.
setOrderByClause()	This method is used to set the **Order by** clause for the current view object.
applyViewCriteria()	This method is used to apply an already created view criteria to the view object to add dynamic query parameters.
clearCache()	This method clears the cached row information in the view object.

Operation	Explanation
`remove()`	This method is used to remove the current view object.
`setMaxFetchSize()`	This method is used to set the maximum fetch size for a view object programmatically.
`executeQuery()`	This method is used to execute the view object's query.

Application module API

Application module APIs are meant for transaction management. Sometimes, we can utilize and expose the methods written in the application module to the view layer. Following are classes of the application module API:

- **Application module**: This class will have all the operations related to maintaining and configuring an application module. The transaction management-related functionalities are built within this class.

- **Application module definition**: This class is used to store metadata information related to the application module. We would not generate this class in real time as it is never used.

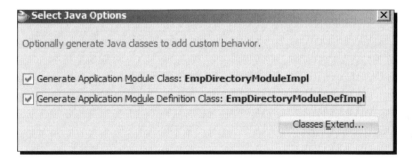

Some of the methods that are common in the application module are as follows:

Operation	Explanation
`createViewObject()`	This method is used to create a view object for an application module.
`findViewObject(String)`	This method will find the view object added to an application module. The `String` parameter will represent the view object's name.
`getTransaction()`	This method is used to get the current transaction object.

`beforeRollback()`	All operations that have to be done before rolling back the transaction are done in this method.
`beforeCommit()`	All operations that have to be done before committing the transaction go in here.

Time for action – learning to override a method

The following steps will show how to override a method from the class and then write our own logic in the method. We will have `EmpDirectoryModuleImpl` as our example here:

1. Right-click on the `EmpDirectoryModuleImpl` class and select the **Source** option.

2. Click on the **Override Methods…** option to override the operations from the base class.

3. Type in the method name, for example `befo`, in the search box that will fetch methods starting with that literal.

4. Check the `beforeCommit()` operation and click on **OK**.

5. Add the following code:

```
ViewObject vo = findViewObject("EmpVO3");
vo.clearCache();
vo.executeQuery();
```

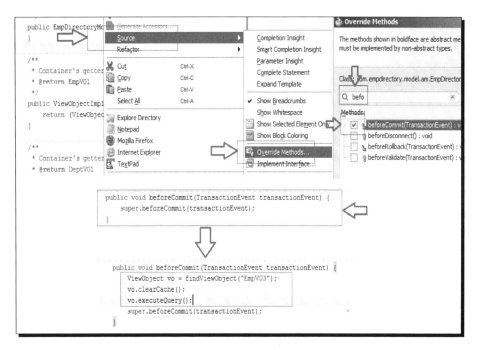

6. This code has to be added before the `super.beforeCommit(transactionEvent)` code statement.

What just happened?

Before committing the transaction:

- We are providing a handle to the `EMPVO3` view object, which is the view instance of the child view object for `DeptVO1`

- The second line clears the cache for the view object and the last line will execute the query.

Have a go hero – more on programming using APIs

Take a look at all the classes that were generated and see how they are different from the others.

Override some of the framework methods and then write some logic to operate on the objects differently.

Managing transactions

An application module is the business service component that encapsulates the logical unit of work. We can have different application modules representing different units of work.

An application module defines database sessions and provides transaction boundaries. It also controls concurrent data accesses. An application module is also responsible for maintaining the connection-pooling mechanism for the available connections.

Configuring transactions

When we create business components, we are asked to create a database connection. We have created `HRSchema` as our connection, and the application module component will use this connection to create the transaction and session. If needed, the application module can also share the transaction.

We will use the **Configurations** tab in the application module to create a configuration for the client to interact with the application modules. Using JDBC Datasource is recommended for the WebLogic server to handle connection pooling.

Time for action – creating configurations

Carry out the following steps for creating a configuration:

1. Click on the **Configurations** tab in the `EmpDirectoryModule.xml` file.

2. Click on the **+** icon to add the configurations.

3. The **Create Configuration** box will open for you to create the configurations in.

4. In order to create the local configuration, provide `EmpDirectoryModuleLocal` as the **Configuration Name**.

5. When you select the configuration type as **JDBC URL** in the application module, the `HRSchema` information will be populated automatically. For the shared connection, you will select **JDBC Datasource**. The data source name will be changed to **jdbc/ HRSchemaDS**.

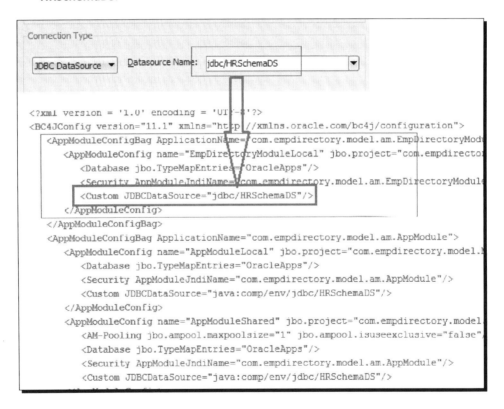

6. Clicking on the pencil icon after selecting the configuration will fetch the **Edit Configuration** box.

7. The **Pooling** and **Scalability** tab will have properties that you can set for pooling and scalability.

8. The **Properties** tab will display the runtime parameters for the configurations.

What just happened?

We have created a configuration using the HRSchema connection for the clients to be able to interact with the deployed application modules. Whenever a configuration is created, we will have a file named bc4j.xcfg to hold the information that has been provided for the configurations. Each of the connections and the configuration information is stored in this file along with other runtime parameters used for pooling and high availability.

Have a go hero – explore the bc4j.xcfg file

Explore the bc4j.xcfg file to know more about the configurations and properties associated with each of the configurations.

Exposing data

We can expose the operation of the business components to the view layer using the *client interface* option. The option to expose the methods from the Java class is explained in the following segments.

Time for action – exposing a method using the client interface

Carry out the following steps to expose a method using the client interface:

1. Open the EmpDirectoryModuleImpl.java file and add the following method:

```
public String getHelloWorld(){
    return "Hello World";
}
```

2. Go to the **Java** tab from the EmpDirectoryModule.xml file, and click on the pencil icon in the **Client Interface** section.

3. The **Edit Client Interface** window will open. Move the `getHelloWorld()` method from the **Available** list to the **Selected** list as shown in the following screenshot:

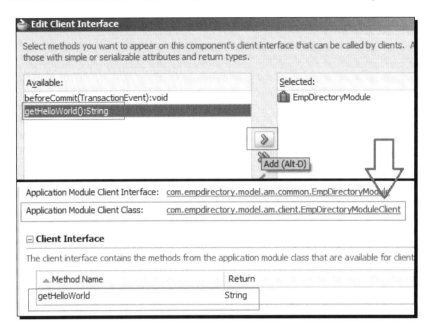

4. Click on the **OK** button to create the interface method.

What just happened?

We now have the client interface defined to expose the `getHelloWorld()` method from the `EmpDirectoryModuleImpl` class to the outside world. The `EmpDirectoryModule.java` interface will be created to expose the method as a service in the data control. The `EmpDirectoryModuleClient` class will implement the interface to invoke the `getHelloWorld()` method from `EmpDirectoryModuleImpl`.

```
/* ----------------------------------------------------------------- ...*/
public class EmpDirectoryModuleClient extends ApplicationModuleImpl implements EmpDi
    /**
     * This is the default constructor (do not remove).
     */
    public EmpDirectoryModuleClient() {
    }

    public String getHelloWorld() {
        Object _ret = this.riInvokeExportedMethod(this,"getHelloWorld",null,null);
        return (String)_ret;
    }
}
```

You can now see the `getHelloWorld()` method exposed to the view layer in the **Data Controls** palette as shown in the following screenshot:

Pop quiz

Q1. _____ and _____ are the validators available only for entity-level validations.

Q2. We can use the following validator to extend the validation using a Java class:

1. `List`
2. `UniqueKey`
3. `Method`
4. `Compare`

Q3. Which of the following is used in a Groovy expression to raise exceptions?

1. `adf.context`
2. `adf.error.raise`
3. `adf.object`
4. `adf.error.warn`
5. `adf.error`

Q4. The entity collection class is used to store metadata information of an entity object.

1. True
2. False

Q5. Which of the following files will hold the information about connections and configurations related to the application module?

1. `connection.xml`
2. `jps-config.xml`
3. `bc4j.xcfg`
4. `jazn-data.xml`
5. None of the above

Summary

Let us recap what we have learned in this chapter. We started with the information related to validations in ADF business components. Also, we learned to use all the built-in declarative validators available in ADF and saw how to use Groovy expression to validate business logic.

We now know how to generate Java classes for the business components and make use of the framework methods used to write complex business requirements. We learned to manage transactions using the application module and related configurations. Finally, we exposed business data as a service to the outside world from the view object and the application module.

In the next chapter, we will see how to expose the business data service to the view layer using data controls and how to bind the data as information to be displayed in the UI.

5
Binding the Data

Validation has been completed for our business components and we are now at the stage where we will expose the underlying business service to the outside world. The components involved in exposing the services to the view layer are simple with the help of ADF data control layer. The data control layer abstracts the implementation logic of business services and provides a common metadata interface to access the operation, data collection, and properties. Data control is based on service-oriented principles to decouple service integration from the view layer. In this way, the service and the user interfaces for the service are separated, and the implementation logic for the business service is abstracted.

In this chapter, we will learn about:

- ADF model layer
- Data control
- Binding the data
- Working together with the data control layer and binding
- Creating page definitions

ADF model layer

The ADF model layer is the architectural element that will allow the UI layer to interact with the data layer. The model layer is responsible for providing the key business services that are available in the view layer. The information is bound to the UI component with the help of the bindings defined in the page definition file. The `PageDef` file that is created for each ADF bound view holds the binding definition for the view's UI components to query data from the business service. The following screenshot explains the relationship between the UI page and the page definition file. Here we can see that the `Empno` column in the UI is mapped to the `Empno` attribute exposed from the `EmpVO1` entity through the **Data controls** pane. The table data displayed in the UI uses the collection model of the `EmpVO1` collection binding. `Collection Model` is the object that holds the collection of rows returned from the VO query in the row set. The binding will make use of the `EmpVO1Iterator` module in the executable section to iterate the data from the `EmpVO1` collection from the data control palette. The data control layer is populated using the data control layer usage information defined in the `DataBindings.cpx` file.

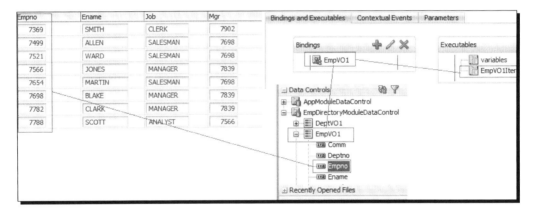

In our `EmpDirectoryApplication` application, we have dragged and dropped the `EmpVO1` instance from the **Data Controls** panel to the `index.jspx` page to display the data them the `EMP` table. The table component is tied up to the `EmpVOIterator` module of the page definition file to collect the data to display in the UI layer. The tree binding `EmpVO1` of the `indexPageDef.xml` file uses the `EmpVO1Iterator` executable to display the data exposed through the data control layer. In our previous chapter, we have exposed the `getHelloWorld()` operation from the `application` module to display the information in the UI page. There are other built-in operations, such as `commit` and `rollback` from the `application` module, that can be exposed through the data control layer using the ADF model bindings. These built-in operations are not exposed in the previous section of the screenshot.

Data Controls palette

The **Data Controls** palette is the component in the IDE that exposes the available `application` module as a data control layer within the application. In our `EmpDirectoryApplication` application, we have two application modules registered in the `Model.jpx` file as highlighted in the following screenshot:

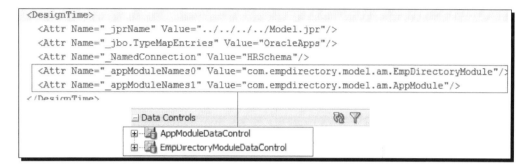

The **Data Controls** palette will have the components explained in the following section.

Data control

The available `application` module is displayed as a data control layer in the palette. The data control layer is a metadata definition that translates the API of the specific business service implementation to a generic format allowing declarative and consistent development. A user cannot drag-and-drop this component to the page because of the reason stated in the previous section.

The view object collection

The `view object` instance that is added to the `application` module is displayed as the `view object` collection in the **Data Controls** palette. All the available attributes in the `view object` collection are contained in the `view object` collection. The collection can be dragged and dropped on the page as a UI component that supports iteration. For example, the `carousel`, `tree`, and `table` components iterate through the collection model to display the rows in the UI. In the following screenshot, we can see that the `EmpDirectoryModuleControl` module is listing the `DeptVO1` and `EmpVO1` view object instances as a collection and source, respectively, to expose the underlying attributes:

Attributes

The attributes are displayed within the `view object` collection. The collection will hold all the attributes available for the `view object` collection. The attributes are dragged and dropped onto the page to display the information of the particular attribute.

Operations

Operations are the actions bounded within the `application` module or the `view object` collection. The exposed operations are mapped to an action component to invoke the action and execute the operation.

For the `application` module, we have the default operations defined. They are the `Commit` and `Rollback` operations.

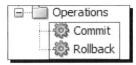

The operations available for the `view object` collection are as follows:

- ◆ `Create`: This operation is available to create a new record for the `table` component. The newly created record will not be inserted and is not displayed in the UI for a table component. For a form-based component, this method will create a new record and will display the information.

- ◆ `CreateInsert`: This operation will create a new record and will also insert a blank record if there is no default value assigned for the attributes of the record. The newly created row is displayed in the UI for the `table` component.

- ◆ `Create with parameters`: This method will allow the user to create a new record with some parameters, and the values passed as parameters will be predefined for the created row.

- ◆ `Delete`: This operation is used to delete the current row from the `view object` collection.

- ◆ `Execute`: This operation will execute and refresh the current collection.

- ◆ `Find`: To find a specific record in the collection object.

- **First**: This method sets the current row so that the first row is shown to the user.
- **Last**: This operation is used to set the last row of the `view object` collection as the current row.
- **Next**: This operation is used to refer to the next row in the collection as the current row.
- **Next Set**: This operation is used to move to the next set in the collection.
- **Previous**: This method is used to set the previous record as the current row.
- **Previous Set**: This method is used to move to the previous set in the `view object` collection.
- **removeRowWithKey**: The key value is provided for this operation to remove the row matching the corresponding key.
- **setCurrentRowWithKey**: The current row in the collection is set to the row matching the corresponding key passed using this operation.
- **setCurrentRowWithKeyValue**: This operation will set the row to the matching key value.

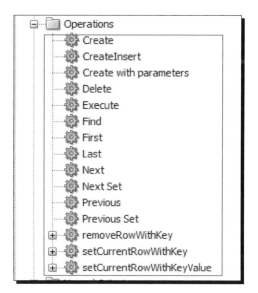

Methods

All the methods exposed in the `application` module or the view objects are displayed as a method element. Users can map the method to a button or a command link or any other action component to invoke the method.

Return

The `return` element will represent the value that is returned from the method displayed.

Parameters

The parameters for the operations are displayed in the **Parameters** section within the operations that expect a parameter to complete the action as shown in the following screenshot:

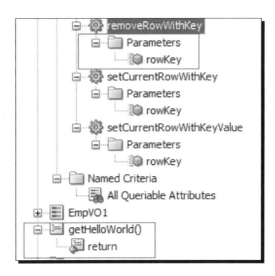

View criteria

For the `view object` collection, the queriable attributes are displayed within the **Named Criteria** section. The available view criteria are displayed in this section, and the user can use this section to create a query component to build a quick search component for the UI layer. The **All Queriable Attributes** element is present by default in the `view` instance collection (which will be displayed to query the attributes within the view object) of the **Data Controls** palette as shown in the following screenshot:

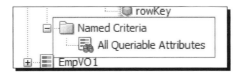

Time for action – adding a Commit button to the UI page

Now we will see how we can expose the built-in `Commit` operation to the UI using the data control layer:

1. In the **Data controls** palette, as shown in the following screenshot, navigate to **EmpDirectoryModuleDataControl**:

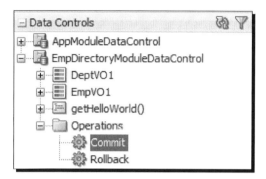

2. Under the **EmpDirectoryModuleDataControl** option, expand the **Operations** section and select the **Commit** operation as shown in the preceding screenshot.

3. Drag this operation to the `index.jspx` page in the **Source** view and place it just after the `</af:table>` tag.

4. Select the **ADF Button** option from the menu displayed. This action will create a **Commit** button to save the changes to the database.

5. The page definition for the `index.jspx` file is accessed by clicking on the **Bindings** section for the page.

What just happened?

In the previous action exercise, we created a `Commit` operation to save the changes made in the UI layer to the database layer. When we select the **ADF Button** option from the menu, a command button is created in the page with the `actionListener` property mapped to the `#{bindings.Commit.execute}` method. Action binding is used to bind the method exposed from the `application` module or the `view object` collection. The `Commit` operation is exposed in the `application` module as shown in the following code:

```
<af:commandButton actionListener="#{bindings.Commit.execute}"
text="Commit" disabled="#{!bindings.Commit.enabled}" id="cb1"/>
```

This is a reference to the action binding that is created in the `indexPageDef.xml` file. To verify this, go to the **Bindings** view and check whether the **Commit** action is added to the page definition file just below the `EmpVO1` instance in the **Bindings** section as shown in the following screenshot:

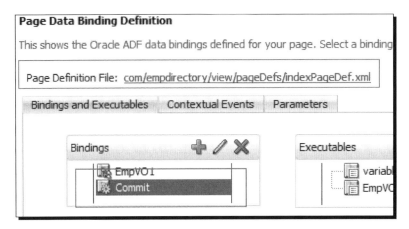

In the page definition file, we can see that the `Commit` action is mapped to the `commitTransaction` operation of `EmpDirectoryModuleDataControl` as shown in the following code:

```
<action id="Commit" RequiresUpdateModel="true"
Action="commitTransaction"
        DataControl="EmpDirectoryModuleDataControl"/>
```

Have a go hero – inserting the records

When you run the `index.jspx` page with the previous changes, you will see a button that is disabled. The button is disabled because we have set the `disabled` property to theEL expression, that is, `#{!bindings.Commit.enabled}`. This means the **Commit** button will be enabled only if there are any modified records available for the entity object.

Now your task is to add the `CreateInsert` operation from the `EmpVO1` instance so that we have an option to modify the record using the `CreateInsert` method available for the `view object` instance.

After adding the button, the page will allow you to create a new record for the `EMP` table, and we can save the changes to the database.

You will have the following screen when you add the `CreateInsert` operation as a button. A record is inserted and committed to the database. The inserted record is highlighted in the following screen:

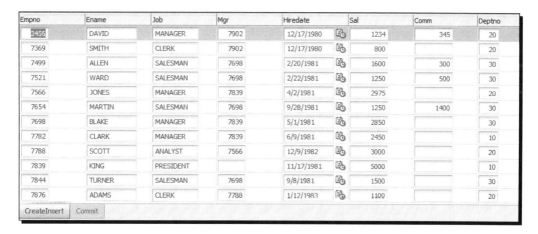

Empno	Ename	Job	Mgr	Hiredate		Sal	Comm	Deptno
9496	DAVID	MANAGER	7902	12/17/1980		1234	345	20
7369	SMITH	CLERK	7902	12/17/1980		800		20
7499	ALLEN	SALESMAN	7698	2/20/1981		1600	300	30
7521	WARD	SALESMAN	7698	2/22/1981		1250	500	30
7566	JONES	MANAGER	7839	4/2/1981		2975		20
7654	MARTIN	SALESMAN	7698	9/28/1981		1250	1400	30
7698	BLAKE	MANAGER	7839	5/1/1981		2850		30
7782	CLARK	MANAGER	7839	6/9/1981		2450		10
7788	SCOTT	ANALYST	7566	12/9/1982		3000		20
7839	KING	PRESIDENT		11/17/1981		5000		10
7844	TURNER	SALESMAN	7698	9/8/1981		1500		30
7876	ADAMS	CLERK	7788	1/12/1983		1100		20

CreateInsert   Commit

Working with the data control layer and binding

When we create a page for the first time, the page definition is not created for the page. The page definition file is created for the page only if the page contains any components bound to the data control layer using the bindings. For example, when we add a text component to display the `Empno` value from the `EMP` table, the page definition file, `indexPageDef.xml`, is created with the corresponding attribute bindings that map it to the underlying `Empno` attribute from the `EmpVO` view object. The page definition file will be created in the `adfmsrc` folder inside the `ViewController` project. For example, the `indexPageDef.xml` file will be created in `\ViewController\adfmsrc\com\empdirectory\view\pageDefs`.

> To go to any file location in the **Application Navigator** window, you just have to right-click on the source file and click on the **Select in Navigator** option on the menu that pops up.

Time for action – accessing the page definition file

We can use multiple means to access the page definition file from the page as follows:

1. Right-click on the `index.jspx` page that is created using the **Create JSF Page** wizard.

2. Select the **Go to Page Definition** option.

3. If you already have the bindings in the page, the easiest way to access the page definition is to select the **Bindings** tab for the page.

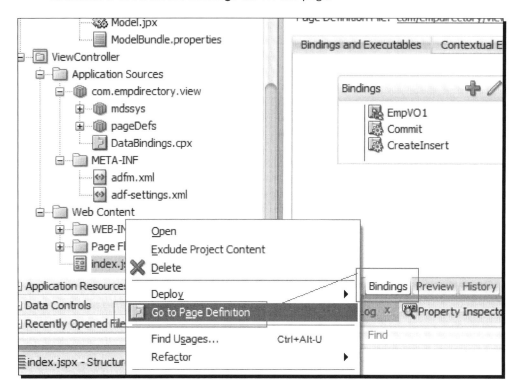

What just happened?

We just found the way to navigate to the page definition from the `.jspx` page. For the new file, the page definition file will not be created. The page definition is mandatory for any bindings that the UI component uses in the page.

Creating the bindings manually

As we know, bindings can be created in the page definition file by dragging and dropping the binding data onto the page from the data control layer. However, sometimes we have to create the bindings manually just to access the underlying data programmatically. In this case, the option available to the user is to create the bindings using the **Add** option in the bindings section, and selecting the **Generic Bindings** category in the **Insert Item** window.

The bindings items available for users are are as follows:

- ◆ `action`: The `action` item is used to bind the operations available from the ADF model layer. The **Data Controls** palette will expose the methods from the `view object` collection or the `application` module, which can be mapped to the `action` item in the page definitions. Some common actions are `Commit`, `Rollback`, `Create`, and so on. These items are used commonly in the `actionListener` property of the **ADF Button** component to execute the actions such as `#{bindings.Commit.execute}`. The **Data Collection** section will list the data controls to select the appropriate operation in the **Edit Action Binding** wizard as shown in the following screenshot:

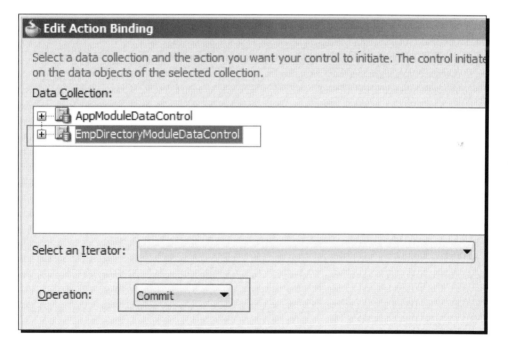

- **attributeValues**: The `attributeValues` item will map to the attributes of the `view object` collection. For example, the `Empno` attribute from the `EmpVO` object is added to the binding section as `attributeValues`. The data source and the attribute are selected in the **Create Attribute Binding** wizard as shown in the following screenshot:

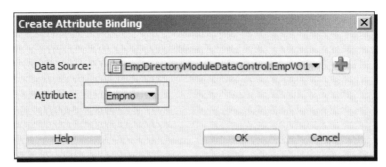

- **button**: The `button` control is there to control the bindings of the selected and the unselected state of the radio button. For example, if we want to map the selection of the radio button to `Yes` and the unselected state to `No`, we can use the button item for the binding.

- **eventBinding**: The `eventBinding` operation is used to control the event for the component. **Contextual events** use `eventBindings` to publish and subscribe to an event. Contextual events are used to communicate between regions using events. When using contextual events, we will use `eventBinding` to register the event. We will refer to the event registered programmatically to raise it, and the subscriber will look for the specific event raised and proceed with the process accordingly.

- **graph**: While using data visualization components, we will use the `graph` binding. Sometimes, to express the results and overview of the progress or performance analysis, we would like to display the result in graphical view. Graphical display will get information from different data sources for which we will use the `graph` binding. ADF data visualizations components are used to display graphical data in the UI. Some of the DVT components are displayed in the following screenshot:

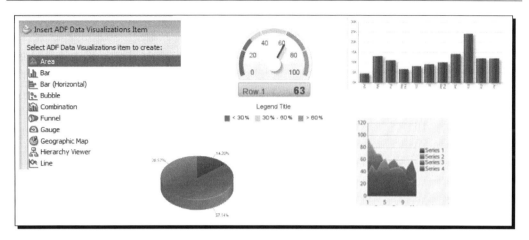

- ◆ `list`: The `list` binding will have the data sources listed in a list of values. The data for the "select one choice" component or "a list of values" component is bound to the list binding in the page definition. The bindings can be as simple as a record navigation or a multiple selection value list. The option for the list is selected from the **Select List Binding Type** wizard as shown in the following screenshot. A `list` binding is used to display a `selectOneChoice` component or any other list component except `inputComboboxListOfValues` in the UI.

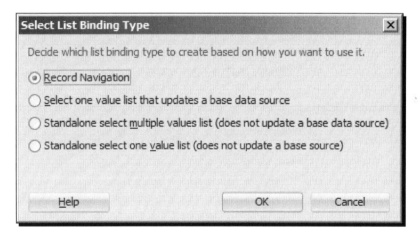

◆ listOfValues: The listOfValues binding is an extension of the list binding, which will display the list from the ADF model layer. The option for listing the values provided for the attribute in the model is displayed in the **List Binding** section to display a list of data sources for the list of values of UI components. The listOfValues binding is used to display inputComboboxlistofValues binding information displayed in the UI.

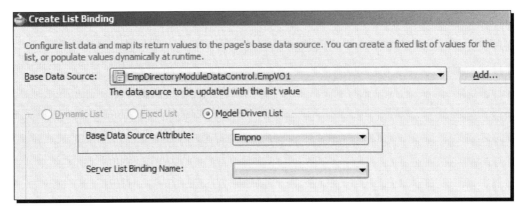

◆ methodAction: The methodAction binding will display the method that is exposed to the client as an interface in the view object or application modules. For example, the getHelloWorld() method in the application module is added as the methodAction binding.

◆ navigationList: The navigationList binding is another form of list binding that is used to traverse the records by specifying the attribute information as a list. For example, the Empno attribute selected for the navigationList list will list all the Empno attributes in the collection of rows within the view object collection.

◆ table: The table binding is used to process the range of rows within the view object binding. To process the range set to display a specific row of the table in a SelectOneChoice component is achieved using a table binding. This binding is for backward compatibility and should never be used.

◆ tree: The tree binding will be used to bind the view object collection in a tree structure displaying the view object rows in a hierarchy. The parent and the child elements will be defined, and the tree binding will take care of displaying the information in a tree node in the UI. The tree binding is useful for displaying the information in a table or a treeTable component in the UI.

◆ treeTable: The treeTable binding is similar to that of a table binding except that the treeTable has a tree structure with a parent-child relationship that is mapped like a tree binding. This binding is for backward compatibility and should never be used.

Time for action – creating page definition bindings

The following steps are used to create page definition bindings:

1. In the **Bindings** section, click on the + icon.

2. The **Insert Item** wizard opens and will list all the bindings options for the page definition file as shown in the following screenshot:

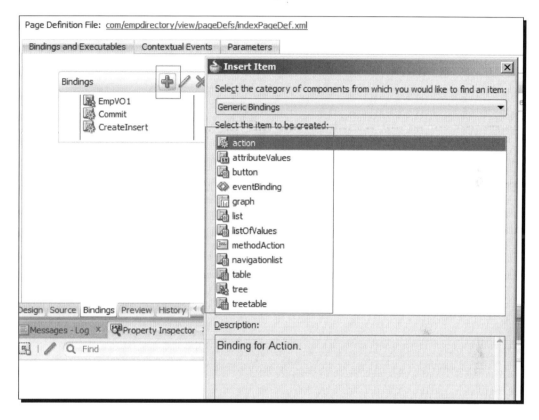

3. Click on the **action** item; this will open a **Binding for Action** palette.

4. Select the **EmpDirectoryModuleDataControl** option; this will populate the **Operation** section with the **Commit** operation.

5. Click on the **OK** button and binding creation is complete.

What just happened?

Using the action performed in the previous section, we learned how to create the bindings in the page definition file. The **Commit** action binding will be displayed in the binding container of the page definition file. In the **Create Action Binding** dialog, the operation is populated automatically because **Commit** and **Rollback** are the options available by default in **EmpDirectoryModuleDataControl**.

Adding executables

Just like creating the bindings for the component, we can add the executable for the page definition by clicking on the **Add** button in the **Executables** section of the page definition file as shown in the following screenshot:

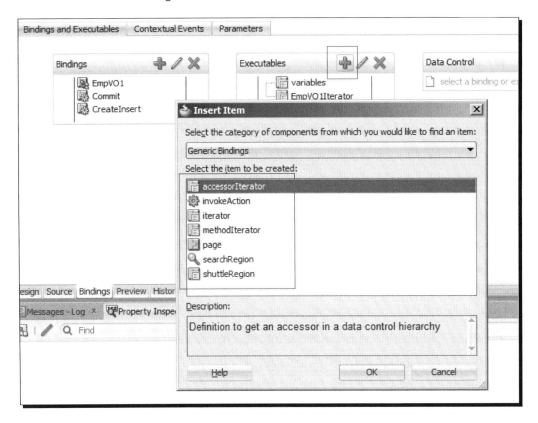

Some of the items in the **Executables** section are as follows:

accessorIterator

`acessorIterator` is used to iterate the **Accessor** hierarchy from the data control layer. The `CacheResults` property will manage the collection between requests. `ChangeEventPolicy` will control the behavior of the `refresh` action. The options available are as follows:

- ◆ `none`: The iterator is refreshed based on the refresh condition provided.

- ◆ `push`: Asynchronous data changes will automatically be refreshed.

- ◆ `ppr`: `ppr` is a partial page rendering, which will refresh only some part of the page. The setting will help the iterator to be refreshed if the current row of the iterator is changed and the `ppr` action occurs.

invokeAction

We create this executable to invoke an action on a specific condition. For example, If we want to invoke the `Commit` action on a condition and on a page load, we will map the `invokeAction` item to the `Commit` operation binding and then move the `invokeAction` item to the top as the first executable in the list of executables in the page definition. The `invokeAction` item provides a `Refresh` property, which will allow the `accessor` method based on the option provided. The options available are as follows:

- ◆ `always`: This option refreshes the executable always.

- ◆ `deferred`: If the refresh is based on another executable, this option refreshes the executable accordingly.

- ◆ `ifNeeded`: The refresh is taken care of whenever needed by the framework. This is the default for executables.

- ◆ `never`: Never refreshes the executable.

- ◆ `prepareModel`: Refreshes every time the binding is prepared.

- ◆ `prepareModelIfNeeded`: Only refreshes if needed and/or if the page binding container is prepared.

- ◆ `refreshAfter`: Sets the dependent executable to execute the current executable after the one mentioned.

- ◆ `renderModel`: Refreshes the executable when the page is rendered.

- ◆ `renderModeIfNeeded`: Refreshes the executable only if it is needed by the framework when the page is rendered.

The `RefreshCondition` item will hold the condition on which the refresh is to happen. `RefreshAfter` will hold the condition after which the executable is refreshed.

iterator

The `iterator` item simply references a collection to traverse the records. We can have the refresh condition and parameters set to change the behavior of the `iterator` item. `Iterator` also has properties such as `Refresh`, `RefreshCondition`, and `cacheResults`. The `RangeSize` property for the `Iterator` item will represent the number of rows displayed in the `Iterator` collection.

page

We can have a nested page definition specified within another page definition as a container using this executable. This is primarily used to ensure that bindings of a template are referenced at runtime.

searchRegion

The `searchRegion` item is an executable for querying the data using view criteria. The query component will make use of the `searchRegion` executable to query information from the database through the view criteria from the model layer.

shuttleRegion

The `shuttleRegion` executable is useful for the `shuttle` component to display the `shuttle` elements. The available and the selected list of elements is maintained within the `shuttleRegion` executable.

Pop quiz

Q1. Changes in the _____ file will display the information in the **Data Controls** palette.

1. `bc4j.xcfg`
2. `.jspx`
3. `.jpx`

Q2. Which of the following is not an executable in the page definition?

1. `Iterator`
2. `SearchRegion`
3. `invokeAction`
4. `tree`

Q3. We can navigate to the page definition of a file from the `.jspx` page.

1. True
2. False

Summary

Let us recap what we have learned in this chapter. We have learned how to expose the service from the ADF model layer. We have also seen how the data control layer is displayed and how to map the service from the data control layer to the UI components. Finally, we have seen how to bind the data using the page definition file. In the next chapter, we will see how to display the data in the UI layer.

6
Displaying the Data

So far, we have the model data exposed to the UI layer and we have seen that the data control is essential in exposing the services. In the real world, the data comes from different sources and is presented in a way that suits the business and simplifies the view layer for the user. For example, a web application for a banking site requires a layout which is appropriate for the user to access the accounts information easily. A dashboard layout with graphs, gauges, and gantt charts are inviting for the user to see an overview of account performance. Some common user layouts are followed in the web application to attract customers and to enhance the user experience. ADF Rich Faces includes more than 150 components to display the information in a user-preferred way. Added to this, the data visualization component's support in ADF will help the user to analyze the data in a graphical way.

In this chapter, we will learn:

- ◆ Creating a page
- ◆ Laying out the page display
- ◆ Adding the UI components
- ◆ Running the page with model data

Creating a page

To display the content of the model layer, we will have to create the page that holds the model layer information bound using the page definition file. We can create a page without the page definition to bind the data to the model layer by just adding static content to the page. We can include the layout information and design the page that will suit the web application context.

`EmpDirectoryApplication` has the `index.jspx` page to display the `EMP` table information. As the `index.jspx` page is the landing page for our web application, we will move the employee information to a separate page named `employee.jspx`. In this way, we have our information separated from the landing page. Categorizing the content of the page is important in creating a web-based application. We will have a layout designed for our `index.jspx` page. The page creation for the `DEPT` table is similar to that of the `EMP` table. We will have the department information displayed in the `dept.jspx` page. Therefore, we will be creating two pages in this section.

Knowing the page template

It is always good to have a standard look and feel for our web application throughout the website. ADF uses the concept of page templates to provide a common layout that defines a uniform look and feel for the application which helps display the content of the page in a more efficient way to the user. For example, the common layout for many of the websites today includes a global menu at the top, navigation menu stacked on the left-hand side of the page along with the content displayed at the center of the page. There are some built-in page templates that come in handy when creating a page. They are **Oracle three column layout** and **Oracle dynamic tabs shell** template. These are the default templates provided by ADF to start with basic web page creation.

Oracle Three Column Layout

This template is used to display three sections in the page and gives room for the user to add contents by providing facets. The layout information uses the `af:pageTemplate` tag with facets defined inside it, as follows:

```
<af:pageTemplate viewId="/oracle/templates/threeColumnTemplate.jspx"
id="pt1">
                    <f:facet name="center"/>
                    <f:facet name="header"/>
                    <f:facet name="end"/>
                    <f:facet name="start"/>
                    <f:facet name="branding"/>
```

```
            <f:facet name="copyright"/>
            <f:facet name="status"/>
        </af:pageTemplate>
```

The facets included are:

♦ `start`: Content added will be displayed to the left-hand side of the page. This section is mostly used to display navigation links. The size of this column can be adjusted using `startColumnSize` in the `af:pageTemplate` tag.

♦ `center`: Most of the web content goes in this section.

♦ `end`: The **Help** section and other useful links are usually displayed here. The size can be adjusted using `endColumnSize`.

♦ `header`: This section will display the title of the page in the top header.

♦ `branding`: This facet is used for backward compatibility.

♦ `copyright`: The facet is used to display the copyright information in the bottom-right corner.

♦ `status`: This section is used to indicate the status of the page upon requests. This is displayed in the top-right corner next to the `af:statusIndicator` component.

Oracle dynamic tabs shell

This template supports displaying multiple pages in a tab that is dynamically generated at runtime when the user clicks on the link from the **Navigation** section. Some additional facets included are `about`, `navigation`, `globallinks`, `globalToolbar`, `globalSearch`, `globalTabs`, `welcome`, and `innerToolbar`. Following is the code in Oracle dynamics tab shell template:

```
<af:pageTemplate value="#{bindings.ptb1}" id="pt1" viewId="/oracle/ui/
pattern/dynamicShell/dynamicTabShell.jspx">
            <f:facet name="copyright"/>
            <f:facet name="about"/>
            <f:facet name="navigation"/>
            <f:facet name="globalLinks"/>
            <f:facet name="status"/>
            <f:facet name="globalToolbar"/>
            <f:facet name="globalSearch"/>
            <f:facet name="globalTabs"/>
            <f:facet name="welcome"/>
            <f:facet name="innerToolbar"/>
        </af:pageTemplate>
```

You can see that the `af:pageTemplate` tag has a binding defined. The reference will be found in the page definition file of the page which uses the following template:

```
<page path="oracle.ui.pattern.dynamicShell.
model.dynamicTabShellDefinition" id="ptb1"
Refresh="ifNeeded"/>
```

This definition will help the page to create dynamic tabs and you can create a maximum of 15 tabs.

Time for action – creating the page template

For `EmpDirectoryApplication`, we can create a template of our own to have a standard look and feel throughout the application:

1. Right-click on the **Web Content** section of the `viewController` project. This will open **New Gallery**.

2. Navigate to the **JSF/Facelets** section under the **Web Tier** section and select the **ADF Page Template** option from the items. You will be using the same steps to create a page by selecting the **Page** option.

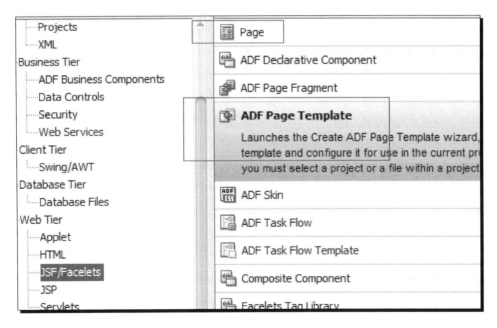

3. Provide the filename as `WebPageTemplate.jspx` and locate the directory for the template in the **Create ADF Page Template** window. The page template name is autopopulated. The document type **Facelets** will have the extension `.jsf` and `JSP XML` will have the extension `.jspx`.

4. Select the **Use a Quick Start Layout** option to browse through the various layouts. Click on the **Browse** button and select the **Three Column** option in the **Categories** section.

5. Select the second item from the **Types** section and select the third option from the **Layouts** section. Select the **Apply Themes** option and click on the **OK** button.

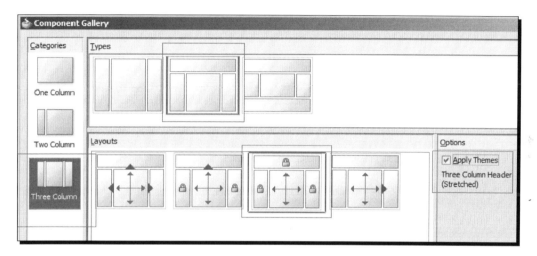

6. Select the **Create Associated ADFm Page Definition** option as shown in the following screenshot to create the page template binding for the template.

7. The **Facet Definitions**, **Attributes** values for the templates can be added to affect the behavior of the template during runtime. The **Add** button is used to create the facets and attributes.

8. A facet is a placeholder which will hold the content of a particular section of the page. An attribute will help you to configure the facet or the page template dynamically at runtime when the template is used in the page. Now, add facets called `content` and `navigation`.

9. Click on the **OK** button to create the page template for the application.

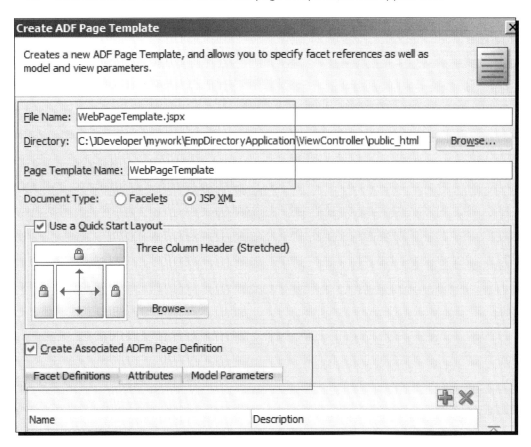

What just happened?

Now we have the `WebPageTemplate.jspx` file created which will have the standard look and feel throughout the web page. The template will have a stretchable container within which we will include the page content. The component for stretching the content is usually a `panelStretchLayout` component. The component includes two facets to include the content in the `top` and `center` portions of the page. The template is designed in such a way that there is another stretchable container within the `center` facet of the `decorativeBox` component to divide the content again into `start`, `center`, and `end` facets.

```
<af:pageTemplateDef var="attrs" definition="private">
    <af:xmlContent>
        <component xmlns="http://xmlns.oracle.com/adf/faces/rich/component">
            <display-name>WebPageTemplate</display-name>
            <facet><facet-name>content</facet-name></facet>
            <facet><facet-name>navigation</facet-name></facet>
        </component>
    </af:xmlContent>
    <af:panelStretchLayout startWidth="100px" endWidth="100px" id="pt_psl1">
        <f:facet name="center">
            <af:decorativeBox theme="dark" id="pt_db3">
                <f:facet name="center">
                    <af:decorativeBox theme="medium" id="pt_db2">
                        <f:facet name="center">
                            <af:panelStretchLayout topHeight="50" startWidth="100px" end
                                <f:facet name="start">
                                    <af:facetRef facetName="navigation"/>
                                </f:facet>
                                <f:facet name="center">
                                    <af:decorativeBox theme="default" id="pt_db1">
                                        <f:facet name="center">
                                            <af:facetRef facetName="content"/>
                                        </f:facet>
```

When the page template is added to the application with the page definition file, the `Databindings.cpx` file is updated with the page definition information. This happens whenever a page definition is assigned to the page. The `pagetemplate-metadata.xml` file will also add the entry of the newly-created template into it.

Have a go hero – adding attributes to the template

While creating the page template, we were asked to add the facets and attributes for the page template.

Now you will add the attributes yourself for a new template to identify the differences as shown in the following list. Remember that this can be added from the **Create** wizard.

1. Add the `height` attribute in the code inside the component section:

```
<attribute>
    <attribute-name>height</attribute-name>
    <attribute-class>java.lang.String</attribute-class>
    <default-value>100</default-value>
</attribute>
```

2. Now go to the `af:declarativeBox` tag with ID as `pt_db1` and add the expression `#{attrs.height}` for the `topHeight` property. This will make sure that the `height` property for `pageTemplate` will map to the `topHeight` property of the `decorativeBox` tag internally. Perform the following in `decorativeBox`:

    1. Observe the page definition file for the template and the changes that are added to the `Databindings.cpx` file.

    2. Observe the changes that are added to the `pagetemplate-metadata.xml` file.

    3. Add a new facet named `header` inside the top facet of the innermost decorative box. You will have to choose the facet definition from the ADF component list and after adding the facet you will have `<af:facetRef facetName="header"/>`.

Creating the page with the template

Let us see how we create a page with the page template and design the layout for our web application. Our task involves creating the `employee.jspx` and `dept.jspx` pages and adding the model layer content to it to display the employee and department information. We will also remove the content of the `index.jspx` page and will add a layout and some static information to welcome the user.

Time for action – creating the dept.jspx file

1. Right-click on the **Web Content** section of the `viewController` project. This will display the **New Gallery** window.

2. Navigate to the **JSF/Facelets** section under the **Web Tier** section and select the **Page** option from the items.

3. Provide the name as `dept.jspx`, and the location for the page can be located in the **Directory** section.

4. Select **Document Type** as the **JSP XML** file to have the extension `.jspx`, facelets will have the extension `.jsf`.

5. Select **WebPageTemplate** that we created in the **Page Layout** section by selecting the **Page Template** option.

6. Managed beans can be added to the page in the **Managed Bean** section. Right now, we will have one backing bean associated with the page. Select the **Automatically Expose UI components in a New Managed Bean** option only if you have a strong reason to bind each of the UI components to the bean, otherwise we do not need to select this option now. Usage of a backing bean rather than a managed bean is applicable if you are creating your own declarative component which is out of the scope of this book.

7. Click on **OK** to create the page.

What just happened?

Now we have our page created which uses the page template for a common look layout. If you have opted to create the backing bean, the Dept.java file will be created for the dept.jspx file. The Java class will have all the bindings for the UI components added to the dept.jspx page. The dept.jspx page currently has af:document and af:form as the UI components in the page. Each of these components will have the binding attribute added to it which will have a binding to the corresponding value in the backing bean. For example, af:form will have the binding as #{backingBeanScope.backing_dept.f1} which means that the form component is bounded to the f1 attribute in the Dept.java file. backingBeanScope is the scope that is very specific for the backing bean. The lifetime of the object in backingBeanScope is within the scope of the backing bean. There are several scopes, but at this time you don't need to worry about them. If you look closely in the Dept bean, you will have the references added to the backing bean.

The getter and the setter for the f1 reference are used to get and set the binding for the form element in the page. This is useful if we have to give reference to the form element in our code at runtime. Also, note that the component reference in bean is of type RichForm and the reference for the document element d1 is of type RichDocument. Each of the UI components will have their own class type API in Java.

The scope of the backing bean can be backingBeanScope, sessionScope, viewScope, pageFlowScope, and applicationScope, and is defined in the **Managed Bean** section of the adfc-config.xml file.

The following statement as the last entry is responsible for updating the backing bean whenever a new component is added or removed from the page:

```
<!--oracle-jdev-comment:auto-binding-backing-bean-
name:backing_dept-->
```

The page template entry in the page will have the binding reference in the `deptPageDef.xml` file and the page definition will also have an entry in the `Databindings.cpx` file.

Have a go hero

The steps for creating `employee.jspx` are similar to that of creating a `dept.jspx` page. Creating the `employee.jspx` page is left for the user as an exercise.

Layout the page display

We have a template and a page now for our web application. The next step is to layout the page so that the information is presentable for the user. Now we will have to add the content of `DeptVO` from the data control and add it to the `dept.jspx` page. We will add model layer content from the data control to the page by dragging-and-dropping the **view object** instance as explained in the previous chapter. Once the content is added to the content facet of the page, it looks like the one shown in the following screenshot:

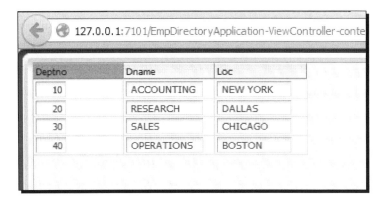

You can see the difference between the `index.jspx` page and the `dept.jspx` in the following screenshot as the new page has a blue border and the content is stretched completely. This is because the `dept.jspx` page is based on the page template and the `index.jspx` page does not have the page template defined for it.

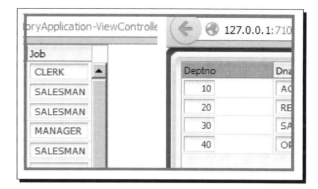

Our next step is to create the layout which contains a navigation menu to the left-hand side of the page and the content will be displayed at the center of the page.

Time for action – creating the layout for the page

1. We will add a link in the `navigation` facet which will display horizontal links. For this, we will add the `af:panelGroupLayout` component to the page with the layout as `vertical`. This can be configured in the property inspector.

2. Most of the time, the components are added to the page using the **Structure** window by right-clicking on the container icon or the section of the page and inserting the component. You may also use the **Component** palette to drag-and-drop the component directly onto the page.

3. Now add two links to the page and change their name to `Employee information` and `Directory information`. These are the text messages that will be displayed for the links.

4. You may notice that for each component added to the page, the backing bean is updated with the references to bind the component reference to the bean. You will have to run the page each time to see the changes you have made.

What just happened?

The previous task was to explain how the page is designed in ADF. Creating the bean with all the components referenced is usually not recommended. The most commonly used layout components are `af:panelGroupLayout` and the other one is `af:panelStretchLayout`. The `panelGroupLayout` component will have the layout attribute to display content horizontally and vertically. It looks good to have the navigation menu displayed in a vertical fashion than in a horizontal structure so we have used the vertical layout for the links.

At runtime, the page is displayed as follows:

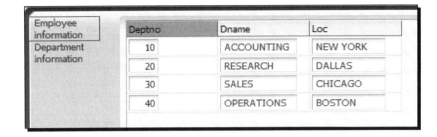

`PanelStretchLayout` is mostly used to stretch the container to the maximum width of the screen. For this reason, we will have the `panelStretchLayout` component added to `pageTemplate` as a container so that the component which is added inside the container will always be stretched when displayed on the screen. Some changes to the page are readily visible at design time.

In 11*g*R2 there is another component called `af:panelGridLayout`, which is used to display a grid layout using one or more `af:gridRow` components. This component will have the `height` and margin defined to align with the grid. Each `af:gridRow` will have one or more `af:gridCell` components with `width` and `margin` defined.

Knowing the UI components

Now it is time for us to think about the UI components that can be added to the web page. To design the web page efficiently in ADF Faces, it is better to know the basics of the UI components available for the framework. ADF Faces consist of more than 150 rich components available for developing rich Internet applications. ADF Faces consist of different components for different purposes. The components are classified based on their behavior and type. For example, some of the component types are `input`, `output`, `layout`, `query`, `popup`, `list of values`, `navigation`, `menu`, `table`, and so on .

Most of the ADF Faces components have some common properties to define the tag elements. The properties are changed using the property inspector available from the **View** menu.

- `id`: The ID to uniquely identify the component in the page.
- `binding`: The reference of the component is added to the backing bean for processing the component in a programmatic way.
- `rendered`: Setting this value to `true` will render the component in the page and this property can be evaluated from the value in the backing bean.

- `visible`: The component is actually available and rendered in the page but can be hidden or displayed to the user with this property.

- `inlineStyle`: The CSS styling is added to this property to change the visual appearance of the component.

- `styleClass`: This property takes the name of the CSS style block defined on the page or from an external CSS file.

- `partialTriggers`: The ID for the triggering components are added to this property to trigger a partial refresh. The component to be refreshed will listen to the corresponding triggering components ID listed and then will trigger an update event.

- `partialSubmit`: This property will be used for a navigation component to partially submit the form in a page for a refresh. This is used in combination with partial refresh.

- `autoSubmit`: When you leave the component whose `autoSubmit` value is `true`, the component sends a notification to other components that are registered to refresh themselves based on the ID provided in the `partialTriggers` property.

- `immediate`: This property will skip `All Validations` phase in the lifecycle and render the page for the `af:commandButton` component. Setting this property for the `af:inputText` component will process and validate the data immediately in the `Apply Request Values` phase. Topics related to ADF phases and lifecycle are explained in the *Chapter 7, Working With Navigation Flows*.

Input components

Input components are the ones used to get the input from the user. The input can be anything such as text, number, color, date, and file. Some of the common input components are explained in the following section.

af:form

`af:form` creates the HTML `<form>` element. This tag is used to pass the data in the page to the server for processing. Some important attributes which are commonly used when compared to other available attributes are `defaultCommand`, `targetFrame`, and `usesUpload`. These are explained as follows:

- `defaultCommand`: This property is used to provide a default action for the form. For example, if the form contains a **Submit** and a **Cancel** button. Providing the ID of the **Submit** button will invoke the **Submit** button as default.

- **targetFrame**: This will define how the new frame will be displayed. The options are _self, _blank, _top, and _parent.
- **usesUpload**: This will be `true` if the form allows uploading the file to the server.

af:inputText

To create an input field in the browser, the `af:inputText` component is used. The behavior of this component is the same as any other input field component. The important properties are:

- **value**: It holds the value for the component.
- **rows**: Number of rows the component will display to support multiline entry.
- **readOnly**: It makes the content not editable.
- **label**: This provides the label for the component.
- **autoComplete**: Setting this property will remember the previous entered values in the form.
- **wrap**: It helps to wrap the text displayed in the `text` component.
- **Secret**: This property will make the component behave like a password field.
- **Required**: This makes a field mandatory in the form. This form cannot be submitted without providing a value in the field.
- **maximumLength**: It sets the maximum length for the field.
- **contentStyle**: This property holds the CSS style property for the content of the field.
- **columns**: It defines the length of the characters to be displayed in the field.

af:inputDate

To input the date, we use the `af:inputDate` component. The `af:inputDate` component will display a calendar to easily select the date by selecting the year, month, and the day of the month. This component is used to enter the time as well:

af:inputFile

To upload a file we will use the af:inputFile component. The file is located using the **Browse** button and the file is uploaded to the server. The upload file configurations are done in the wcb.xml file.

af:selectOneChoice

The list of options that have to be selected by the user is displayed in the af:selectOneChoice component. The user can select a single item from the list of items of the components. The component may contain the <f:selectItems> element or the <af:selectItem> element.

af:selectOneRadio

A single option is selected from the items defined as a series of radio buttons. The components will help to select a single item at a time.

af:selectBooleanCheckbox

The af:selectBooleanCheckbox component is like an HTML checkbox component, which has selected and unselected states. The selected state is set to true and the unselected state corresponds to false.

Output components

The output components are used to display the content of the page. The components are widely used to display a read-only content in the page or a popup.

af:outputText

af:outputText is used to display the text in the page. The component supports styles and the escaped text.

af:message

To display a message inside a popup we use the af:message component. To display global messages for the page, we use the af:messages component with the globalOnly attribute set to true. The af:message type can be configured as fatal, info, error, warning, and confirmation. The for attribute will identify the component for which the message has to be shown. The message attribute will hold the message that is displayed to the user.

Showing the message programmatically

ADF allows you to programmatically show a message. ADF uses the JSF messaging API to display the messages. FacesMessage is added to the FacesContext object by adding the message using the addMessage(String clientId, FacesMessage message) method.

Use the following snippet to show the af:message component globally. If we pass a client of the component, the message will be shown for the component.

```
String messageString="Info Message";
FacesMessage fm = new FacesMessage(messageString);
fm.setSeverity(FacesMessage.SEVERITY_INFO);
FacesContext context = FacesContext.getCurrentInstance();
context.addMessage(null, fm);
//to show for the component use this code
context.addMessage(getInputComponent().getClientId(context),
fm); // getInputComponent is the binding for the component
that you would like to show the message.
```

af:outputFormatted

The af:outputFormatted component is just like the af:outputText component but supports the HTML mark-ups and formatted results.

Layout components

Layout components are mainly used to arrange the content of the page in a standard way so that the view of the content is presentable and fits perfectly for the user. The layout components sometime act as a container to hold the elements collectively or separately to utilize the space in the page uniformly.

af:panelGroupLayout

The af:panelGroupLayout component is used as a container which will hold other components in a horizontal or vertical fashion. The items inside the group layout are separated by the space defined in the separator and the Layout property will have horizontal, vertical, and scroll options to arrange the child components.

af:panelStretchLayout

This component will stretch the components inside it. The component will act as a container to stretch its children with options to place the components in the start, center, end, top, and bottom facets.

af:panelGridLayout

This layout is to show the grid structure. It uses one or more af:gridRow components which hold one or more af:gridCell components.

af:panelFormLayout

This component will display the content more or less as a form layout. The label and the fields are displayed side by side and the columns of the layout are configured using the columns property. This container has the fieldWidth and labelWidth properties to change the field attributes based on the user's needs.

af:panelHeader

The af:panelHeader component will display a header panel with an option icon at the top of the section. The supported facets for the panelHeader component are info, help, context, legend, menuBar, and toolbar.

Query components

To query the backend with the criteria, the ADF query component is used. The view criteria for view object is dragged-and-dropped on to the page to create a query component. QueryEvent is fired when the user clicks on the **Search** button.

af:query

The component will help to perform the query for a particular record in the table by providing the search criteria. A search panel will hold the filters for the query. af:query contains the resultComponentId property to specify the ID of the component in which the result of the query will be displayed. The result component must be a table component.

Popup components

To display information or a warning to the user, we use the `popup` component.

af:popup

The `popup` component is used to display a menu or a message to the user which is hidden and is displayed on a specific event. For example, to display a message in a popup using the **Context** menu.

af:dialog

The `dialog` component is enclosed within a `popup` component to show a message or a warning to the user. This will be an invisible layer in the page that is activated on an event. The `dialog` component more or less looks like a window with buttons and icons as shown in the following screenshot:

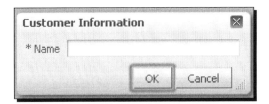

Time for action – showing a popup to the user

Now we will see how to create a popup from scratch in ADF:

1. Go to the `index.jspx` page and then select the **Command** button that holds the `commit` operation from the **Structure** window.

2. Right-click on the **Command** button and select the **Insert inside the af:commandButton –Commit** option and the select the **Adf Faces** option.

3. Click on the **Show Popup Behavior** option in the **Insert ADF Faces Item** window:

4. Now a af:showPopupBehavior component is added to the commit operation. Now add triggerType as action, which is the event that should invoke the popup. The id value of the **Command** button cb1 is provided for the alignId component, that is, the popup relative to the **Command** button. The align property is set to beforeStart to align the popup next to the af:commandButton component.

5. Now we will create an af:popup component and add an af:dialog component to it. Add a message saying Do you really want to commit the data? inside the af:dialog component.

6. Provide the ID of the popup p1 to the popupId property of the af:showPopupBehavior component. Now the dialog will be shown to the user whenever the **Commit** button is clicked on in the UI.

What just happened?

We have created a confirmation popup for the user to confirm if the **Commit** button is clicked on by the user. So every time the **Commit** button is clicked, the popup will be shown to the user. The dialog will have a Type property, which will allow the user to select the buttons that will be shown to the user inside the dialog box. The default buttons are **Ok** and **Cancel**. Here the user input is important which means clicking on the **OK** button in the dialog should commit the record. Clicking on the **Cancel** button should not commit the record.

To implement the previous scenario we would have to:

◆ Remove the commit operation from the **Command** button, which is added to the actionListener property.

◆ af:dialog has a property called dialogListener, which will help to determine the user selection by getting the dialog outcome from the dialogEvent component in the managed bean, as shown in the following code:

```
public void dilaogListener(DialogEvent dialogEvent) {
    String outcome = dialogEvent.getOutcome().toString();
    if(outcome.equals(DialogEvent.Outcome.ok)){
        //ok logic
    }
    else{
        //cancel
    }
}
```

◆ The ok logic should commit the data by calling the commit operation.

List of values components

The list of values is the list of items which are populated from the model data. The data source for the list is fetched at runtime and is displayed to the user in a list.

af:inputComboboxListOfValues

The combobox feature is included in the af:inputcomboboxListofValues component with which the user can select or search an item from the list displayed from a data source.

Navigation components

To navigate from one page to another we will use the navigation component. ActionEvent is raised when the **Component** button is clicked on. When the **Component** button is clicked, the client event is raised at the client side.

af:commandbutton

af:commandbutton corresponds to an HTML input type button element. Navigation occurs when the user clicks on the button.

af:commandLink

`af:commandlink` is more or less similar to a command button but instead of a button the link is used.

Menu components

Menu components are used to select features from an option when the user clicks on it. The **Menu** popup opens for the users to choose the submenu items. The submenu may or may not have a child menu.

af:menu

The menu is displayed using the `menu` component. The menu is displayed in a vertical popup container, which will hold a submenu, which will invoke an action upon clicking on it. The menu is displayed in a vertical popup as shown in the following screenshot:

Table components

The table components are used to display the content of the data source. The data source is defined in the page definition file as a binding and the component will display the data in columns.

af:table

The `af:table` component will display information from the binding using the `collectionModel` component of the table data source. The component consists of rows and columns and each row is represented using the `#{row}` variable.

af:treeTable

The `af:treeTable` component is similar to the `table` component but differs with a hierarchical information display as a tree. The parent row is always collapsed and each of the nodes is displayed by collapsing the node, as shown in the following screenshot:

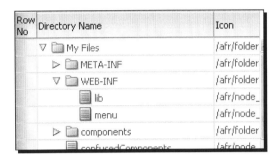

Miscellaneous components

Some components in ADF are used to support other components which involve rendering other components conditionally or looping through the components.

af:forEach

This component is used to display components in iteration. The `varStatus` property of the tag will expose the status during iteration. This component does not contain an `id` attribute The properties includes:

- ◆ `items`: It gives the collection or list for iteration.
- ◆ `begin`: It gives the index at which the loop begins.
- ◆ `end`: It is the index at which the loop ends.
- ◆ `step`: This is the number to increment on each iteration.
- ◆ `var`: It gives the name of the variable available inside the loop.
- ◆ `varStatus`: It gives the loop status available on iteration. This can have variables such as `index`, `count`, `step`, `first`, `last`, `begin`, and `end`.

af:iterator

`af:iterator` will use the `collectionModel` component to iterate through the content just like the `table` component. The rows processed by the `af:iterator` component are adjusted using the `rows` property. For example, the user might want to display some text next to the `Ename` attribute of each row of the `EmpVO1` collection in an output component. Here, `af:iterator` can use `EmpVO1 collectionModel` as a `value` to iterate to get the individual row and append the desired message.

af:switcher

The ternary operator with the `if` and `else` condition is satisfied by the `af:switcher` component. This component uses the facets to display information based on some condition. The `defaultFacet` and `facetName` components can have the expression to toggle the facets.

Data visualization components

These are sets of components which are used to visualize the information from the data source. Some components of this type are `dvt:gauge`, `dvt:graph`, `dvt:area`, `dvt:pvotTable`, and so on.

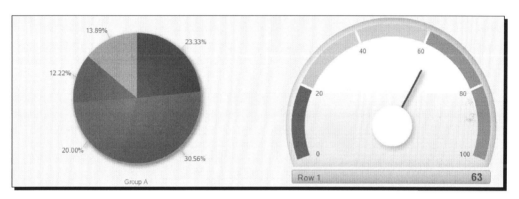

Other tags

There are other tags in ADF which are used to support other components. Adding these tags to the components will modify how the component behaves. Some tags will add extra features to the component to which it is added:

- **Behavior**: It adds a special behavior to the component. For example, the `af:autoSuggestBehavior` tag added to the `af:inputText` component will display an autosuggestion on typing the text in the input field.

- **Converter**: It adds the `converter` tag to the input or output component and will convert the data displayed to the user. For example, a number displayed in an input field will be displayed in groups and decimals can be achieved using these tags.

- **Listener**: These tags will add a listener to the component to listen for special events. Adding a `af:setActionListener` component to `af:commandButton` will set the value when the `action` event fires for the **Command** button.

- **Validator**: These tags are added to validate the information displayed in the component. These are the UI validators which are different from the declarative validators available from the ADF business components.

- **Drag and drop**: These tags are added to the container component to support drag-and-drop capabilities.

Only the important and most commonly used components and tags are explained in the previous list.

You can visit the following URL to get a better understanding about the ADF components. The ADF demo site is also added for reference:

- `http://jdevadf.oracle.com/adf-richclient-demo/docs/enhanced-tagdoc.html`

- `http://jdevadf.oracle.com/adf-richclient-demo/faces/index.jspx`

- `http://docs.oracle.com/cd/E24382_01/apirefs.1112/e17490/toc.htm`

Have a go hero – working with the components

You can now learn about some components and their usage to get some practice by yourself:

1. Analyze all the components explained previously and check how they behave at runtime. Try out all the components in each of the type and familiarize yourself with them.

2. Note down the component's properties and see how it differs from the properties of other components.

3. Add a welcome message and use the page template to the `index.jspx` page. Display some information in the `index.jspx` page using the components that we have learned.

4. Add the employee information to the `employee.jspx` page and lay out the page properly with the components that you have learned.

EL expression

Almost all the properties in the ADF Faces components will accept values in an expression language commonly called the EL expression. The value is evaluated at runtime and the output is dynamically assigned for the property. EL expression usage in ADF will extend the dynamic capabilities of ADF to another level.

Let us now add an EL expression to the page that we have created. Here we are going to use the `af:switcher` component to display two sections in the `employee.jspx` page. One is to display content that displays the employee information. The other facet will display the department information.

Time for action – adding an EL expression

1. Add the `af:switcher` component to the page from the **Component** palette.

2. Select the `switcher` component in the page from the **Structure** window or from the `design` view.

3. From the **Structure** window right-click on the `af:switcher` component and then select **Insert** into the option to insert a facet.

4. Provide the `facet` name as `first`. Repeat the same step to add another facet named `second`.

5. In the property inspector, provide the value as `first` for the `defaultFacet` property.

6. Inside the first facet, add the employee information from the **Data Controls** palette. Drag-and-drop the `EmpVO` information on to the first facet.

7. Add the `DeptVO` to the second facet. Surround the table with a group layout or a stretch layout based on the requirements of the page.

8. Now add the following EL expression to the `facetName` property of the switcher:

    ```
    #{bindings. EmpVO1.estimatedRowCount > 0 ? 'first' : 'second'}
    ```

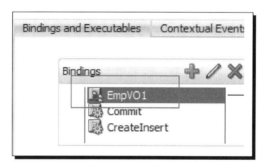

What just happened?

The previous expression will render the `first` facet if there is any row available for the `EMP` table. If there is no row, the `second` facet is rendered and processed. The `bindings` component will get the reference to the binding context for the page definition. `EmpVO1` instance is the tree binding to the `EMPVO.xml` view object. The `estimatedRowCount` will get the count of the rows available for the `EmpVO.xml` file.

Partial page rendering

ADF framework has the feature of refreshing the content or a section of the page without refreshing the complete page. Only the component that is registered will be refreshed. This is called partial page rendering. For the `navigation` components, we will use the `partialSubmit` attribute to send notification for changes and `partialTriggers` will specify the ID of the component on which the current component should listen for notification. For other components, we will use the `autoSubmit` property to send a `refresh` notification.

Have a go hero – completing the page

Now we will move on to practising something that we have learned:

- Create a new page named `Employee Search`. Add a `query` page to it which will search for an employee and then the result will be displayed in a table.

- Add a `command` button that will display a popup message **Hi good morning** in a dialog.

- Add another `command` button that will display a message in the page in an output text. When the button is clicked on again, the message should display a number which gets increased every time the button is clicked.

Pop quiz

Q1. _____ is responsible for a uniform look and feel of the entire web application.

1. page
2. page template
3. page definition file

Q2. What is the extension for the facelets?

1. `.jspx`
2. `.jsff`
3. `.jsf`
4. `.xml`

Q3. Backing bean will hold all the references of the UI components in the page.

1. True
2. False

Q4. _____ and _____ are the two commonly used layout components.

1. `PanelStretchLayout` and `PanelBorderLayout`
2. `Document` and `Form`
3. `PanelGroupLayout` and `Decorativebox`
4. `PanelStretchLayout` and `PanelGroupLayout`

Q5. _____ component in the following is categorized as a `navigation` component.

1. `inputText`
2. `outputText`
3. `commandLink`
4. `toolbar`
5. both 3 and 4

Summary

Let us recap what we have learned in this chapter.

We saw how to create the page template for a standard look and feel throughout the web application. We have seen how to use the page template to create the page and then properly layout the content for a presentable view.

We have seen about the backing bean and how it is bound to the UI. We have seen various options to display the content of the model data in the UI layer.

In the next chapter, we will see the controls and task flows for navigating from one page to another.

Working with Navigation Flows

Many of the web applications that are available in the market involve complex tasks and approval processes to provide a secure way of controlling the navigation between web pages. For example, imagine you are in an online bookstore and you want to check out a book. The lists of options available to you are to log in to your account, browse through the books available, add to the shopping cart, and then check out the product. There are four separate flows involved in this process to buy a product. Each flow is individual and has a specific entry and exit points. ADF controller introduces the concept of task flows to simplify the navigation and to reuse the flows for any number of times.

In this chapter, we will learn about:

- Task flows
- Control flows and activities
- Task flow parameters
- The ADF lifecycle

Task flows

The main advantage of the ADF controller is the support for task flows. It helps us to break our complex web application into smaller reusable flows. The task flows are simple XML files which support a diagram view to drag-and-drop the activities involved in a particular user scenario. Each of the pages that are involved in the task flow is added as a view activity and the control flows between the pages describe the navigation. The components in the task flows are called as activities and each of the control flows will have an outcome to define the navigation.

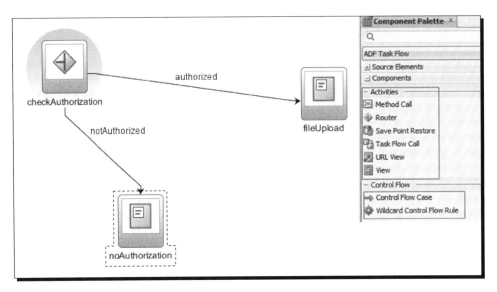

In the previous screenshot, the activities are **checkAuthorization**, **noAuthorization**, and **fileUpload**. The control flows are **authorized** and **notAuthorized**. The activities are dragged from the **Component Palette** pane and dropped onto the task flow to define the page flows.

Task flow types

There are two types of task flows available in the ADF controller. They are unbounded task flow and bounded task flow.

Unbounded task flow

As the name goes, the unbounded task flows has no defined entry and exit point. The activities and control flows added to the unbounded task flow will not be included in the bounded task flow.

An ADF application contains at least one unbounded task flow and may contain zero or more bounded task flows. `adfc-config.xml` is the unbounded task flow that is used to specify the unbounded activities for the application. This file will hold the task flow call activity that would call another bounded task flows in the application. The unbounded task flows have multiple entry points, which allow them to be bookmarked.

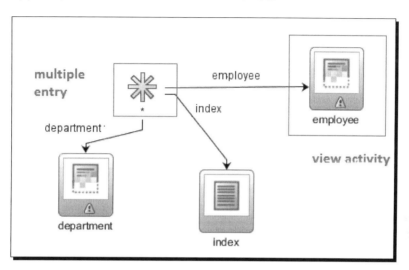

The previous screenshot has the wildcard activity to represent the multiple entry points. The control flows are defined to navigate the respective pages. The warning for the view activity is to represent the missing physical file for the application. Any pages added to the unbounded task flow are URL-accessible.

By default, the ADF application is provided with an `adfc-config.xml` file which acts as an unbounded task flow. An unbounded task flow can have activities and control flows which are considered public for the application. The activities used are explained.

Bounded task flow

This task flow will enclose a set of private activities and control flows that are reusable within an application. They have a single entry point and zero or multiple exit points. The advantages of the bounded task flow over the unbounded task flows are as follows:

- **Single point of entry**: There is no multiple entry for the flow and it uses a default activity which will get executed before any other activity in the task flows.

- **Accept parameters and return values**: The task flow accepts parameter values to be processed within the task flow and returns a value to the calling task flow.

- ◆ **Reusability**: Task flows can be reused within the application to perform common tasks.

- ◆ **Re-entry supported**: Users can re-enter the task flow based on the task flow re-entry setting.

- ◆ **Rendered within ADF region in a page**: A task flow can be added to a `jspx` page as a region.

- ◆ **Own memory scopes (page flow scope)**: The task flow contains the `pageFlowScope` variable as a unique variable to store the data that exists within the boundary of the task flow instance.

- ◆ **Transaction management**: The task flow can manage transactions. It can create or join an existing transaction.

- ◆ **Security**: Task flows can be secured by providing privileges and granting and restricting access in an application.

Time for action – adding a bounded task flow to EmpDirectoryApplication

So let us see how to add a bounded task flow to the application:

1. Right-click on `the web content` folder and select the **New** option from the menu. The **New Gallery** window can be accessed by navigating to **File | New** also.

2. Under the **Web Tier** section, select the **JSF/Facelets** category.

3. Scroll down to select the **ADF Page Flow** and click on the **OK** button. The **Create Task Flow** window is to be displayed to the user.

4. Provide the file name as `createEmployeeFlow.xml`.

5. Locate the directory where you want to store the task flow file.

6. Check the **Create as Bounded Task Flow** option to create the task flow as a bounded task flow. Later, we have an option to toggle between the task flow types.

7. The **task flow id** is the same as the flow name, which will uniquely identify the task flow.

8. Check the **Create with Page Fragments** option to allow the creation of page fragments inside the task flow. Page fragments are small units of information in an incomplete JSF page added to the task flow. The purpose of creating page fragments is reusability. The complete page is a `jspx` page with `af:document` enclosed within an `f:view` tag. Page fragments represent a small portion in a complete page.

9. The **Create Train** option will allow the task flow to behave like a train. It defines a train model that allows you to use implicit navigation cases to navigate views in a bounded task flow following a wizard style approach. The **Base on Template** option is used to base the task flow template to inherit standard functions from the template. We will see this option in the later chapters.

10. Click on the **OK** button to create the task flow.

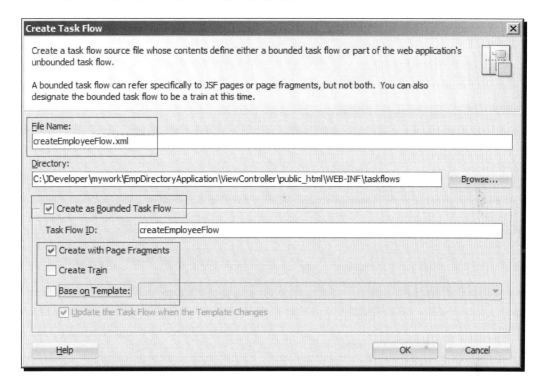

What just happened?

We have created a bounded task flow named `createEmployeeFlow.xml`. This task flow will be used to create the employees and can be reused whenever the employee creation process is needed for the application.

Any bounded task flow can be converted to unbounded task flow by right-clicking on the task flow and selecting the **Convert To Unbounded Task Flow** option. This holds good for unbounded task flows also.

Task flow components

ADF task flows consist of components which can be added to the task flows to define the application scenario.

Method call

The method call is the activity available for the task flow to add a method from the managed bean or from the business components such as an application module or view object. The method call is added to the task flow by dragging and dropping it onto the task flow. We can have the method call as the placeholder, even if the method is not available at design time. Later, we can double-click the activity to create a method in the managed bean.

Time for action – adding a method call activity

Now we will see how a method call activity is added to the task flow:

1. Drag the **Method Call** activity from the **Components** section of the **Component Palette** to the `createEmployeeTaskflow` task flow to see that **Component Palette** is available from the **View** menu or use the default keyboard shortcut *Ctrl + Shift + P* to invoke the palette.

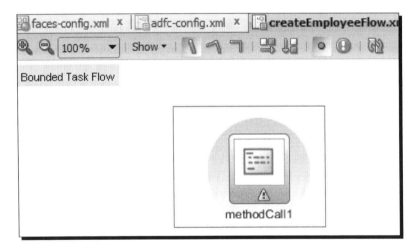

2. In the task flow, we will have the entries as follows:

```
<task-flow-definition id="createEmployeeFlow">
    <default-activity>methodCall1</default-activity>
    <method-call id="methodCall1">
    </method-call>
```

```
    <use-page-fragments/>
  </task-flow-definition>
```

- ❏ `fixed-outcome`: When this method is called, the outcome of the **Method Call Activity** button is provided in the `fixed-outcome` property from the property inspector.

- ❏ `to-string`: Setting this option to `true` for the method activity will navigate the outcome to the specified outcome, just like calling the `toString()` method from the Java Object API.

- ❏ `method`: This will represent the method that is wired to the activity.

3. Double–click on the **Method Call Activity** button to open a pop up which will ask us to select the method.

4. Click on the **New** button and provide the information as follows:

    - ❏ **Bean Name**: `employeeBean`
    - ❏ **Class Name**: `EmployeeBean`
    - ❏ **Package**: `com.employee.ui`
    - ❏ **Scope**: `pageFlow`

The `pageFlowScope` **is used as we want to make** `EmployeeBean` **available within the** `createEmployeeFlow` **task flow.**

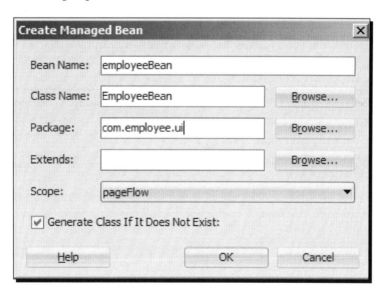

5. Check the **Generate Class If It Does Not Exist** option and then click on the **OK** button.

6. Now the `employeeBean` name is added to the managed bean list in the **Select Method** dialog.

7. Add a method named `prepageEmployeeQuery()` in the method section and click on **OK**.

8. Now the **EmployeeBean.java** will be opened with the `prepageEmployeeQuery()` method.

9. Inside the method, change the return type to `String` and then just type
    `return "employee";`

10. Now change the name of the method call activity to `prepageEmployeeQuery`. This is optional, but it is a standard to have the same name as the method for the method call activity.

11. So now whenever you double-click on the method activity, it will take you to the `prepageEmployeeQuery()` method from the Java class.

> The green circular border for the activity indicates that the activity is the default activity. This can be toggled by right-clicking on the task flow and navigating to **Mark Activity | Default Activity**.

What just happened?

We have now created the task flow with a method call activity that calls a method from `EmployeeBean.java`. The `prepageEmployeeQuery()` method returns a string variable as `employee`.

We have kept the scope of the managed bean as `pageflowScope`, which means that the bean is visible only within `createEmployeeFlow`.

Have a go hero – explore the task flow

Now just look at the task flow that you have created and then do the following:

◆ Find out what are the tags available for the task flow

◆ Identify the `fixed-outcome` and the `toString` attributes

Router

Now we have the **Router** activity, which is used to check for a condition and then direct the control to the appropriate flow. When you drag-and-drop the router component, the **Router** activity is added to the task flow which has the following properties:

◆ `default-outcome`: This determines the default outcome of the router.

◆ `expression`: This is used to provide the expression that will be evaluated at runtime to determine which outcome has to be chosen for the flow. There can be many `expression` properties, but there will always be one `default-outcome`. The EL expression is used at design time to provide the expression. For example:

```
<expression>#{pageFlowScope.employeBean.count == 1}</expression>
        <outcome>department</outcome>
```

If the count variable in employeeBean is evaluated to 1, then the control is taken to the department flow as outcome.

Save Point Restore

The **Save Point Restore** activity is used to restore the save point that is already saved in the user's previous transactions. The controller will have the snapshot of the application at a particular point and then we can restore the system to the saved state of the application. **Save Point Restore** uses `save-point-id` to store each of the states uniquely and then restores the state by providing a `save-point-id`.

Task Flow Call

The **Task Flow Call** activity is used to call another task flow from within the same task flow. You can call the task flow from either unbounded or from a bounded task flow. Task flows may accept parameters and then may return a value to the calling task flow.

To create the task flow, you will have to use the steps that were explained earlier and then drag-and-drop the task flow directly to the current task flow. You can also add a new task flow by adding the **Task Flow Call** activity and then double–clicking on the activity to create a new task flow.

If the task flow is expecting a parameter, then we will have to provide the parameter for the task flow by selecting the task flow.

Now `createEmployeeFlow` looks as follows:

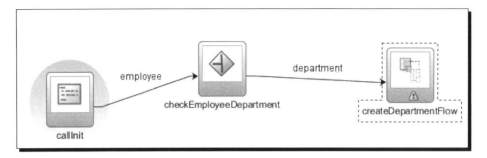

The following options are available for the task flow call in the property inspector.

- **Run As Dialog**: We can make the task flow run as a dialog from the parent task flow by selecting the **true** option.

- **Display Type**: If the task flow is running in a dialog, then the window should open in either an inline pop-up or an external window.

- **Remote Application URL**: This option is used to call the task flow when the application is called remotely from a web application.

Task Flow Return

Task Flow Return is used in a task flow to return to the calling task flow after completing a process within the task flow. For example, in the previous screenshot, we have a task flow call `createDepartmentFlow`, which will call the corresponding task flow and the flow continues within `createDepartmentFlow`. However, at some point, the `createDepartmentFlow` task flow ends and the control has to come back to the calling `createEmployeeFlow` task flow for further processes within the current task flow. This option is available only for a bounded task flow.

Time for action – adding a Task Flow Return

Now we will see how to create a **Task Flow Return** activity within the task flow:

1. Double–click on **createDepartmentFlow** to open a **Create Bounded Task Flow** dialog.

2. Accept the default entries by clicking on the **OK** button. The dialog box is similar to that of the create task flow dialog that we saw earlier to create the `createEmployeeFlow` task flow.

3. The previous action will create the bounded task flow.

4. Select and then drag-and-drop the **Task Flow Return** activity from the component palette to the task flow.

5. Name the **Task Flow Return** activity as `return`.

What just happened?

In the previous action, we have seen how the task flow will return to its calling activity. The task flow return activity will have the following options available:

♦ **Reentry**: This attribute will represent whether the re-entry is allowed for the task flow or not. The available options are **reentry-allowed** and **reentry-not-allowed**.

♦ **End Transaction**: **commit** and **rollback** options are available for the task flow to commit or rollback the transaction to the database. This is available if the task flows are configured to always require an existing transaction. **Transaction** options in the task flow will be covered later in this chapter.

♦ **Restore Save point**: When this is set to **true**, this option will help to restore the state of the task flow upon entering next time to the point when it exited the last time.

Parent Action

We know that a task flow can be added to a page as a region. A region will be a section in the page which acts as a placeholder for the task flow. In an ADF region, if the bounded task flow needs to trigger navigation, then we would see **Parent Action**. The outcome will be used to navigate the task flow containing **Parent Action** instead of navigating the task flow of the ADF region. The options available are as follows:

♦ **Parent Outcome**: This will allow the outcome to navigate the parent action to the parent view activity. It allows the region to force navigation in the parent task flow. It is the immediate view owning the region.

◆ **Root Outcome**: This will navigate the parent action activity to the root page of the application. Parent outcome and root outcome are mutually exclusive.

◆ **Outcome**: This will allow the control flow to the ADF region when the parent or root outcome is queued.

URL View

URL View activity is used to redirect the view port to an external application. This activity is used to redirect the current view port to a bounded task flow or the view of another unbounded task flow. A view port is the area that allows independent navigation to other view ports. A browser or a region can be considered as a view port. The URL attribute can take EL expressions also. The **URL View** activity also accepts parameters.

View

The **View** activity is the important activity to add page fragments to the task flow. For the bounded task flow, adding a **View** activity will create a page fragment for the user to interact. Page fragments will have an extension .jsff for bounded task flows and .jspx documents are top-level complete pages without any fragments. The Facelets can also be added to the bounded task flow with .jsf as an extension for the file. Facelet is added only for a full page.

◆ **Redirect**: Setting this attribute to **true** will redirect the page from the current view. The GET request is used for navigation to a different view activity.

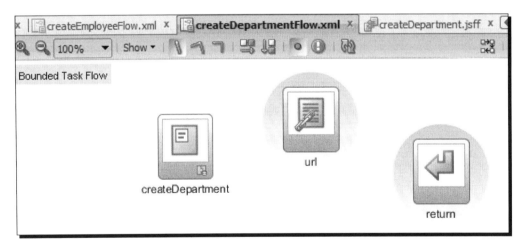

Time for action – adding a View activity to the task flow

Now let us see how to add a view activity to the task flow:

1. Drag-and-drop the **View** activity from the component palette to
   `createDepartmentFlow`.

2. Double–click on the view to open a **Create ADF Page Fragment** dialog.

3. Provide the **File Name** as `createDepartment.jsff` and locate the **Directory**
   to save the file.

4. Select the **Page Template** option as **WebPageTemplate**. This is similar to the
   creation of an `index.jspx` page in the previous chapter.

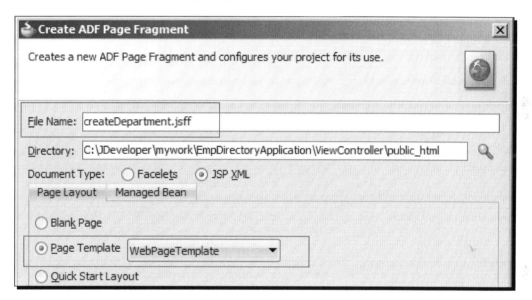

What just happened?

The view activity is added to the task flow which will represent the view port that is included
within the task flow. The view activity can be a page fragment or a facelet.

 The **Use Page Fragments** option in the **Overview** tab for the task
flow is used to allow whether the task flow can support a page
fragment or not.

Control flow

To navigate between activities inside the task flow, we use the control flow. The control flow will connect the activity using the arrows in the diagram view. The control flow will have three sections defined, namely, `from-activity`, `to-activity`, and `from-outcome`.

- `from-activity`: This represents the activity from which the control flow initiates.
- `to-activity`: This represents the activity to which the control flow is mapped.
- `from-outcome`: This represents the activity from which the control flow is directed. This is the outcome from `from-activity`.

Wild card

Wild card activity can be added to bounded or to unbounded task flows. We use the wild card activity if we want to navigate the control flow from any outcome. The outcome and the flow can be anything to reach an activity targeted in the task flow. For example, in the next screenshot, the control flow will navigate to **createDepartment** from any outcome, which starts with **foo** and any number of characters after that.

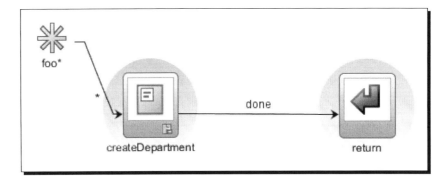

Task flow options

The task flow options are available to support different configurations for the task flow. The options can be changed from the **Overview** tab or from the property inspector by selecting the task flow. Let us see the options available for the task flows in detail.

General

The options available in this category are as follows:

- **Task Flow ID**: This is a unique task flow ID used to identify the task flow when used within another task flow within an application, or when the task flow is included in a library for reuse.

- **Default Activity**: This is the default activity which will set any one of the activities available in the task flow as the default one.

- **Exception Handler**: Any page view activity can be made an exception handler by right–clicking on the activity and selecting **Mark Activity Exception Handler**. This property can be set for any activity in the task flow using the property inspector. This setting for the activity is to handle exceptions. This is the only property available for the unbounded task flow in the general section.

- **Initializer**: This will specify the Java method that is called when the task flow is initialized.

- **Finalizer**: This will specify the Java method that is called when the clean up takes place for the task flow.

- **Save Point Restore Finalizer**: This specifies the Java method that initializes the task flow state when it is restored from the save point.

- **Use Page Fragments**: This will allow the use of page fragments in the task flow.

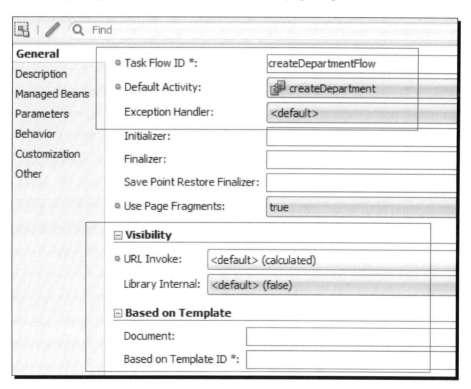

Visibility

The options available in this category are as follows:

- **URL Invoke**: This will allow the bounded task flow to be called directly from a URL link. The three properties supported are `calculated`, `url-invoke-allowed`, and `url-invoke-disallowed`. The `calculated` option will allow a URL to invoke the bounded task flow if there is no initial URL specified.

- **Library Internal**: Sometimes we package the task flow as an ADF library for reusability. If this value is set to `true`, then the bounded task flow will be considered internal to the library.

Based on a template

The options available in this category are as follows:

- **Document**: The template will be based on a task flow template to have standard and common activities and additional activities. The task flow template file is specified for this property.

- **Based on Template ID**: The task flow ID is provided to base the bounded task flow on a task flow template.

Managed beans

A managed bean is similar to a backing bean, but can have higher scopes. Backing beans are special uses of managed beans. Unlike a backing bean, the fields and methods of the managed beans are added by the user and not all the components are tied up to a property in the bean. A managed bean can be added to the unbounded or the bounded task flow. `pageFlowScope` is just one of the scopes in ADF. To add a managed bean to the task flow, we need to provide the three values that are mandatory:

- **Name**: The name of the managed bean, which we will use in our application to refer to the bean object.

- **Class**: The actual Java class that represents the managed bean.

- **Scope**: This attribute will define the lifespan of the managed bean object at runtime. You will see memory scopes explained later in this chapter.

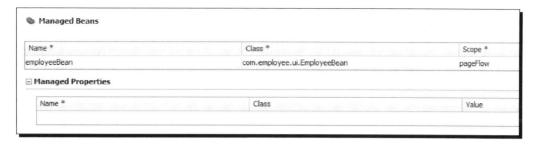

Managed properties

Managed properties are used to store information in a variable that is available to use within the task flow. For example, we would want to store the value of a class object in a property for which we do not want to write the code. We can simply have the managed property defined to access the value.

- ◆ **Name**: The name of the managed property
- ◆ **Class**: The class for which the property is defined
- ◆ **Value**: The value that you want to store for the managed property

Parameters

To pass information from one page to another, we use parameters. Only bounded task flows can accept parameters. For example, in our application, we have two task flows created up till now. One is createEmployeeFlow.xml and the other one is createDepartmentFlow. xml. The second task flow is added to the first task flow as a task flow call. Therefore, if createDepartmentFlow.xml is expecting a parameter, then the parameter has to be passed from the createEmployeeFlow task flow.

Time for action – passing parameters to a task flow

Let us see how to pass a parameter to createDepartmentFlow from the createEmployeeFlow bounded task flow:

1. Go inside createDepartmentFlow in the ViewController project of EmpDirectoryApplication.
2. Click on the **Overview** tab and select the **Parameters** section from the left-hand side.
3. Click on the + icon to add a parameter in the **Input Parameter Definitions** section.
4. Provide the **Name** as deptIdParam and tab out of the **Name** column. The **Value** section will be auto populated with **#{pageFlowScope. deptIdParam}**.

5. Provide `java.lang.String` in the **Class** column to define that the parameter that we are passing will be of a `String` type.

6. Select the **Required** option to make the parameter as the required value for the task flow. The task flow will expect the parameter to be populated or user to provide a value when the task flow is used as a region in a page fragment.

7. Now go back to `createEmployeeFlow` and select the `createDepartmentFlow` task flow call.

8. In the **Parameter** section of the task flow property inspector, the `param` that we have inserted in `createDepartmentFlow` will be visible.

9. Here you will have to provide **Value** as `#{pageFlowScope.employeeBean.value}`. This will be a reference to the value attribute in the `EmployeeBean` class with getter and setter for the value field in the class file. Any field that is added to the managed bean can be exposed by providing the `get` and `set` methods to access the field. You can also provide the string literals like `#{'employee'}` as parameters.

What just happened?

We have now passed the parameter from `createEmployeeFlow` to the `createDepartmentFlow`. The parameter that we have passed is coming from the `EmployeeBean` class, which has to be populated in the bean before passing the value to `createDepartmentFlow`.

Have a go hero – explore the task flow

Now it's time for us to check the task flow thoroughly and identify which option is used and for what reason:

1. In the `createEmployeeFlow` task flow, have a creation flow for the `EMP` table.

2. Similarly have the `DEPT` creation flow in `createDepartmentFlow`.
   Pass the employee number as a parameter from `createEmployeeFlow` to `createDepartmentFlow` and display the information specific to the employee.

3. The departments added in the `createDepartmentFlow` should automatically populate for the employee with the number that is passed as a parameter.

Behavior

The behavior section is available in the property inspector of the task flow. This section will hold all the properties that are related to the behavior of the task flow.

- **Train**: Setting this option to **true** will make the task flow behave like a train component with progression of the task. The train stop is provided to complete individual tasks using the page fragment.

- **Task Flow Reentry**: Setting this option will let the task flow determine whether the task flow will be allowed to re-enter when the browser back button is clicked by the user. The options available are as follows:
    - **Reentry-allowed**: The task flow is allowed to re-enter from any of the task flows within the view activity.
    - **Reentry-not allowed**: The reentry for the task flow is not allowed by throwing the `InvalidTaskFlowReentry` exception to the user.
    - **Reentry-outcome-dependent**: This option is evaluated on the task flow where the return activity is located. It depends on how the task flow had been existing before.

- **Critical**: If you set this option to **true** to save the transaction within the task flow, then it performs an implicit save.

Transactions

A bounded task flow supports transactions, which makes it unique when compared to unbounded task flow. The options available for transaction management within the task flow are as follows:

◆ **No controller Transaction**: This is the default option, which means that the task flow will not take part in any transaction. There will always be a transaction if we use the ADF Business components.

◆ **Always Use Existing Transaction**: The transaction which is already in use is taken by the task flow always. This requires the calling task flow to start a transaction.

◆ **Use Existing Transaction If Possible**: This option will look for available existing transactions when the task flow is called. If it is available, then the transaction is taken, otherwise, a new transaction is created.

◆ **Always Begin New Transaction**: This option will always create a new transaction, regardless of whether a transaction already exists or not. The created transaction will end when the task flow starts exiting.

◆ **Share data control with calling task flow**: The data control can be shared between task flows using this option. The called task flow can change or modify the data from the data control owned by the calling task flow.

◆ **No save point on task flow entry**: This option will restrict the transaction to create the ADF model save point on the task flow.

Task flow as a region

By now, you will have understood clearly the usage of task flows as a powerful component in building interactive flows in the web application. For example, the `createDepartmentFlow` task flow can be added to the page fragments so that the entire content of the bounded task flow can be utilized inside the fragments itself. Bounded task flows added to the page fragments as `af:region` will have the reference in the page definition file as task flow bindings. The reference to the task flow is added as a value pointing to the `RegionModel` framework API. You can pass a parameter to the task flow using the task flow bindings.

Time for action – adding a task flow as a region

Now we will see how to add a task flow to the page fragment file:

1. Double–click on the `employee.jspx` file from the **Structure** window. This will open up the file for you.

2. Now select `createEmployeeFlow.xml` from the application navigator.

3. Drag the file and place it inside the content facet, as marked in the following image:

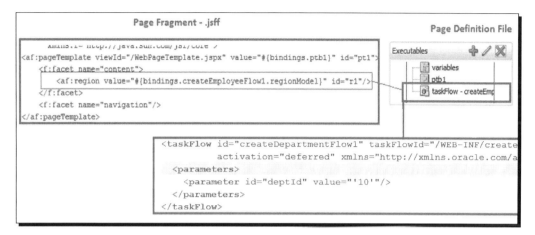

4. A small pop up will be shown to select a **Region** or a **Dynamic Region**. A **Dynamic Region** will dynamically determine which task flow will be displayed at runtime based on a value set in the managed bean. Select the **Region** option from the pop up.

5. A pop up will be displayed for you to provide a value for the parameter. Provide a value for the parameter. You can enter the value `'10'`.

What just happened?

We have added a task flow to the page. You can now see that the page definition file will have a task flow binding added to it, as shown in the previous screenshot. The task flow will have the parameter `deptId` and the value as `10`. The department ID passed to the task flow is `10` and the task flow will be displaying the information related to department `10`.

ADF life cycle

When the ADF page is requested from the client by the user in a web application, it will undergo some phases to process the request and respond to the client. The phases which are involved in ADF to respond to the client are known as the ADF life cycle. The life cycle is involved in every request that happens for the page: request a page, refreshing the page, throwing an exception, displaying the UI message, all involve the ADF life cycle.

As ADF is built on top of JSF, it would share some of the life cycle phases from JSF:

- **Restore View**: When the URL is requested by the client, the ADF faces component tree is built from scratch for the page, or it will be restored from the previous request. During this phase, the URL requested is passed to the `bindingContext` object, which will locate the page definition file for the requested page.

◆ **Initialize Context**: In this phase, the `LifeCycleContext` object is instantiated and initialized with the associated request, binding container, and the life cycle. At runtime, the page definition file is created for the requested page, which is used to create the `bindingContainer` object. The `initializeMethodParameters` method is called as part of the life cycle.

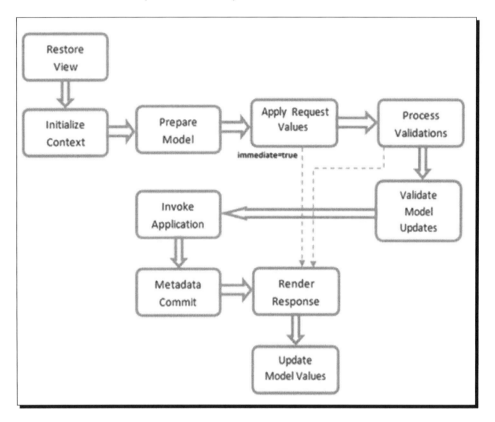

◆ **Prepare Model**: This phase prepares and initializes the model. The page parameters are set and the methods in the executable section of the page bindings are executed. The `prepareModel` method is called in this phase.

◆ **Apply Request Values**: The values for the components are applied and the associated events are queued. These values are later used in the **Update Model Values** phase. If the immediate option for the component is set to **true**, then the validation, conversion, and updating of model values are skipped. The life cycle directly goes to the **Render Response** phase. The `buildEventList` method is called in this phase.

- **Process Validations**: The validation for the applied values takes place in this phase. If there is an error while doing validation, then the life cycle directly moves to the **Render Response** phase.

- **Validate Model Updates**: This phase is to verify the model updates that occurred previously. The `validateModelUpdates` method is called.

- **Invoke Application**: The application is invoked using the action binding components.

- **Metadata Commit**: This phase is used to commit the runtime metadata for the model.

- **Render Response**: The components in the tree are rendered with the updated values. The state of the view is saved for further request processing.

- **Update Model Values**: After the validation is successful, the model values are updated for the components. In this phase, the `processUpdateModel` method is called. This method will update the model with the submitted values in the request.

Memory scopes

At runtime, we have the bindings and the managed bean instantiated and these objects have a specified life time to live after which the access to these objects is not possible. If you want to store an object in a specific scope, we will use the scope to store the value, such as #{requestScope.param}, which means that the object param is stored in requestScope. The scope will determine how long the objects are to be made available for access. There are six scopes available for us to use.

- **Application Scope**: The object will be stored for the duration of the current application and it is across user sessions.

- **Session Scope:** The object is available for the current user session and will not be available if the user exits out of the session. We will use the SessionScope API to store the object in the session. In an EL expression we used it as #{sessionScope. param}. You should not reference or use the standard servlet scopes such as session, application, or request to refer to the managed bean. Referring to the managed bean with a standard prefix will fail to instantiate the bean.

- **Page Flow Scope**: The object is available for the duration of the bonded task flow. We use #{pageFlowScope.param} to access the object stored in pageFlowScope.

- **Request Scope**: The object is available only from the HTTP request and the response time is sent back to the client.

◆ **Backing Bean Scope**: The scope is just like **Request Scope** and is only used for a managed bean and for developing custom components. Each page can have more than one page fragment or a declarative component and we would want to separate the scope instances from each other. The scope is used as `#{backingBeanScope.param}`.

◆ **View Scope**: The object is available only for the time the view ID is available and it is unavailable if the ID changes. If we want to store information that needs to be available only for a single page, we will use the **View Scope**. It is used as `#{viewScope.param}`.

Relationships between the scopes

The following diagram will explain the relationship between the various scopes that are available in ADF:

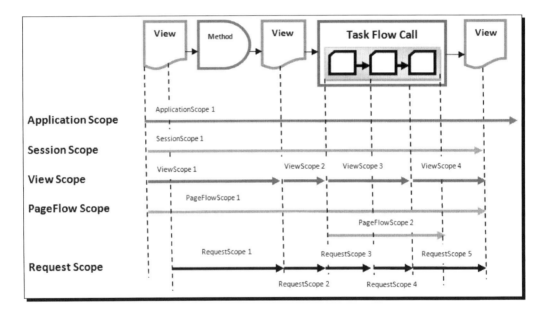

The previous image explains the scopes using the `.jspx` page in an unbounded task flow. The **View** activity, **Method** call activity, and **Task Flow Call** activity are included in the flow.

Application Scope is available throughout the application.

Session Scope ends at the last **View** activity.

Page Flow Scope within an unbounded task flow is available till the last **View** activity. **PageFlowScope2** is available within the **Task Flow Call** activity.

Request Scope is available only between two control flow requests. **RequestScope1** is available between first **View** and the second **View** activity. **RequestScope2** is available between the second **View** and the **Task Flow Call** activity. **RequestScope5** is available from the **Task Flow Call** to the last **View** activity.

View Scope is available separately for each of the **View** ports involved in the flow.

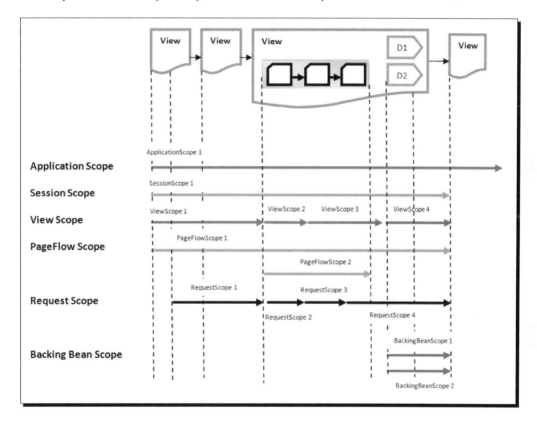

The previous image will explain the scopes within a bounded task flow. All the views involved are page fragments in the task flow. The third **View** contains a task flow as a region. **D1** and **D2** are the two components defined in **Backing Bean Scope** for which two backing bean scopes are available for each of the components. **PageFlowScope2** is available within the task flow inside the page fragment of the third **View**.

Pop quiz

Q1. _____ and _____ are the two types of ADF Task Flows available.

1. Unbounded, bounded
2. Call, return
3. Managed, unmanaged

Q2. Which of the following is considered as the usage of Bounded Task flows?

1. Reusability
2. Security
3. Single point of entry
4. Pass parameter
5. All of the above

Q3. **Router** activity is useful to display the ADF faces components in the page conditionally.

1. True
2. False

Q4. Which of the following is not defined as the ADF memory scopes?

1. Page flow scope
2. Application scope
3. Backing bean scope
4. Flash scope
5. Request scope

Q5. We would use which of the following component to display bounded task flow in the UI page?

1. `af:inputText`
2. `af:outputText`
3. `af:commandLink`
4. `af:region`
5. `af:panelGroupLayout`

Summary

Let us recap what we have learned in this chapter. We have learned about the ADF task flows and its types. We saw how to use the task flow activities and the options available for the task flows. We have also learned how to pass parameters to the task flow and how task flows are displayed in the UI. Finally, we have learned about the ADF life cycle and the memory scopes in ADF.

- In the next chapter, we will see how to enhance the UI look and feel using the CSS skins and themes.

8
Layout with Look and Feel

The main advantage of having a web application is being able to provide business services directly to the customer without physically going and shopping at the vendor's location. Nowadays, e-commerce has evolved to the extent that everything is done online just with a couple of clicks. As online activities count a lot for business, the presentation of a web layer is increasingly important to drive traffic to the website. User traffic will increase based on the look and feel of the web page. A user will prefer to visit a web page that is visually appealing.

One of the reasons for Facebook's success is its simple layout, with a uniform look and feel throughout the website. Skins and themes are vital for any web application to become a success.

In this chapter, we will learn:

- Skinning essentials
- Using the skin editor
- Skinning a web application

Skinning essentials

ADF 11gR2 provides a skinning framework to allow the developer to change the look and feel of the page easily and consistently. With the introduction of the skin editor in JDeveloper Release 2, the skinning experience with ADF web application development is taken to a different level.

Skinning is an important task in any web application because styling makes the application presentable and will attract user traffic. CSS customizes the appearance of the web application and allows a consistent look and feel throughout the website.

What is a skin?

A skin is a stylesheet based on a CSS 3.0 standard defined for the entire application. The skin will provide a visual change in the appearance of the application at runtime.

Some of the advantages of skinning are as follows:

◆ Styling the application

◆ Customizing the web components

◆ Changing the runtime labels

In ADF 11gR2, we have a skinning editor IDE that is used to skin and style the application visually. The skin editor is used to create a skin for the web application without writing its code manually. All the actions in the IDE add the necessary content in the `.css` file, and the skin is made ready for our use.

In the following screenshot, we can see the different types of skinning that is possible using ADF 11gR2:

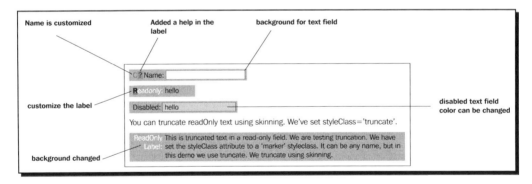

ADF 11gR2 uses the `fusionFx` skin for all applications by default. ADF allows the user to change the skin that has to be applied for the application. The skins are configured using the `trinidad-config.xml` file to use the user-defined skins for the application. The ADF Faces component provides a wide range of skins to be selected for the application. They are `simple`, `fusion`, `fusionFx`, `blafplus`, `blafplus-medium`, `blafplus-rich`, `fusion-simple`, `fusionFx-simple`, and so on. The simple skin will have minimal formatting and the blafplus skins will have a modest skinning and formatting style. The fusion skins will define the default ADF Faces component styles. Each of these skins will inherit some styles from the parent skins.

In the following hierarchy, we can see that `blafplus` and `fusion-base` are the two skins that inherit the features of the simple skin. `blafplus` again gets extended to `blafplus-medium` and `blafplus-rich`. `fusion` and `fusion-simple` are derived from `fusion-base` that gets extended to the `fusionFx` and `fusionFx-simple` skins.

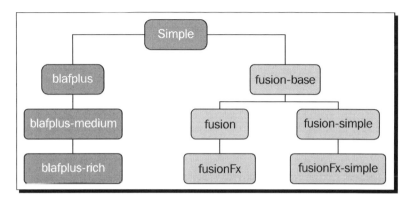

Time for action – adding a skin file to the application

Let us see how to create a skin file for our `EmpDirectoryApplication` application.

1. Right-click on the `WEB-INF` folder from the `ViewController` project of your `EmpDirectoryApplication` application, and select the **New** option from the **Context** menu.

2. From the **General** section in the **New Gallery** window, select the **File** item.

3. Provide the **File Name** value of the file as `trinidad-skins.xml` and click on the **Ok** button to create the file.

4. Add the following entry in the `.xml` file:

```xml
<?xml version="1.0" encoding="ISO-8859-1"?>
<skins xmlns="http://myfaces.apache.org/trinidad/skin">
    <skin>
        <id>empSkin.desktop</id>
        <family>empSkin</family>
        <extends>fusionFx-simple.desktop</extends>
        <render-kit-id>org.apache.myfaces.trinidad.desktop
</render-kit-id>
        <style-sheet-name>skins/empSkin/empSkin.css</style-sheet-
name>
        <bundle-name>myBundle</bundle-name>
    </skin>
</skins>
```

5. Now we will have to create the CSS file referenced in our skin file.

6. Follow steps 1 through 3 and provide the **File Name** value as `empSkin.css`; the location of the file has to be `ViewController/public_html/skins/empSkin/`.

7. Click on the **Ok** button when finished.

What just happened?

To have your own skins, you will have to create a file named `trinidad-skins.xml` in the same folder as that of the `trinidad-config.xml` file. A typical `trinidad-skins.xml` file will have attributes, such as ID, family, render kit, and the stylesheet location for the custom skin file. In the previous section, we have created the `trinidad-skins.xml` file with the following elements:

◆ `<skins>`: This is the root that will contain one or more skin definitions.

◆ `<skin>`: This element is used to identify individual skins.

◆ `<id>`: This is the unique ID given to the skin reference that you are creating. Usually, the ID is the skin family value suffixed with `.desktop`.

◆ `<family>`: This is to configure your skin for a particular family of skins. Each skin must belong to a family that is referenced from the `trindad-config.xml` file.

◆ `<extends>`: This element is used to extend the skin by its family name.

◆ `<render-kit>`: This is used to define which render kit has to be used for the skin.

◆ `<style-sheet-name>`: This is used to refer to the location of the skin file. In our case, we have created our skin stylesheet at the location specified in the file.

◆ `<bundle-name>`: This element will define the resource bundle that has to be used for the skin. The bundle name can refer to the fully qualified name of the Java resource bundle.

◆ `<version>`: This option is used to version the skin that is added to the file. An application can have different versions of the same skin.

The `trinidad-config.xml` file is located in your `ViewController/public_html/WEB-INF` folder. The file will have a reference to the skin that was used in the web application. The `<skin-family>` tag will refer to the skin name and the `<skin-version>` tag will have a reference to the version of the skin that has to be used for the application. The file in our `EmpDirectoryApplication` application should have entries such as the following:

```
<?xml version="1.0" encoding="windows-1252"?>
<trinidad-config xmlns="http://myfaces.apache.org/trinidad/config">
  <skin-family>empSkin</skin-family>
```

```
    <skin-version>1.0</skin-version>
</trinidad-config>
```

Skin selectors

A cascading stylesheet includes identifiers and properties to describe the appearance of the components inside the applications. Following are the types of selectors used in ADF for styling the components:

- **Global selectors**: These are selectors that affect more than one component. If the property ends with `:alias`, the selector will affect more than one component. For example, having a property like the following will affect all the components, which includes the selector as well:

```
.AFDefaultFontFamily:alias {
  font-family: Tahoma, Verdana, Helvetica, sans-serif;
}
```

- **Component selectors**: This selector is applied to a single ADF Faces component. For example, if you want to change the background color of an `af:inputText` component, you will be writing the style selector as:

```
af|inputText::content {
        background-color: red;
}
```

- **Standard selectors**: This selector is a generic selector defined to represent the component directly. The styles and properties of the component used in the CSS are:

```
af|inputText {
        font-family: Tahoma, Verdana, Helvetica, sans-serif;
}
```

Pseudo classes in the ADF skinning framework

Pseudo elements are supporting elements representing the component state that are styled in CSS. For example, the command link has two states that are `:hover` and `:active`. They are applied to almost every ADF Faces component. Even the `:alias` state that was explained in the previous section is defined as a pseudo class. Some common pseudo classes used by ADF are:

- **Drag and drop**: `:drag-source`, `:drop-target`
- **Standard**: `:hover`, `:active`, and `:focus`
- **Right to left**: `:rtl`

- ◆ **Inline editing**: `:inline-selected`
- ◆ **Message**: `:fatal`, `:error`, `:confirmation`, `:warning`, and `:info`

Using the skin editor

The skin editor is a visual IDE with all the key features helpful for creating skins and themes for the web application. The skin editor within the **Property** window is very helpful for editing styles and skin properties.

You can download the skin editor for 11gR2 from the following URL:

`http://www.oracle.com/technetwork/developer-tools/adf/downloads/index.html`

Extract the `skineditor.zip` file to a new folder inside the middleware folder and name the folder as `skineditor`.

Time for action – creating an ADF skin using the skin editor IDE

Let us see how to create an ADF skin using the skin editor. Open `skineditor.exe` from the location in the `skineditor` folder where you have extracted the `skineditor.zip` file. Perform the following steps to create an ADF skin using the skin editor IDE:

1. Click on **New Application**; it will open **Create ADF Skin Application**.

2. Provide the **Application Name** value as `SkinApplication` and locate the directory for the application.

3. Click on the **Next** button; it will open the next screen where you can provide the **Project Name** and **Directory** values for the project.

4. Provide the **Project Name** value as `EmployeeDirectory` and locate the directory for the project. The **Target Application Release** value is set to `11.1.2.0.0/11.1.2.1.0/11.1.2.2.0`.

5. Click on the **OK** button to create the project.

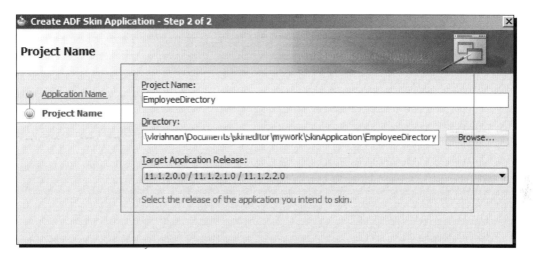

6. Now you will see the added **EmployeeDirectory** project in the **projects** section. Now right-click on the **EmployeeDirectory** project and select **New**, and then select **ADF Skin File** from the option.

7. Now the **Create ADF Skin File** dialog will open where you can create the skin file. Provide the **File Name** value as `empSkin.css` and the **Directory** name for the skin is autopopulated with the skin name.

8. The **Family** name is autopopulated with `empSkin`; do not change it.

9. Select the `fusionFx-simple-v2.desktop` file as the selection in the **Extends** option list.

10. The **Skin Id** value is autopopulated as `empSkin.desktop`. Click on **OK** to create the skin file for the `EmployeeDirectory` project as shown in the following screenshot:

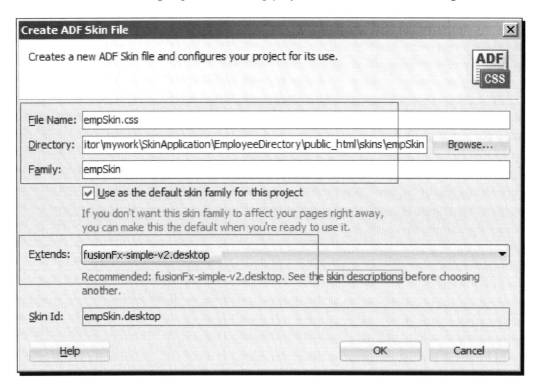

What just happened?

Now we have created a skin using the skin editor, which can be used to build both the styling and theme for the application. When the **OK** button for the **Create ADF Skin File** dialog is clicked, the `empSkin.css` file will be created in the `empSkin` directory. The `skinBundle.properties` file is also created to provide resource information for the skins. The `trinidad-skins.xml` file is created with the skin details that we created in the previous sections. The `trinidad-config.xml` file is updated with `empSkin` information as shown in the following screenshot:

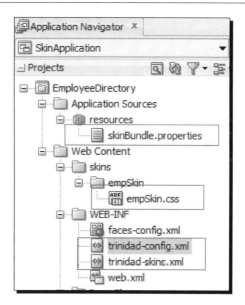

When you open the empSkin.css file in the **Design** view, all available selector information is provided to make the skin creation experience simple for users. The skin will have the following sections displayed to implement the styles and properties for the components in the ADF Faces application.

Extended skins

The empSkin.css file extends the fusionFx-simple.desktop file; this means that all the styles and properties defined for the fusion skin will be inherited by the empSkin.css file, and the user can add or define more styles to prepare a skin for the application. The **Extended Skins** dropdown in the skin editor with the folder icon for the skin will list all the available skins for the application to extend.

Style classes

The **Style Classes** section will have the style class defined for most of the components used in ADF Faces. This section will have the Miscellaneous folder in which most of the common styles for the components are categorized. The Note Window folder will contain the styles that can be applied only for the ADF note window component. The Popup folder will have the styles required for the Popup component.

You can select the style from the list, and a preview of the component style will be displayed in the right pane with or without themes as shown in the following screenshot:

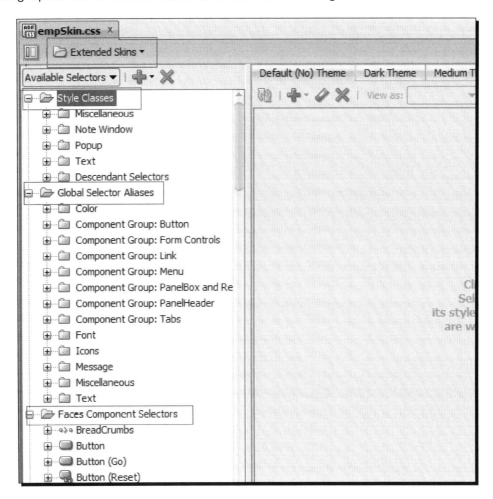

The `Text` folder will be helpful in providing visual styles for the text that appears with the component. For example, the `af:inputText` component that accepts only numbers can be displayed visually in a style different from the one that accepts alphanumeric characters. The + button in the skin editor will help you to create additional style changes to the component. A user can change the properties of a component using the properties inspector. Any changes made through the property inspector will be updated in the `empSkin.css` file. The style class contains one more folder called `Descendant Selectors` that will highlight the styles of one or more components separated by whitespaces. These selectors will allow you to configure the style of one component when they render within another component.

Global selector aliases

Global selector aliases will list the styles that affect most components based on their common properties. These styles are as follows:

- `Color`: This section will list the selectors that affect the color scheme of the component, for example, `.AFBrightBackground:alias`, `.AFDarkBackground:alias`, and so on.

- `Component Groups`: This section will have the selectors applicable for specific component groups, such as **Button**, **Form Controls**, **Menu**, and **Link**.

- `Font`: This section will have the global font selector for controlling the fonts of the application. `.AFDefaultFont:alias` is a typical example of this type.

- `Icons`: This section will have styles such as those defined for icons in the application. `.AFChangedicon:alias` and `.AFErrorIcon:alias` are examples of this type. You can create a new selector wherever you want by clicking on the **+** button and selecting **New Alias Selector** from the menu option as shown in the following screenshot:

- `Message`: This section will list the selectors for the common messages displayed for the application.

Faces component selectors

This section will have all the selectors, such as a button, textbox, table, menu, and so on, that are related to individual components. Each component will have their respective selectors to represent the styles. For example, `af:inputText` will have `af|inputText`, and `af:commandButton` will have selectors such as `af|commandButton`. Components will have the `Pseudo-elements` folder and the `Descendant Selectors` folder to determine how they behave visually when combined with another component. Some components will have `Component Style Classes` specific to the type of the component.

The `af:inputText` component will have a customized style to display the address and phone number.

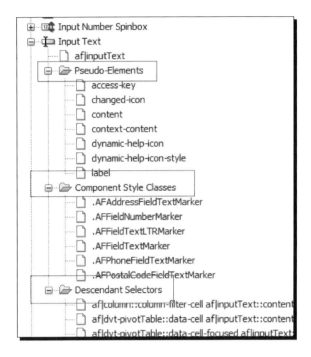

Applying skins

After creating the skins for the application, we will have to test the application to cross-verify whether the skin that we have created is appropriate for the application or not, and modify the style information until the skin is satisfactory. To test the skin, we will have to add the following information into the `context-param` section of the `web.xml` file in your `EmpdirectoryApplication` application:

```
<context-param>
    <param-name>org.apache.myfaces.trinidad.CHECK_FILE_MODIFICATION</
param-name>
    <param-value>true</param-value>
</context-param>
<context-param>
    <param-name>org.apache.myfaces.trinidad.DISABLE_CONTENT_
COMPRESSION</param-name>
    <param-value>true</param-value>
  </context-param>
```

The CHECK_FILE_MODIFICATION parameter is used to check whether the file is modified externally or not, and will apply CSS style changes without restarting the application. At runtime, the CSS style will cause a compression and change the name of the classes for performance reasons. We will use the DISABLE_CONTENT_COMPRESSION parameter to disable the CSS style causing this compression to identify the style classes at runtime. This parameter is mainly used to debug the skin used for the application.

Deploying skins

The empSkin.css file will contain the stylesheet information and properties for styling our web application. Deploying the skin is as easy as creating the skin for the application. As we are using the skin editor IDE to create our skin file, we will have to deploy the information into the ADF library for our EmpDirectoryApplication application to use the skin.

Time for action – deploying the skin file

Now we will see how to deploy the skin file to make it available for our EmpDirectoryApplication application:

1. Right-click on the EmployeeDirectory project in the SkinApplication application, and select the **New Deployment Profile** option in **Deploy** from the **Menu** option.

2. In the **Create Deployment Profile** dialog, select **ADF Library JAR File** for the **Profile Type** option.

3. Provide the **Deployment Profile Name** value as adfEmpSkin.

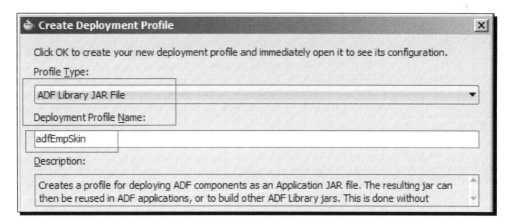

4. Click on the **OK** button to open **Edit ADF Library Jar Deployment Profile Properties**.

5. Select the **Jar Option** section, and locate the **Jar File** location using the **Browse** button.

6. Click on the **OK** button and then right-click on the `EmployeeDirectory` project to select the `adfEmpSkin` file from the **Deploy** option.

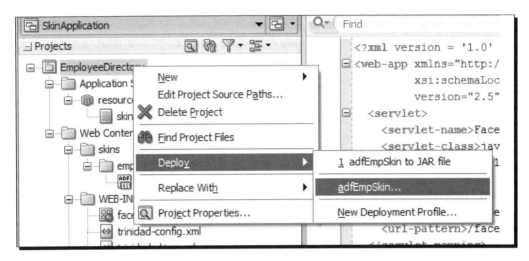

What just happened?

We have created the skin file for the `EmpDirectoryApplication` application and deployed it as an ADF library. The `adfEmpSkin.jar` file that is deployed to the deployment location was added as a library to the `ViewController` project of the `EmpDirectoryApplication` application; we need the `adfEmpSkin.jar` file to use the `empSkin` file.

Pop quiz

Q1. ADF skinning is helpful for which of the following reasons?

1. Customizing the application

2. Styling the components

3. Adding images for the components

4. Maintaining resource strings for the components

5. All of the above

Q2. Global selectors are used to define the style property of a particular component.

1. True
2. False

Q3. The _____ file is used to define the skin of the application.

1. `trinidad-config.xml`
2. `faces-config.xml`
3. `adf-config.xml`
4. `trinidad-skins.xml`
5. None of the above

Q4. The _____ tag is used on the `trinidad-config.xml` file to refer to the skin that has to be used for the application.

1. `<skins>`
2. `<family>`
3. `<skin-family>`
4. `<family-skins>`
5. `<render-skins>`

Q5. Which property is used to provide the styles for the ADF Faces component?

1. `styleClass`
2. `contentStyle`
3. `inlineStyle`
4. Both a and c
5. None of the above

Summary

Let us recap what we have learned in this chapter. We have learned about skinning and the skin editor. We have learned how to create skins and their components for an application. Finally, we have learned how to skin the web application that we have developed.

In the next chapter, we will see how to implement the security for a web application that has been developed using ADF11gR2.

9
Implementing Security

Nowadays, the increase in the use of web applications also increases the demand for securing these applications. Security plays a vital role in a web application to restrict unauthorized access to it. Hacking and phishing are some kinds of unauthorized access faced by web applications. They enable the intruder to gain complete control of the application and track sensitive information. To overcome security breaches, most websites have arranged to secure their pages efficiently.

ADF provides an in-built security feature that is handy and is simple for developers to implement without much coding involved. With a few clicks, ADF allows you to implement a basic set of security features for the application.

In this chapter, we will learn:

- ◆ Implementing security
- ◆ Applying security and permissions
- ◆ Creating a login page
- ◆ Creating roles and groups

Introduction to security

The ADF security framework provides authentication and authorization for web applications. This security framework is built on top of **Java Authentication and Authorization Services** (**JAAS**). Security can be applied to objects, task flows, page fragments, and the page, by giving permissions and grants. The framework also supports the enforcing of policies and grants for the application to tighten security for the web application.

Basic security

Security using ADF is set up for the entire application and implementing it is in fact very easy. The ADF security wizard will be used to provide the security for the entire application. Later, the application can be tuned, and policies and grants can be introduced to increase the level of security for the application.

Time for action – implementing basic security

Now let us see how we will implement the basic set of security features for the **EmpDirectoryApplication** application using the security wizard:

1. Right-click on the **EmpDirectoryApplication** application and select the **Secure** option from the menu displayed. This can also be accessed from the **Application** menu or the list icon next to the application name.

2. Select the **Configure ADF Security** option from the submenu.

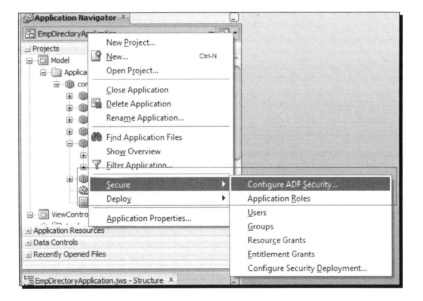

3. Select the **ADF Authentication and Authorization** option from the **Security Model** section. You will find another option that is used for ADF authentication, authorization, and to disable security for the application.

4. On the next screen, you will have an option which will allow you to select the **Authentication Type** options, namely, **HTTP Basic Authentication**, **HTTP Digest Authentication**, **HTTPS Client Authentication**, and **Form Based Authentication**. **HTTP Basic Authentication** will display a login box to enter the username and password for security. We will select **HTTP Basic Authentication** now.

5. Click on the **Next** button, which displays the grants to the user to choose from the **Enable Automatic Grant** section. The options are **No Automatic Grants**, **Grant to Existing Objects Only**, and **Grant to All Objects**. These options define whether existing objects are granted to work for everyone or whether they are locked down until proper granting happens.

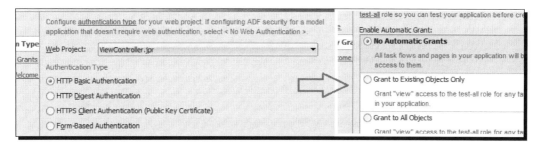

6. In the next screen, you will have to choose the welcome page. Click on the **Redirect Upon Successful Authentication** checkbox. Checking this option will redirect you to a page when the authentication is successful. Checking the **Generate Default** option will generate a default `welcome.jspx` script. You can create your own welcome page by clicking on the magnifying glass icon.

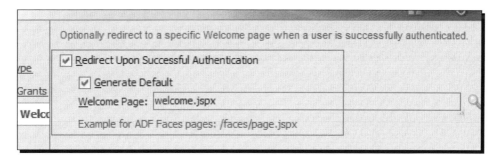

7. The **Summary** page will list down the summary of options selected. Click on the **Finish** button to secure your application.

What just happened?

After clicking on the **Finish** button, you get a message saying that the security infrastructure is created. Authentication will prompt for a login to enter into the website and authorization will make sure whether the user logging in is the right person to access the resource provided in the website. When you enable security for the ADF application, some files get updated to make the security feature work for the application.

web.xml

This file can be found in the `public_html/WEB-INF` folder. `web.xml` is the deployment descriptor for the entire application. The changes that are made as part of enabling security are:

- The initialization parameter `remove.anonymous.role` is set to `false` for the `JpsFilter` filter as this filter is the first filter defined in the file.

- Filter mapping for `adfBindings` along with `adfAuthentication` is added. This is added for the authentication servlet.

- The servlet and the servlet mapping are added for `adfAuthentication`.

- The security constraint is added for the authentication servlet so that when the framework invokes it, authentication gets triggered.

weblogic.xml

This file is used as the deployment descriptor for the web application deployed in the WebLogic server. The security role is assigned in the `weblogic.xml` file, which is located in the same folder as that of the `web.xml` file, using the following code:

```
<security-role-assignment>
    <role-name>valid-users</role-name>
    <principal-name>users</principal-name>
</security-role-assignment>
```

adf-config.xml

The runtime configurations for the ADF web application are added to this file. The metadata for the UI page is configured using `adf-config.xml`. The `JaasSecurityContext` element is added for the file located in the `.adf/META-INF` folder. The `authorizationEnforce` and `authenticationRequire` options will be set to `true` for the property using the following code:

```
<sec:JaasSecurityContext initialContextFactoryClass="
oracle.adf.share.security.JAASInitialContextFactory"
jaasProviderClass="oracle.adf.share.security.providers.jps.JpsSecurity
Context"authorizationEnforce="true" authenticationRequire="true"/>
```

jps-config.xml

This file is located in the `src/META-INF` folder. The security service is provided and the service instances are defined in this file. **Oracle Platform Security Services (OPSS)** are defined for different security stores. `Credential Store Service Provider`, `Login Module Service Provider`, `XML-based IdStore Provider`, `XML-based PolicyStore Provider`, and `Anonymous Service Provider` are the service providers added to the file. Different login modules are added. The equivalent file in the WebLogic server is used for security.

jazn-data.xml

This file is primarily a policy store. The default security realm is added to this file in the same folder. The security realm is determined by the file in the WebLogic server domain using the following code:

```
<jazn-realm default="jazn.com">
    <realm>
      <name>jazn.com</name>
    </realm>
</jazn-realm>
```

When you run the `EmpDirectoryApplication` application, you will get a dialog box prompting the user to enter the login information. Since we have not configured any username and password, we will provide `weblogic` as the username and `weblogic1` as the password. Remember that we entered the username and password when the integrated server was started for the first time.

When you log in, you will get the **Error 401--Unauthorized** message, which means that you do not have permission to view the page you are trying to get access to. This error is seen because we have set the **No Automatic Grants** option from the **Enable Automatic Grant** section. The following topic will help you understand the security permissions.

Applying security permissions

The applying of security permissions is done by providing the user with the access to view or by modifying the content in the page. For example, employees are given `view` access to a page on the website but are restricted from having `edit` permission . This means they can view the page as read only and cannot personalize the page or modify its content.

Security permissions for an ADF web application are given to business objects, task flows, pages, and page fragments. Pages and page fragments are protected through the respective page definition files.

Security for business objects

Security for business components is added directly to the entity to restrict `read` access or to update or remove the entity. The **Security** option is available in the **General** section for the **Entity** object as shown in the following screenshot. To apply security, there are three operations available for an entity. They are **read**, **update**, and **removeCurrentRow**. These operations are enabled based on the security requirement.

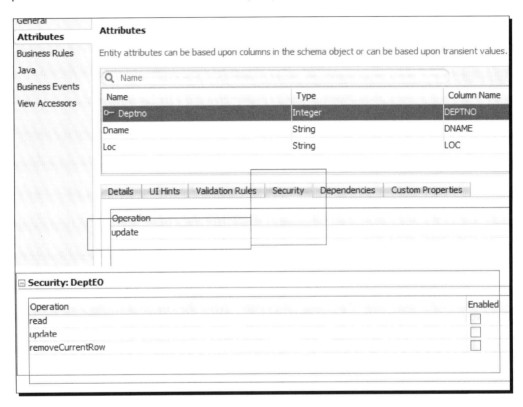

In the same way, we can apply security for the **Entity** attribute from the **Security** tab of the attribute as shown in the previous screenshot. Click on any attribute that you want to secure, and then click on the **Security** tab. Only the **update** operation is available as a security option for the attribute `Deptno`.

Security for task flows and page-related files

Security for task Flows, web pages, and page definition files is configured in the `jazn-data.xml` file. To secure these artifacts, we have to have the `jazn-data.xml` file available for the `ViewController` project. This file is created in the `src/META-INF` folder when we configure the application for security.

Time for action – adding permissions

Now we will see how to provide permissions for the available resources:

1. Double-click on the `jazn-data.xml` file from the `META-INF` folder in **Application Resources | Descriptors**.

2. Go to the **Resource Grants** section in the `jazn-data.xml` file. Set the **Source Project** value to `ViewController`.

3. From the **Resource Type** list, select the **Web Page** option.

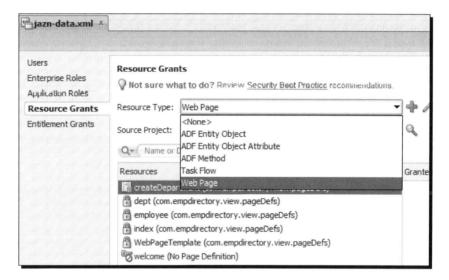

4. When you select the **Web Page** option, you will see that all the page resources for the application are listed below.

5. Now we will have to give permission for our `index` page so that we can see the page instead of getting the **401 --Unauthorized** error after login.

6. Select the `index` page from the **Resources** list and then click on the + icon from the **Granted To** section. We are going to grant permission for the `index` page to anonymous role as shown in the following screenshot:

7. After clicking on the + icon, we select the **Add Application Role** option from the menu. This will open the **Select Application Roles** pop up.

8. In the pop-up window, select the **anonymous-role** option and click on the **OK** button.

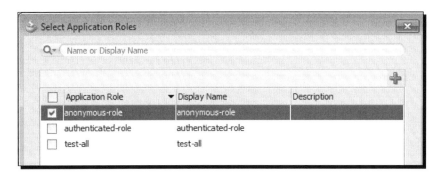

9. Now the **Granted To** section will have the **anonymous-role** application role added to it, and you can see the change in the icon of the `index` file in the **Resources** list.

10. The **Actions** section on the right-hand side will list actions such as **Customize**, **Grant**, **Personalize**, and **View**.

11. Select the **view** action and start running the `index.jspx` file.

12. Now you should be able to view the page, and the **401 --Unauthorized** error will have gone.

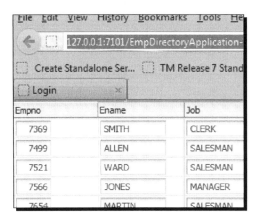

13. Now go back to `jazn-data.xml` and the **Granted To** section and uncheck the **anonymous-role** option.

14. Add **authenticated-role** from the **Add Application Role** option.

15. Go to the **User** section and click on the **+** icon. This will allow you to create a new user.

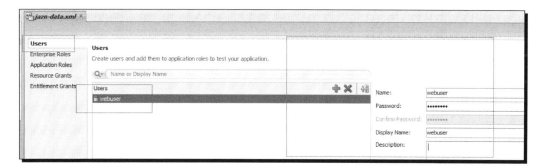

16. Provide webuser as the value for **Name**, welcome1 as **Password**, confirm the password, and provide webuser as the **Display Name** value. Ignore the **Description** field.

17. Now run the index.jspx page by right-clicking on and selecting the **Run** option. You will be prompted to log in.

18. Provide webuser as the **Username** value and **Password** as welcome1 to view the page.

What just happened?

We created security permissions for the index.jspx page. If we open the jazn-data.xml file, we will see the following entries that were added for the page:

```
<permissions>
  <permission>
    <class>oracle.adf.share.security.authorization.
RegionPermission</class>
    <name>com.empdirectory.view.pageDefs.indexPageDef</
name>
    <actions>view</actions>
  </permission>
</permissions>
```

The permission to view the index.jspx page has actually been added for the index page definition file. In the same way, security permissions can be given to task flows and page fragments.

Have a go hero – checking options for authentication in the Security wizard

Now check each and every option under **Authentication Type** in the **Security** wizard. The options that have to be tried are **HTTP Digest** and **HTTPS Client** .

- ◆ Check the changed files and analyze the changes made to the security settings
- ◆ Try out the **test-all** grant that is available for the **Application Role** section and observe the difference

Creating a login page

In our previous exercise, we saw how to create basic security infrastructure for **EmpDirectoryApplication**. Now we will see how to create a login page for our application.

The simplest way of creating a login page is to use the form-based authentication available as part of the wizard that is used to secure the application.

Time for action – creating a login page

A login page can be created by following these steps:

1. Right-click on **EmpDirectoryApplication** and select **Configure ADF Security** under **Secure**.

2. In the **Configure ADF Security** wizard, select **ADF Authentication and Authorization**.

3. Under **Authentication Type** , select **Form-Based Authentication** and check **Generate Default Pages**.

4. As you can see, **Login Page** will be named login.html and **Error Page** is named error.html. These files will be created at the root of the web application.

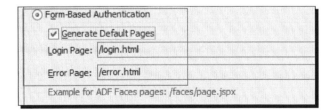

5. Continue until you click the **Finish** button as explained before.

6. Now when you run your `index.jspx` page, you will be redirected to the `login.html` page. Provide the correct password to enter into the application, otherwise you will be redirected to the `error.html` page.

7. With **HTTP based Authentication** selected, the login prompt cannot be asked for unless you restart the server. In **Form based Authentication**, the user is redirected to the login page if the user's session expires.

What just happened?

Now we have the login page ready for our application. Whenever the page is accessed by the user, he/she will be redirected to the login page before entering the web application. The `web.xml` entry will change from BASIC to FORM as shown in the following code:

```
<login-config>
    <auth-method>FORM</auth-method>
    <form-login-config>
      <form-login-page>/login.html</form-login-page>
      <form-error-page>/error.html</form-error-page>
    </form-login-config>
</login-config>
```

And for the user that gets added, the changes will be in the `jazn-data.xml` file as follows:

```
<users>
        <user>
          <name>webuser</name>
          <display-name>webuser</display-name>
          <credentials>{903}hUdKmD5fW+iPvOj6ssYILvxD/eZNB5Tf
          </credentials>
        </user>
</users>
```

The `login.html` file will have the following entry to get the username and password from the user. The name of the text field is important as the value is processed based on the name of the text field. For example, in the following code, the username is retrieved by the text field that has `j_username` as the username:

```
<input type="text" name="j_username"/>
```

In the same way, the password field is represented as `j_password`:

```
<input type="password" name="j_password"/>
```

The form will have the method `POST` and the action `j_security_check`.

```
<form method="POST" action="j_security_check">
```

When login succeeds, `j_security_check` will be redirected to the `login.html` page. If login fails, the error page is shown.

Creating roles and groups

Roles are created to separate a section of users from the rest within the application. Application roles are defined inside the application, and the mapping of application roles to enterprise roles happens at deployment. Enterprise roles for users in JDeveloper exist only to simulate a real-world environment. Enterprise roles represent the user groups defined in corporate identity management. In the `jazn-data.xml` file, enterprise roles are created for testing to mimic the identity management system.

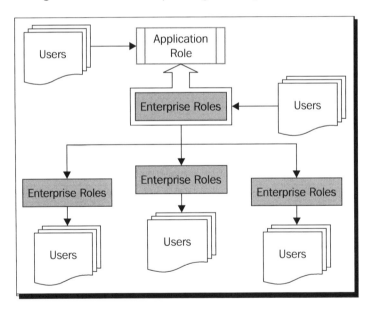

For example, application roles can be `OPERATIONS_DUTY` and `MARKETING_DUTY`, and enterprise roles can be `VP_JOB` and `CHANNEL_MANAGER_JOB`. The hierarchy can have an application role that can directly have users and some of the enterprise roles as well. Enterprise roles can further have enterprise roles and can directly have users.

Time for action – creating roles and assignments

Now we will create the roles and assign them accordingly:

1. Open the `jazn-data.xml` file. Open the **Users** section and make sure that you have `webuser` added to the **Users** list.

2. Click on the **+** icon, and create the `marketinguser` and `operationsuser` users just like we did in the previous exercise by providing `welcome1` as **Password**.

3. Now move to the **Enterprise roles** section, and click on the **+** icon to create a role. Create three roles, namely, `VP_ROLE`, `MANAGER_ROLE`, and `EMPLOYEE_ROLE`.

4. In the **Members** section, add `operationsuser`.

5. For `VP_ROLE` in the **Assigned Roles** tab, click on the **+** icon to go to the **Assign Enterprise Role** page and select `MANAGER_ROLE` and `EMPLOYEE_ROLE`. A VP can act as a manager and as an employee.

6. Now select `MANAGER_ROLE` and `EMPLOYEE_ROLE` as **Assign the Enterprise role**:

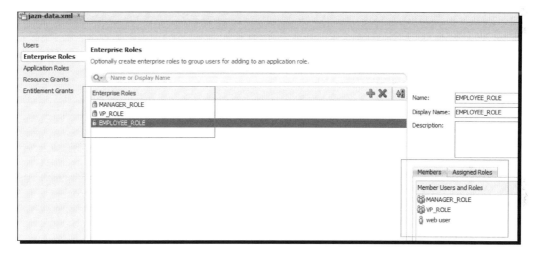

7. Now select `EMPLOYEE_ROLE`, and in the **Members** section, add `webuser` to it using the **Add User** option.

8. Now go to **Application Role** and add `MARKETING_DUTY` and `OPERATIONS_DUTY` as new application roles.

9. Under `MARKETING_DUTY`, add two more roles by selecting **Add to Existing Roles** after right-clicking on the `MARKETING_DUTY` role.

10. Within the `ADMIN_ROLE` section, click on the **+** icon in the **Mappings** section as shown in the following screenshot. Click on the **Add User** option and add `marketinguser`.

11. For USER_ROLE, add operationsuser and webuser.

12. For the MARKETING_DUTY role add EMPLOYEE_ROLE and MANAGER_ROLE as the application roles. OPERATION_DUTY will have only MANAGER_ROLE assigned as the application role. Application roles are those which end with _DUTY, and the enterprise roles end with _ROLE.

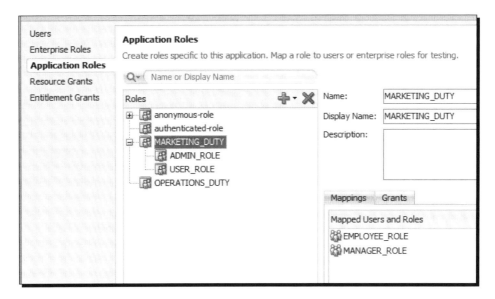

13. Now move to the **Resource Grants** section and click on the index page. In the **Granted To** section, we have authenticated-role already added to it. Click on the **+** icon and add **Application Roles**.

14. Now select the OPERATION_DUTY role in the **Select Application Roles** window.

What just happened?

When we run the index.jspx file and try to log in with marketinguser. You will get the **401 unauthorized** error, and you will not be allowed to enter the page. However, when you log in using operationsuser, you will be redirected to the correct page because operationsuser alone fits into the hierarchy as shown in the following diagram:

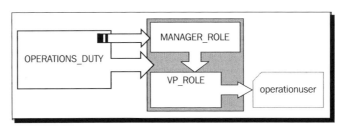

The OPERATION_DUTY application role has a mapping to MANAGER_ROLE as enterprise role. MANAGER_ROLE has VP_ROLE as a member in the **Enterprise Roles** section. VP_ROLE has operationuser as a member. So operationuser will resolve the security constraint and will provide access to the page.

Have a go hero – assigning different application roles to users

Now you can have different users and try out different users assigned to different application roles and enterprise roles and check whether the users have proper access to various pages:

- ◆ Create some users then add them to application roles and enterprise roles and observe the difference in the role assignments.

- ◆ Know the hierarchy and research each of the options available for you to explore in the jazn-data.xml file.

Disabling ADF security

We have now secured our page properly. However, if you do not want the security in place later, for testing purposes, you will have to remove it. You don't have to worry about the changes that get added while removing security. ADF takes care of modifying all the files that are affected, and your application will be unsecured in couple of clicks.

Time for action – disabling security for ADF applications

Now let's disable ADF security by using the following steps:

1. Right-click on **EmpDirectoryApplication** and select the **Secure** option or select the **Secure** option from the **Application** menu.

2. Select **Configure ADF Security** from the submenu.

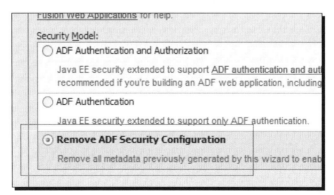

3. Select **Remove ADF Security Configurations** and click on the **Next** button.

4. Click on the **Finish** button to remove security from the application.

What just happened?

We just removed security from EmpDirectoryApplication. All the entries related to security in the web.xml, jazn-data.xml, and jps-config.xml files will be removed. You can reapply security to the application by following the steps described earlier in this chapter.

Pop quiz

Q1. ADF security is configured by _____.

1. writing code
2. using a configuration wizard
3. a declarative way
4. All of the above
5. None of the above

Q2. A single user can have different roles.

1. True
2. False

Q3. The _____ file is important in defining the security roles for the user in ADF web applications.

1. cwallet.sso
2. jps-config.xml
3. jazn-data.xml
4. web.xml
5. None of the above

Q4. The _____ authentication type is used to provide login.html and error.html for user login authentication.

1. BASIC
2. HTTPS
3. FORM
4. KERBEROS
5. CLIENT

Q5. Which servlet is used for ADF authentication?

1. `FacesServlet`

2. `AuthorizationServlet`

3. `AutoServlet`

4. `AutheticationServlet`

5. None of the above

Summary

Let us recap what we have learned in this chapter. We have learned about ADF security. We have learned how to create security permissions for the pages and their related files. Finally, we have learned how to create users and enterprise and application roles, and how to assign policies and grants to the roles.

In the next chapter, we will see how to deploy a web application to the server in ADF 11gR2.

10
Deploying the ADF Application

Once the web application is designed, developed, and tested, the next task is to make it available for the public to access and experience the user interface and interactions. The web application is deployed to a server that can be accessed by users from any location using a web browser. The application hosted on a web server will be accessed through a request made by the user using the HTTP protocol. For any application lifecycle, deploying the application to the server is important to make it accessible from anywhere.

In the case of the ADF web application, we will normally deploy the application as a J2EE application. The deployed application inside the web container of the server will serve the user requests.

In this chapter, we will learn:

- ◆ ADF application deployment
- ◆ Preparing for deployment
- ◆ Deployment to the WebLogic server

ADF application deployment

The ADF web application files are packaged into archives and deployed to the server for user access and interaction. Normally, in a development environment, JDeveloper 11*g*R2 comes with an integrated WebLogic server to test the application. The ADF application can be deployed to different servers such as WebLogic and WebSphere which are provided with the ADF runtime libraries, and the shared libraries related to the web application are available for the server. Using JDeveloper, the user can deploy the current application and test it with the use of the integrated WebLogic server.

Overview

Deploying an application is as important as developing the application. The WebLogic server 10.3.5.0 is integrated with JDeveloper 11.2.2.0. There is an option for us to deploy the application to a different application server provided that the server contains all runtime libraries to support the ADF application. The ADF runtime libraries, which are called **Java Resource Files** (**JRF**), are provided by default for the WebLogic server, WebSphere, and GlassFish. The ADF application is deployed to the server as a packaged enterprise archive which contains the required web content and related resource files. All the deployment library properties are configured from the **Deployment** option in the **Project properties** and **Application properties** options. The different archives that are helpful at different stages of the ADF web application deployments are as follows:

- Java **Archive (JAR)**: Java archive is a Java specific archive that is used to package all the Java class files related to the project. For example, we can bundle all the utility class files as a Java archive file and then use it in any other project. JAR files are used as libraries in the `Model` and `Viewcontroller` projects. The file structure includes a class file and a `META-INF` folder that contains the `MANIFEST.MF` file.

- **ADF library (JAR)**: The ADF library is an archive that is specific to the ADF framework. The ADF library is different from a Java archive file because the ADF library will pull all related libraries referenced by the files and add it to the manifest file. The dependent libraries are pulled by JDeveloper and added as a secondary import. The ADF library will expose the ADF task flows and other ADF-specific metadata files that are not exposed by a normal Java archive file. ADF libraries may contain task flows but are also used for declarative components and page templates. Using the ADF library, we can drag-and-drop the task flow onto the page as a region. The structure includes the `META-INF` folder containing the manifest file along with the `jar-connection.xml` and `jar-adf-config.xml` files specific to the ADF library. The ADF library can contain configuration files for the ADF application.

- **Web Application Archive (WAR)**: Web archive is a package of all the web-related files. The **Web Archive** option is available from the `Viewcontroller` project that contains the web resources. All files such as `.html`, `.jspx`, `.jsff`, and `.jsf` are packaged as WAR files. The file structure contains a `WEB-INF` folder that contains `adfc-config.xml`, `web.xml`, `weblogic.xml`, `faces-config.xml`, `trinidad-config.xml`, and so on. The `classes` folder contains the Java classes such as `backing` or `managed bean` added in the UI project. The `lib` folder will include all the dependent libraries that are required to compile the web archive file.

- **Metadata Archive (MAR)**: This archive will package all the metadata files needed for the customization of the web pages. Customization includes a few XML files that will have the delta details for different users. The metadata archive will package the XML files along with the configuration files to support the user customization. More about this will be discussed in *Chapter 11, Advanced Features of ADF*.

- **Enterprise Archive (EAR)**: Most of the web applications which involve model data interaction will be packaged using the enterprise archive. The business logic which interacts with the data layer and the presentation layer is collectively bundled into a single archive. The presentation layer information is bundled internally using the web archive and then it is added to the enterprise archive. The folder structure of an EAR will be as follows:

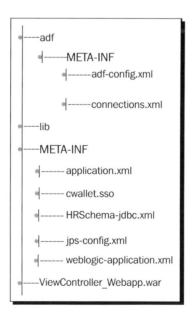

Preparing for deployment

Before deploying the ADF application to the application server, we have to make sure that the following tasks are set up correctly in order to deploy the application:

◆ Connection

◆ Deployment profiles

◆ MDS configuration

◆ Deployment descriptors

◆ Security

◆ Data source

Connection

The database connection is essential for deployment. The **ADF Business Components** section in the Model project will display the database connection information for accessing the data from the DB layer. In EmpDirectoryApplication, we have the HRSchema connection added to the Model project as the database connection. The connection information is stored in connections.xml. The connection name alone can be deployed by selecting the **Connection Name Only** option for the deployment profile of the Model project. You also have an option to deploy the **Connection Details** option in the same location.

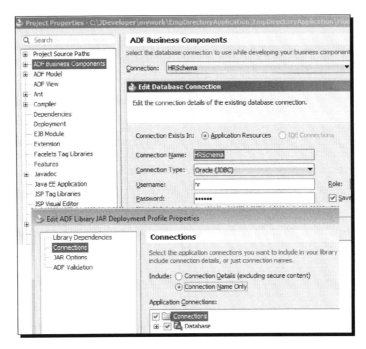

Deployment profiles

The deployment profile is the setting that is added to the project to configure the project for deployment. Deployment will package the project related files and archive it as a library. The profile information will include the dependent libraries, archive location, filter option for the files to include, and so on.

Time for action – creating the deployment profile

Now we will see how to create a deployment profile for `EmpDirectoryApplication`. First, we will create the profile for the `ViewController` project and later we will create a profile for the application. Creating an ADF library is explained in *Chapter 8, Layout with Look & Feel*.

1. Right-click on the **ViewController** project and select **Deploy** from the menu options.

2. Select the **New Deployment Profile** from the **New** button in the **Deployment** section of the **Project properties** pane, which will create a new deployment profile.

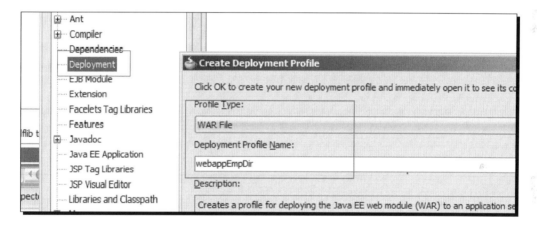

The **Create Deployment Profile** dialog box is displayed to the user. Select **WAR File** from the **Profile Type** options and then provide **Deployment Profile Name** as `webappEmpDir` as shown in the previous screenshot.

3. Click on the **OK** button to open the **Edit WAR Deployment Profile Properties** page. The **General** section will allow the user to specify the WAR file's location and the web application's context root.

4. The **Profile Dependencies** and **Library Dependencies** sections are used to provide the dependencies for the WAR file. Check the `adflibModel` library from the **Profile Dependencies** section under the **Model** section.

5. Click the **Ok** button to create the WAR file for the `ViewController` project. This action teaches how to create the WAR file, because every `Viewcontroller` project will have a deployment profile by default, which will deploy to a WAR file and will be deployed to the server when the application starts running from the integrated server.

6. In a similar way, create the deployment profile for `EmpDirectoryApplication` by clicking on the **Application** menu and then selecting the **New Deployment Profile** option from **Deploy**.

7. In the **Create Deployment Profile** window, select **EAR** as **Profile Type** and then `EmpDirectory` as the **Profile Name**.

8. Click on the **Ok** button to configure the profile. In the **Application Assembly** section, select the `webappEmpDir` project under the respective projects.

9. Click on the **Ok** button when finished.

What just happened?

We have created a deployment profile for the `ViewController` project and for `EmpDirectoryApplication`. The deployment profile is helpful in creating the archive file as part of the deployment process. The profile information will configure the archive with related information such as which files to add, where the archive is to be deployed, and which libraries are to be added. The deployment process will read this information to deploy the archive as desired.

Have a go hero – analyze the deployment profile configurations

Now you are going to analyze the configurations in the deployment profile:

1. Analyze the **File Groups** section.
2. Why do we have library dependencies?
3. What is the significance of profile dependencies?

MDS configuration

Metadata Services (**MDS**) is used to customize the web application based on the user role. The customization allows the user to change the content of the web application at runtime for visual preferences and retain them for the next session. The customization is stored in the MDS repository. The customization is stored in a metadata archive file in the server directory. The MDS repository directory is configured from the application properties as shown in the following screenshot:

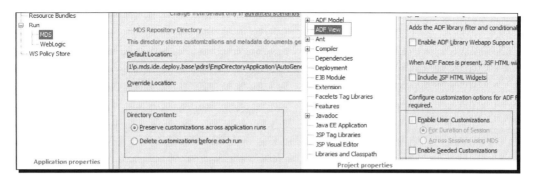

The `adf-config.xml` file will hold the configuration information for the MDS customization. The `customization` class is added to the file using the following code:

```
<adf-mds-config xmlns="http://xmlns.oracle.com/adf/mds/config">
    <mds-config xmlns="http://xmlns.oracle.com/mds/config"
version="11.1.1.000">
        <cust-config>
          <match path="/">
            <customization-class name="oracle.adf.share.config.UserCC"/>
          </match>
        </cust-config>
      </mds-config>
    </adf-mds-config>
```

Deployment descriptors

These are the files that will have the configuration and deployment information that is essential to deploy an application to the server. For every JEE web application, we will have a dedicated deployment descriptor to manage and maintain the way the web application runs. The common deployment descriptor for the ADF web application is `web.xml`, which is found under the `WEB-INF` folder of the application.

web.xml

`web.xml` is the deployment descriptor that will store all the configurations needed to deploy and start the application in the WebLogic server. This file will store the session timeout, security features, and welcome files for the web application. Some of the configurations are:

- **Context initialization parameters**: These are the values that are available at the start of the application. Sometimes we use the option available to toggle between the logic in our application. For example, `javax.faces.PARTIAL_STATE_SAVING` can be set to `true` or `false` based on whether the application will enable or disable partial state saving. These parameters are defined inside the `<context-param>` element under the `<param-name>` and `<param-value>` tags.

♦ **Filters**: Filters are used to bypass some operations when the application is initialized. Some custom filters are added to make the application behave in a way the user wants. `<filter-name>` and `<filter-class>` are used to define the filters. The `<filter-mapping>` elements are used to map the filter name with the servlet and the patterns required to filter the URL are added. The `<dispatcher>` element will make sure that the URL is forwarded to a proper flow in the application.

♦ **Listeners**: Listeners are added to an application to listen and execute based on some action performed in the application life cycle.

♦ **Servlets**: These are the controller elements for the web application that will forward and request the page for the user. The `<servlet-name >` and `<servlet-class>` elements are enclosed in the `<servlet>` element to define the servlet information. The `<servlet-mapping>` element will define the URL pattern that has to be applied to process the page using the specific servlet class.

weblogic.xml

`web.xml` is more of a file that holds configuration and deployment information related to the web application. `weblogic.xml` is a descriptor file that describes how the web application files have to be configured and compiled inside the WebLogic server. The **Overview** tab has separate tabs defined for each of the sections to be configured. A common configuration includes **Context Root**, **Authentication Filter**, **Logging**, **Request Handling**, **Directory Mapping**, **JSP compilation**, **Library definitions**, **Security**, **Servlets**, **Session**, and so on.

The **Logging** section will allow you to configure logging for the web application. The **JSP** section will allow you to precompile the JSP file. **Request Handling** in the **Container** section will allow you to redirect with absolute URL and filter dispatched requests.

weblogic-application.xml

`weblogic-application.xml` is the file that is responsible for the deployment details of an enterprise application in the WebLogic server. Some of the configurations include **Application Parameters**, **Class Loading preferences**, **Shared Libraries**, **Listeners**, **Security**, **Session configurations**, and so on.

In the **Session** section you would find options such as **Enable session tracking**, **Enable session sharing**, and **Enable cookies**. It also allows configuring the persistent store by selecting the store type as a memory, file, JDBC, and so on. The `adf.oracle.domain` library will be added by default in the **Library** section.

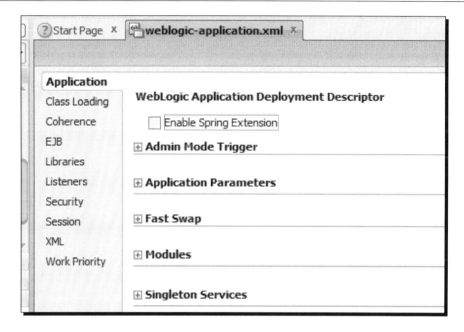

Security

Security is important for the application and it plays a vital role in any web application. In ADF, the security is taken care of by a file called `jazn-data.xml` that is used to configure different users with different roles. The deployment of the security information to the WebLogic server would help the web application to authenticate and authorize the user accessing the application.

jazn-data.xml

This file is responsible for storing the security information for the application. `jazn-data.xml` will hold the information related to the roles used in the web application at design time. The content will be merged into the `system-jazn.data.xml` file during deployment of the application. Every user in the web application will be assigned to single or multiple roles. We can create a new user in the `jazn-data.xml` file, but it is not recommended.

We create users in the server for application roles. The users defined in the `jazn-data.xml` file are displayed in the **Users** section as shown in the following screenshot:

For example, the user `John` from the `Operations` department is given an `EMPLOYEE` role that has the privilege to view all the employee information, but modify only his information. However, an employee `Victor` with an HR role can view and edit information related to any employee except deleting an employee record. An `Employee` named `Matt` who is given an `HR_ADMIN` role can view, edit, and delete any record from the employee database.

The permission for each of the files in the application is also configured in `jazn-data.xml`. `jazn-data.xml` is merged with the server as `system-jazn-data.xml`, which holds the information related to the user roles, application roles, and enterprise roles. If the organization is huge then LDAP or other powerful user profile directories are used.

Data source

Data source for the ADF application is stored in the `connections.xml` file, which is an essential deployment asset for smooth application deployment. In the WebLogic server, the database connection information in the `connections.xml` file is added as a data source and is used by the application at runtime. Our `HRSchema` database connection will be converted into the `jdbc/HRSchemaDS` data source in the WebLogic server for the integrated server. This is configured in the **Connections** section from the `Model` project deployment profile.

Deployment to the WebLogic server

After archiving the application as an EAR file, we will have to deploy the application to the server. Before the deployment, we will have to make sure that all the shared libraries are available in the server to support the deployment and compilation of Java classes at runtime. The libraries are listed at the following URL:

```
http://docs.oracle.com/cd/E35521_01/admin.111230/e16179/ap_jdevlibs.
htm
```

You will have to make sure that you have the correct `web.xml` and `weblogic-application.xml` files, and the data source connection defined correctly in your `connections.xml` file for a successful ADF application deployment.

The application can be deployed to an integrated server or a standalone server. Deploying to a standalone server can be done either through the **Administration Console** page or through **Enterprise Manager**.

Integrated server

Deploying to an integrated server is automatically taken care of by JDeveloper and most of the time the developer will be running or debugging the application that will start the server, create the archive file, and deploy it to the server. If there is any error or exception in parsing any of the information specified in the `web.xml` or `weblogic-application.xml` files, the deployment will not be successful.

Time for action – creating a default domain for integrated server

For any WebLogic server, it is essential to create a domain in which all the server instances will be running. A domain defines the configuration for a single server instance that may have managed servers on the same or other remote machines. The following are the steps for creating a default domain for the integrated server:

1. Select the **Start Server Instance (IntegratedWeblogicServer)** option from the **Run** menu. Now the **Create Domain** dialog will be displayed to the user.

2. Provide the **Password** value as `weblogic1` and repeat the same for the **Confirm Password** textbox as shown in the following screenshot. Leave other options as they are.

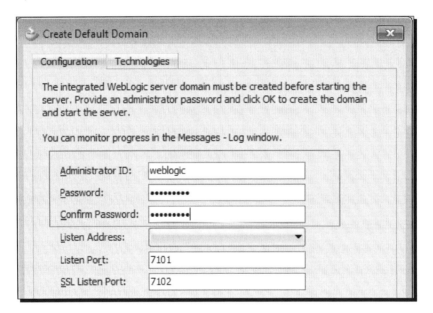

3. Click on the **OK** button to see the following message in the **Console - Log** window:

[Waiting for the domain to finish building...]

[10:17:29 AM] Creating Integrated Weblogic domain...

[10:18:40 AM] Extending Integrated Weblogic domain...

Wait until you get the following message to confirm that the server has been started:

IntegratedWebLogicServer startup time: 49776 ms.

IntegratedWebLogicServer started.

What just happened?

We just have created a new default domain for the integrated server. A domain is considered as a room equipped with all the necessary configurations for the server to run in.

Time for action – deployment to integrated server

Make sure the deployment profile is already added for the `Model` and `ViewController` projects. If needed, the `ViewController` project is made dependent on the `Model` project. Following are the steps for deploying to the integrated server:

1. Go to the **Run** menu and select the **Start Server Instance (IntegratedWeblogicServer)** option if the server is not already running. This will start the integrated server for you. Make sure that you see the **Integrated Server started** message in the console before proceeding to the next step.

2. With `EmpDirectoryApplication` open in JDeveloper, click on the **Application Menu** option.

3. Select the **Deploy** option from the menu and click on the deployment profile that you created for the application. This will open up a dialog to deploy the application to the application server or to an EAR file.

4. Select the **Deploy to Application Server** option and click on the **Next** button.

5. The **IntegratedWeblogicServer** option will be listed in the **Application Servers** list. You can add an application server if you want by clicking on the **+** button. Select the **IntegratedWeblogicServer** option to proceed to the next screen.

6. In the WebLogic server's **Options** section, the **Deploy to all instances** option in the domain will deploy the application to the entire server instances running inside the domain. To deploy to a particular instance we have to select the server that is listed by selecting **Deploy to selected instances in the domain**.

7. After the selection, the **Deploy as Standalone Application** option will be checked to deploy the application. The **Deploy to shared Library** option will deploy the archive as a library in the WebLogic server so that it will be available at runtime for some other applications to access. It is best suited for skin files and dependent Java classes that are archived as a JAR file.

8. Clicking on the **Next** button will summarize all the actions. Click on the **Finish** button to deploy the application to the integrated server.

What just happened?

We have just deployed our `EmpDirectoryApplication` to the integrated server. The application will be accessible from the following URL link:

`http://127.0.0.1:7101/EmpDirectoryApplication-ViewController-context-root/faces/index.jspx`

The port number is defaulted to `7101` for the integrated server and `EmpDirectoryApplication-ViewController-context-root` is the context root for the JEE web application.

Have a go hero

The **Administration** console for the integrated server can be accessed from `http://127.0.0.1:7101/console`. Perform the following to analyze the deployment to the integrated server:

- Log in to the console using the username and password that you have provided while creating the integrated server.
- Go to the **Deployment** section and find `EmpDirectoryApplication` deployed as an EAR file.
- Try to find and analyze the options available in the **Deployment** section.

Standalone server

A standalone server is just like an integrated server but they are not created automatically by JDeveloper. We have to create the server using a wizard or script. We will use the configuration wizard that is shipped with JDeveloper to create the standalone server. Usually in Windows the location for invoking the standalone server will be `Start Menu/Oracle Fusion Middleware 11.1.2.3.0/Weblogic Server 11gR1/Tools/Configuration Wizard`.

Or simply run `C:\Oracle\Middleware\wlserver_10.3\common\bin\config.exe`.

This can be invoked from JDeveloper's **Quick Start** wizard also.

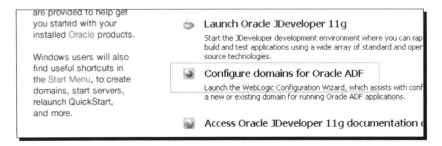

Time for action – deploying to the standalone server

1. Now we will see how to deploy the application to the standalone server. To create the standalone server we have to use **Configuration Wizard**. After opening the **Configuration Wizard** page you are given an option as **Create New Weblogic Domain** or **Extend an existing Weblogic Domain**. Click on the **Next** button with the default options for creating a new domain.

2. In the **Select Domain Source** screen, the **Generate a domain configured automatically to support the following products** option is defaulted. You may select the components to support. In the next screen provide the **Domain name** value as standaloneDomain and leave the **Domain location** value to default.

3. Provide the **Name** value as weblogic, **User password** as weblogic1, and confirm the user password once again. Click on **Next** to proceed.

4. In the **Configure Server Start Mode** list, select the **Production Mode** option and the default JDK file will be selected. Selecting the **Production** mode will ask for the username and password every time you start the server.

5. Click on the **Next** button on the **Select Optional Configuration** page. The Admin server is defaulted to run with 7001 as the port number. If you have chosen **Administration Server** then you have an option to change the port number and the name of the server. Other options such as **Managed Servers**, **Clusters**, and **Machines** can be selected to configure the respective configurations.

6. Proceed until the **Configuration Summary** page and click on the **Create** button.

7. At the end of the domain creation, check the **Start Admin Server** option and click on the **Done** button.

8. The server will be started and then you will have to access the URL http://127.0.0.1:7001/console.

9. Provide the username and password and then login to the **Administration** console.

10. Select the **Deployment** option and click on the **Install** option. Select the **upload your file(s)** link to locate the EAR file:

11. Click on the **Next** button and select the default option of **Install this deployment as application**.

12. Set all the options to default and click on the **Finish** button. Now you will have the deployed application.

13. You will have to click on the **Activate Changes** button to complete the deployment.

What just happened?

We have deployed the ADF application onto the standalone server. You can access the application by using the URL http://127.0.0.1:7001/EmpDirectoryApplication-ViewController-context-root/faces/index.jspx.

The EmpDirectoryApplication-ViewController-context-root context root can be set from the **Java EE Application** option in the ViewController project's properties.

Pop quiz

Q1. When you deploy the application to the application server, the connection information is converted to a data source to be used at runtime.

1. True
2. False

Q2. Identify the archive file that is not used in ADF deployment.

1. MAR (Metadata Archive)
2. EAR (Enterprise Archive)
3. WAR (Web Archive)
4. RAR (Resource Adapter Archive)
5. None of the above

Q3. _____ element is used to define the servlet information in the deployment descriptor file.

1. `<servlet>`
2. `<servlet-info>`
3. `<servlet-name>`
4. `<servlet-class>`
5. `<servlet-param>`

Q4. Identify the file which is very commonly used to hold configuration and deployment information for a typical JEE web application

1. `weblogic.xml`
2. `weblogic-application.xml`
3. `adfc-config.xml`
4. `web.xml`
5. None of the above

Summary

Let us recap what we have learned in this chapter. We have learned about application deployment. We have learned how to prepare for deployment and have understood various deployment files that would affect deployment. We have learned how to deploy an application in an integrated and a standalone server.

In the next chapter, we will see some of the advanced topics in developing applications using ADF 11*g*R2.

11
Advanced Features of ADF

Now we have come to the stage where we know the basic concept of creating an ADF application. We started from ADF business components and then learned about the data control used in the model layer. We learned about the important concept of ADF Task Flow and ADF Faces. Finally, we learned how to implement security for an ADF application, and learned to deploy a web application.

In this chapter, we will learn more on the advanced and complex topics of ADF.

In this chapter, we will cover the following topics:

- Advanced topics on entity objects
- Advanced topics on view objects
- Application module state management
- Complex data control
- Complex task flows
- Complex usage of a managed bean
- Debugging an application
- The Metadata Services framework
- The Active Data Services framework
- WebLogic server configurations
- Creating extensions

Advanced topics on entity objects

In the earlier chapters, we saw the basic features of entity objects and learned how to use them for our web application. In this chapter, we will see some advanced features of the entity object, which is more powerful in building a robust and scalable ADF web application.

Tuning

The **Use Update Batching** checkbox in the **Tuning** section of an entity object's **Overview** tab is used to update the underlying tables for the entity object, and to use a statement that has minimal queries for the INSERT, DELETE, and UPDATE operations. One bulk CRUD statement is used for transactions involving independent statements. When this option is checked, you will have to provide a value in the **When Number of Entities to Modify Exceeds:** box. The default option is 1, which will enable update batching when the number of entities exceed one.

The **Retain Association Accessor Rowset** option in the **Tuning** section is used to retain the association accessor when the entity is involved in retrieving the rowset from the association accessor. When this property is not checked, a new rowset is created whenever the entity retrieves information using the association accessor.

Enabling this option will reduce additional query executions because the creation of rowsets will happen only for the first time, and the same rowset is accessed the next time. Programmatically, you will use the setAssociationAccessorRetained() method to set the value in your EntityCollImpl class.

If we need to iterate through the rowset programmatically, we use the following code:

```
RowSet rs = (RowSet)getAccounts();
rs.reset();
while (rs.hasNext()) {
  AccountImpl r = (AccountImpl)rs.next();
//do custom logic
}
```

For more information, go to the following links:

- `http://docs.oracle.com/cd/E35521_01/web.111230/e16182/`
  `bcentities.htm#CEGCJFDA`
- `http://docs.oracle.com/cd/E35521_01/web.111230/e16182/`
  `bcentities.htm#autoId119`

Custom properties

Add custom properties for the entity object to retrieve and set some property at runtime. For example, if you would like to change the value of a tooltip at runtime for a particular attribute, let's say `DeptNo` in `DeptEO.xml`, you will add a custom property and retrieve the property using the following snippet in your custom `EntityImpl` class file:

```
AttributeDefImpl attr =
    gctEntityDef().getAttributeDefImpl("Dept");
attr.setProperty("tooltip", "Simple value");
attr.getProperty("tooltip");
```

The following screenshot shows the **Custom Properties** page:

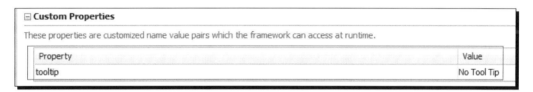

Property sets

Property sets are a grouped collection of properties and references used to differentiate from other business components. You can store properties, error messages, tool tips, control hints, and others in a property set, and make it translatable using the resource bundle.

Property sets are added to the business object attribute by using **New Gallery** and navigating to **Business Tier | ADF Business Components | Property Sets**.

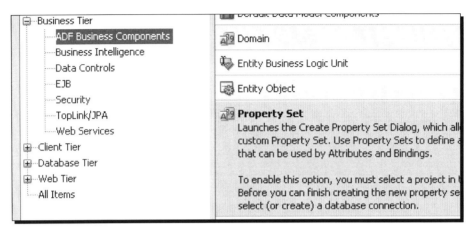

More information on this is available at the following link:

```
http://docs.oracle.com/cd/E35521_01/web.111230/e16182/bcentities.
htm#BABDAAJG
```

A resource bundle

A resource bundle is used in ADF business components to support translatable strings. String references such as attribute names, error messages, tool tips, control hints, and others are stored in a resource bundle to support *internationalization* and *localization*. These are configured in the **Resource Bundle** section in **Project Properties**.

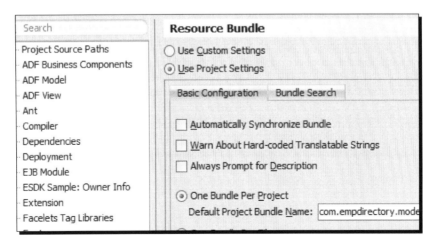

There are three types of resource bundles that can be created, as follows:

◆ XLIFF: The resource key and value will be represented in an XML file

◆ Properties: The `properties` file will have the key and value defined

◆ List: The key-value pair will be defined in a Java file that extends the `ListResourceBundle` API

You can configure the resource bundle to be a part of the project, or to be created for every file. The information from the resource bundle can be accessed programmatically in any of the implementation classes using the following code:

```
String bundle= "com.view.ViewControllerBundle";
ResourceBundle resourceBundle = BundleFactory.getBundle(bundle);
resourceBundle.getString("id");
```

For more information, please go to http://docs.oracle.com/cd/
E35521_01/web.111230/e16182/bcentities.htm#BABJACFB.

Business logic groups

Business logic groups are used to separate business components logically based on their functionality. The group can encapsulate related objects, validations, custom logic, and resource bundles. These can be enabled dynamically based on the context of a row. For example, HR units can have a set of validations that differ from the validation logic for operation managers. Customers can view certain details and validations that do not apply to staff. The group is created in the **Business Logic Group** section by providing a **discriminator** attribute.

The **Business logic unit** is created to separate the validation logic for business objects. For example, in an organization, CUSTOMER, SUPPLIER, STAFF, and SUPPORT can each be an individual business unit that can have different validations, hints, default values, and business logic specific to their respective business. All business units are added to the base entity object to maintain the business group list. The value of the discriminator attribute will determine the corresponding business logic units to be loaded.

Domain

ADF allows you to create a validation for the data type that is used in the attribute. A domain is created to wrap the primary data type in order to apply validation based on the domain. For example, if you have `PhoneNumber` as an attribute with the data type as numbers, you can wrap the attribute with the `PhoneNumber` domain and use it as a data type for validation. The `validate()` method for the domain is used for the validation. The domain type is created in the **New Gallery** section by navigating to **Business Tier | ADF Business Components | Domain**.

The Custom validation rule

ADF comes with default declarative validation rules that are used in the **Business Rule** section of an entity object. In most business cases, we would like to have our own validation rule to be applied to business objects. ADF allows users to create a custom validation rule by going to **Business Tier | ADF Business Components | Validation Rule | New Gallery**. The `validate()` method is used to raise an exception based on the business condition. The validation will be displayed in the **Business Rule** section of an entity object.

The following is a sample validation code:

```java
public boolean validateValue(Object value) {
    return true;
}
public void validate(JboValidatorContext ctx) {
    if (!validateValue(ctx.getNewValue())) {
        throw new ValidationException(
          "com.empdirectory.model.view.BasicValidationRule
          validation failed");
    }
}
```

The following screenshot shows the **Create Validation Rule Class** pane:

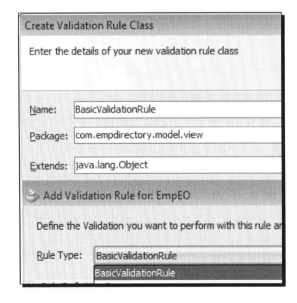

Custom error messages

At times, you will want to display a custom message for error messages that are triggered from the framework. For example, if the precision of an attribute is not met, the framework will throw an error saying **Invalid precision/scale**.

In order to display a different message for this message, you will have to define a custom error message in the project's properties. Go to **Project Properties | Business Components | Options** to define a new class named `MessageBundle.java`.

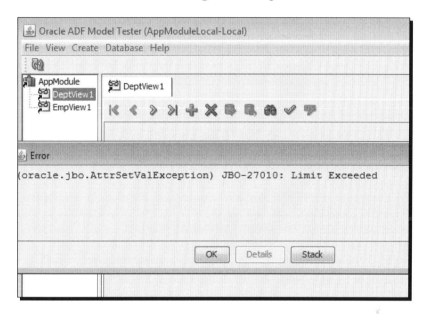

The bundle class will have the definition shown in the following code:

```
public class MessageBundle
  extends ListResourceBundle {
    private static final Object[][]
      sMessageStrings = new String[][] {
        {CSMessageBundle.EXC_VAL_PRECISION_VALIDATOR,
            "Limit Exceeded"}
      };

    protected Object[][] getContents() {
      return sMessageStrings;
    }
}
```

Advanced topics on view objects

In a view object, you will have the custom logic to work on SQL queries and the data that is displayed in the UI layer. The following are some of the advanced concepts for view objects:

- **Tuning**: View object tuning plays an important role in the performance of an application. Some of the common tuning concepts are discussed here in this section.

- `MaxFetchSize`: `MaxFetchSize` is the maximum number of rows fetched from a database for the current view object. `-1` will retrieve an unlimited number of rows or all the rows returned from a query. The value `0` will cause no query execution and no rows will be returned.

- `FetchSize`: This is the number of rows that is returned on a single database round trip. This setting will determine how many rows will be returned for a particular view object at runtime on a single query.

- `FetchMode`: This is the mode that controls how the rows are retrieved in a JDBC result set. Some of the modes allowed for this function are as follows:

  - `FETCH_ALL`: This mode will fetch all the rows at once

  - `FETCH_AS_NEEDED`: This mode will fetch the number of rows defined by `FetchSize` first, and the rows are again fetched upon further request

- `RowFetchLimit`: This option is provided in the `adf-config.xml` file to limit the number of rows fetched by the view object query, and it is applied to the entire view object in an application.

- **Forward-only mode:** This setting is used to manage one row and the next row. The navigation proceeds in a linearly forward manner.

- `ListRangeSize`: This is the setting for the list of values that are added to the attribute in the view object. The value of this setting will be set to a lesser value to reduce a large number of rows being returned unnecessarily. The value `-1` will retrieve all the rows.

- `RangeSize`: This is the setting that is added in combination with the `ListRangeSize` setting in the UI binding iterator. A value of `-1` will include all the rows to be displayed in the iterator range.

- AccessMode: This defines how the row is accessed in a view object. The modes are as follows:

  - SCROLLABLE: This mode is used to cache rows in a collection.

  - FORWARD_ONLY: This mode is used for sequential access to rows in a collection.

  - RANGE_PAGING: The paging is done based on the defined value of RangeSize. If the rows that are requested are not in the range, the rows are fetched from the database using the ROWNUM query.

  - RANGE_PAGING_AUTO_POST: The rowset will post any changes in the transaction for rows out of the current range.

- **Query Optimizer**: These are hints added to a query to help retrieve the record efficiently. This will influence the execution plan of the query. The modes are as follows:

  - ALL_ROWS: This mode fetches all rows as quickly as possible

  - FIRST_ROWS: This mode fetches the first row as quickly as possible

- **SQL Mode**: Use the view object SQL mode to control the area from which the rows have to be retrieved. You can combine the following query modes to retrieve records efficiently:

  - QUERY_MODE_SCAN_DATABASE_TABLES: This mode is used to scan rows from the database. This is the default mode.

  - QUERY_MODE_SCAN_VIEW_ROWS: This mode is used to scan rows from the view cache. This mode uses the existing rows and will not go back to the database.

  - QUERY_MODE_SCAN_ENTITY_ROWS: This mode is used to scan rows from the entity cache. This mode uses the entity object rows that are valid for entity-based view objects.

- **Association Consistent**: When using two view objects that have the same entity type, one view object is notified about the changes made to an entity through the other view object via the flag to view link consistency. The flag to view link consistency is jbo.viewlink.consistent in the AM configurations, which can be performed programmatically using setAssociationConsistent(true).

Avoid getRowCount, getEstimatedRowCount

It is advised not to use `getRowCount()` or `getEstimatedRowCount()` for a view object, as this will fetch all the rows in memory, use `getCappedRowCount(n)` instead.

The `getCappedRowCount(n)` method executes the query and a count up to to n number of rows. If the row count is less than n, it returns a positive integer. It returns a negative ID if the row count is greater than n.

Working with Rowsets

When working with a view object, it is possible to open many rowsets and forget to close the rowsets that are cleared on garbage collection. Use the `RowSet.closeRowSet()` method to close the rowset opened previously, so that you do not need to wait until the object is garbage collected. This would improve the performance by utilizing the space and the amount of work done on garbage collection.

List of values

View accessors are added to display the list of values for an attribute. For example, if you want to show a list of values of department names instead of department IDs, you will have to use the view accessor section to add a view object that will list all the department names.

Time for action – creating a list of values of a department

Carry out the following steps to create a list of values:

1. Add a view accessor mapping to the `DeptVO.xml` file, in the `EmpEO.xml` file.

2. Go to the `EmpVO.xml` file and then select the `Deptno` attribute.

3. Select the **List of Values:** section to add a new list of values, as shown in the following screenshot:

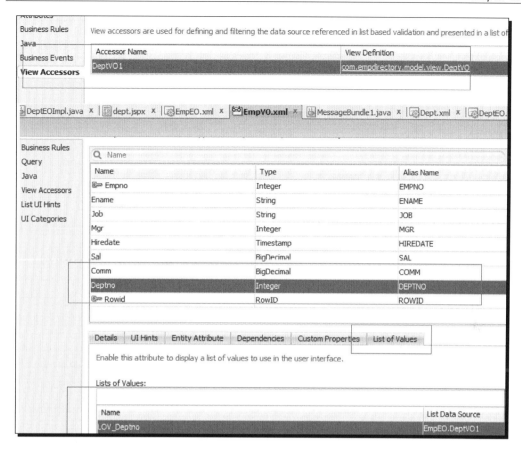

4. Select `EmpEO.DeptVO1` as **List Data Source** and `Deptno` as **List Attribute** to map the `Deptno` attribute of `DeptVO` to the `EmpVO` attribute.

5. Go to the **UI Hints** tab and move the `Dname` attribute from the **Available:** section to the **Selected:** list.

6. Select **Combo Box with List of Values** as the value for **Default List Type**, as shown in the following screenshot:

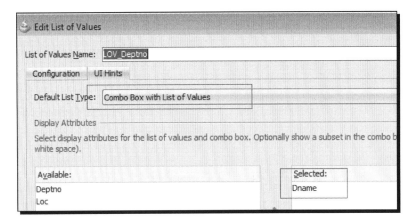

What just happened?

We created a list of values for our view object attribute, which will create a list of department names for the Deptno attribute. The list of department names is displayed based on the result of the query executed by the DeptVO1 view object.

In this way, we can display valid values in the list for the attribute. When the user selects a department, the corresponding deptno will get assigned to the attribute.

UI categories

You can define the UI category for attributes that are listed in a view object. For example, the FirstName, MiddleName, and LastName attributes are collectively added to the **Name** category.

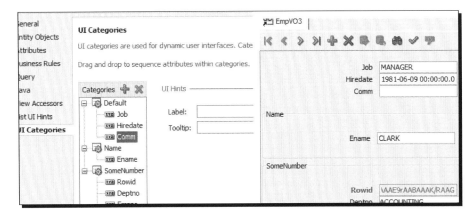

More information can be found at the following link:

```
http://docs.oracle.com/cd/E35521_01/web.111230/e16182/bcadvvo.
htm#sm0331
```

Application module state management

Since an application module is responsible for the transaction management of an application, it includes some of the settings and configurations for high availability and to maintain the state of the application. **High availability** is a concept in which the state of an application is maintained even when the handshake between servers occurs in a clustered environment. In this context, a handshake means that when a server goes down, the clustered server gets another server up and running to maintain the state of the application.

For example, a user connects to a website that is hosted on a clustered server and gets connected to Server1 of that cluster. The user starts creating a new record at the same time that Server1 goes down for maintenance. At such a time, the user data should not be lost, and the user should be allowed to continue with the creation of the record. For this to happen, the state of the application has to be maintained so that the state of the application is transferred from Server1 to Server2, and the user will not see the change in the state of the application. The following screenshot explains this:

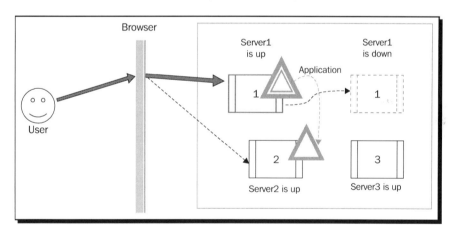

Passivation is done in the server to store the state of the application, and the passivation state can be stored in a flat file or a database. Activation reloads the state of the application at the point where it was left. The two APIs that are helpful in the application module for high availability are `assivateState()` and `activateState()`.The failover feature is enabled by setting the value of `jbo.dofailover` to `true` in the application module. With this setting, the passivation state will occur at the end of every request.

For more information, please refer to the following link:

```
http://docs.oracle.com/cd/E35521_01/web.111230/e16182/bcstatemgmt.
htm#sm0318
```

Complex data controls

In our previous chapters, we have seen the usage of basic data controls that are used to provide an interface between the model layer and the UI layer. There are other data controls that ADF supports for integration and interoperability. All these data controls are created by going to **New Gallery | Data Control**. The following are some of these data controls:

- **URL data control**: We can create a data control that is based on a URL. Basically, we can have an Excel spreadsheet uploaded in a URL, and based on the information in this spreadsheet it is possible to create a data control in ADF. Files other than Excel spreadsheets that are supported are XML and REST services.

- **Web service data control**: In ADF, it is possible to create a data control based on the WSDL information of a web service running on a server. The service definition is provided to define a data source for the data control.

- **Java and EJB data control**: JavaBeans can be converted to a data control by simply right-clicking on the bean and selecting the **Create Data Control** option. An EJB session bean can also be used to create a data control.

- **JMX data control**: ADF also allows us to create a data control based on JMX Mbeans found on the server.

Complex task flows

Some of the complex and advanced features of the task flow are discussed in the following sections:

- **Trains**: One of the reasons for using a task flow is that an ADF task flow allows the user to add trains to a web application, as shown in the following screenshot:

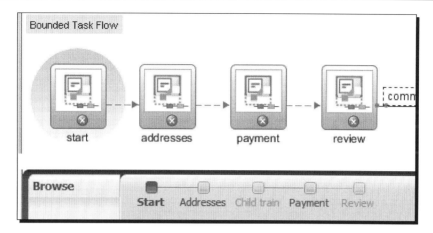

Each of the page fragments is added as a train stop and is linearly linked to provide a wizard-like feature in the web page. Checking the `train` option for the task flow will enable the task flow to support train stops. One common expression used with the train is as follows:

```
#{controllerContext.currentViewPort
  .taskFlowContext.trainModel.getNext}"
#{controllerContext.currentViewPort
  .taskFlowContext.trainModel.getPrevious}"
```

- ◆ **Template**: The task flow template is another useful feature that will enable the task flow to behave like a template, to add and support other task flows. A base task flow template is created for a repeated process and then it is reused by the consuming task flow to build a complex task flow.

- ◆ **Menu model navigation**: ADF supports a feature that will let the task flow be displayed in a menu. The task flow navigation is represented in a `TreeModel` feature or in an `XMLMenuModel` feature in a `root_menu.xml` file. Later, the XML file is processed to display a menu structure, using the menu component in the page, by identifying the corresponding node that represents the task flow for navigation. The menu model is added to the `adfc-config.xml` file as a menu, and each of its task flows will be displayed in a separate tab in the UI page. The following code is an example of the `root_menu.xml` file:

```
<menu xmlns="http://myfaces.apache.org/trinidad/menu">
  <itemNode id="itemNode_home"
    label="label_home"
    action="adfMenu_home"
    focusViewId="/home"/>
```

```
        <itemNode id="itemNode_help"
          label="label_help"
          action="adfMenu_help"
          focusViewId="/help"/>
        <itemNode id="itemNode_preferences"
          label="label_preferences"
          action="adfMenu_preferences"
          focusViewId="/preferences"/>
        <itemNode id="itemNode_shop"
          label="label_shop"
          action="adfMenu_shop"
          focusViewId="/shop"/>
    </menu>
```

More information about complex task flows is available at:
`http://docs.oracle.com/cd/E35521_01/web.111230/e16182/taskflows_complex.htm#BABBEECE`

Contextual events

ADF supports event-driven development, where an *event* is raised to mark a status of the process, and the component will subscribe for the event to proceed with the process. For example, consider a page in which a component in a page fragment inside a task flow is to be refreshed whenever the command button in that page is clicked. In this case, we cannot use `partialTriggers` and `partialSubmit` because the ID of the component will not be available in the page fragment inside the task flow that holds the component to be refreshed. In this case, the `commandButton` option in the outside page will raise an event named `REFRESH` and publish it. The component inside the page fragments will subscribe for the `REFRESH` event, refresh the component, and display the updated value.

Time for action – publishing an event and subscribing it

Use the following steps to publish and subscribe an event:

1. Select the component that is raising the `REFRESH` event.

2. Go to the property inspector and create a contextual event.

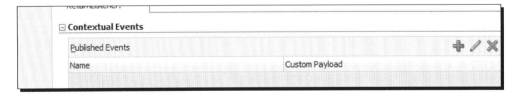

3. In the **Publish Contextual Event** dialog, select the **Create New Event** option and provide the name REFRESH in the text field provided.

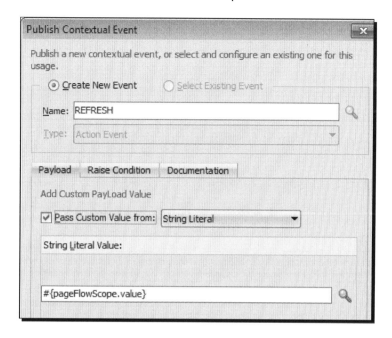

In the **Payload** section, select the **Pass Custom Value from:** option and then the **String Literal** option. You are provided with other options such as **Page Data** and **Managed Bean method return**. Please note that we can refresh the page without any payload value. The payload example provided here is only for you to learn how to pass the values.

4. You can set a condition to raise the event in the **Raise Condition** section of the dialog.

5. Click on the **OK** button. Now go to the page definition, and you can see the REFRESH event added to the **Contextual Event** section, as shown in the following screenshot:

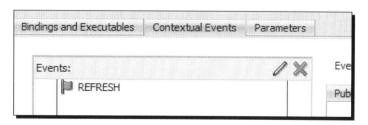

6. Now go to the page where you want to subscribe the REFRESH event. Add a method binding that handles the `action` event named `payload` because we are using the `Command` tag to raise the event. The method will look like the following code:

```
public void handleEvent(ActionEvent payload){
        // do the logic
}
```

The following screenshot shows how the `payload` event is added in the `handleEvent` binding:

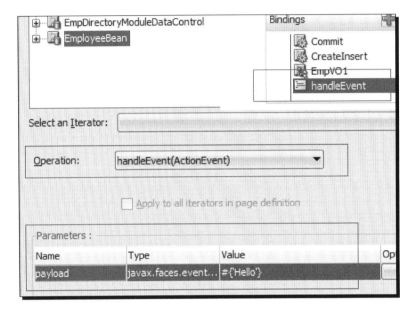

7. Now go to the page where you are raising the REFRESH event. Go to the page definition file, right-click on the structure window, and select **Edit Event Map**. This will open an **Event Map Editor** window. Again, note that the payload provided here is just an example as we do not need a payload to refresh the page.

8. Click on the **+** icon to create an event map. Provide the corresponding details and run the application by right-clicking on the `index` page.

What just happened?

The component outside the task flow will publish the REFRESH event, which is subscribed by the component in the page fragment.

Refer to the following link for more information:

```
http://docs.oracle.com/cd/E35521_01/web.111230/e16182/contextual_
events.htm#BABFCAFI
```

Complex usage of a managed bean

A managed bean is the place where the complex UI logic is added for an ADF web application. Complex bean logic involves listener logic for the components, page load logic, component-initialization logic, and so on. Some UI use cases involve other operations that have to be performed In the managed bean. The following are some of the use cases, snippets, and implementations that involve writing logic in a managed bean:

- Getting the iterator information:

  ```
  BindingContainer bindings =
    BindingContext.getCurrent()
    .getCurrentBindingsEntry();
  DCIteratorBinding dciterContainer =
  (DCIteratorBinding)bindings.get(iteratorName);
  ```

- Getting the current row from the iterator:

  ```
  DCBindingContainer bc =
    (DCBindingContainer)BindingContext.getCurrent()
    .getCurrentBindingsEntry();
  DCIteratorBinding iterator =
    bc.findIteratorBinding("VOIterator");
  Row r = iterator.getCurrentRow();
  String val = (String)r.getAttribute("fieldName");
  ```

- Accessing scope variables:

  ```
  AdfFacesContext context =
    AdfFacesContext.getCurrentInstance();
  Map pfScope =
    context.getPageFlowScope();
  pfScope.get("paramName");
  FacesContext fctx =
    FacesContext.getCurrentInstance();
  ExternalContext ectx =
    fctx.getExternalContext();
  ```

```
Map sessionScope =
  ectx.getSessionMap();
sessionScope.get("paramName");
```

◆ Check if the transaction is "dirty":

```
BindingContext bctx =
  oracle.adf.controller.binding
  .BindingUtils.getBindingContext();
if (bctx.findDataControlFrame
  (bctx.getCurrentDataControlFrame())
  .isTransactionDirty()) {
    //show the timestamp
}
else{
    //don't show
}
```

◆ Scroll to a specific row on the loading of a page:

```
this.tableBinding.setRowIndex(rowIndex);
RowKeySet ps =
  this.tableBinding.getSelectedRowKeys();
ps.clear();
ps.add(this.tableBinding.getRowKey());
AdfFacesContext.getCurrentInstance()
  .addPartialTarget(this.tableBinding);
```

◆ Reset the value of InputText:

```
RichInputText input = (RichInputText)
  JSFUtils.findComponentInRoot(id);
input.setSubmittedValue(null);
input.resetValue();
AdfFacesContext.getCurrentInstance()
  .addPartialTarget(input);
```

◆ Refresh the component:

```
AdfFacesContext.getCurrentInstance()
  .addPartialTarget(component);
```

◆ Show the pop-up window:

```
RichPopup.PopupHints ph =
  new RichPopup.PopupHints();
myPop.show(ph);
```

Debugging the application

JDeveloper 11*g*R2 supports the debugging feature, which will allow a developer to debug the application code to fix an issue or isolate a problem in the production environment. Some of the common debugging practices are discussed in this section.

Debugging practices

Some of the debugging practices are as follows:

- **Resolving compilation errors**: This is very simple to resolve as part of the issues will be related to the coding issue. Compilation issues can occur during Java compilation, XML parsing, XML validations, and so on.

- **Print values**: The basic debugging technique that is known to any Java developer is to print the values using `System.out.println` statements in the console to verify if the program behaves as expected. This, however, is not recommended and a `Logger` API is used instead. The ADF recommendation is to use the `ADFLogger` API, which is configurable to print the values in the logfile.

- **Breakpoints**: Another way to debug is to insert a breakpoint next to the statement and debug the code. When the corresponding statement is about to process, the breakpoint is highlighted and the control is given to the developer to inspect and analyze the variable values, statuses of the object at that time, and so on. We have to start the application in debug mode and then utilize the **Inspect**, **Smart Data**, and **Watch Windows** features to debug the code efficiently.

- **Conditional debugging**: Conditional debugging is the option provided to highlight the breakpoint, only when a particular condition becomes valid. In order to set the conditional breakpoint, you will have to hover over the breakpoint and enter the condition, as shown in the following screenshot:

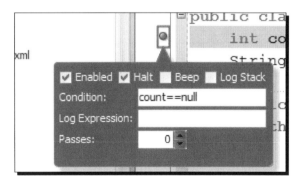

Exception handling

Exception handling in Java is a very common practice for handling the exceptions and errors occurring in the application. Some of the exception-handling processes are as follows:

- **Try-catch**: A Java developer uses the `try-catch` statement to gracefully handle an application's exception. We can use the `finally` statement to include closing operations after the occurrence of the exception.

- **Task flow exception handler**: We can have an exception handler for the task flow that will navigate to the error page, or display an error message or process the error flow for the page. You can mark an activity in the task flow as error-handler.

- **Databindings (DCErrorHandler)**: In the `Databindings.cpx` file, you can add an error handling class for handling errors in the ADF controller layer. You will have to use the `ErrorHandlerClass` property to specify the `ErrorHandlerImpl` class that extends the `DCErrorHandlerImpl` class. In this way, you can handle the exception at the controller layer. The following code snippet explains this:

```
import oracle.adf.model
  .binding.DCBindingContainer;
import oracle.adf.model
  .binding.DCErrorHandlerImpl;
class ErrorHandlerImpl
  extends DCErrorHandlerImpl {
    public ErrorHandlerImpl()
      { super(true); }
    @Override
    public void reportException
      (DCBindingContainer dCBindingContainer,
        Exception exception) {
      super.reportException
        (dCBindingContainer, exception);
    }
}
```

You can also create a text file of the name `oracle.adf.view.rich.context.ExceptionHandler` in the `.adf/META-INF/services` folder. In this file, provide the fully qualified class that will define your exception handler. The handler class should extend the `ExceptionHandler` class as shown in the following code snippet:

```
import oracle.adf.view
  .rich.context.ExceptionHandler;
public class CustomExceptionHandler
  extends ExceptionHandler {
```

```
        public MyCustomExceptionHandler() {
           super();
        }
   public void handleException
     (FacesContext facesContext,
     Throwable throwable, PhaseId phaseId)
     throws Throwable{
        //handle exception
   }
```

Debugging the lifecycle

ADF allows a developer to debug the lifecycle method. When the application is in the debug mode, the JDeveloper IDE will show the ADF lifecycle method to the developer, in order to debug issues with the lifecycle of the page. You can set breakpoints for both before and after a lifecycle.

The following screenshot shows the debugging of the lifecycle method by setting the breakpoint at the **JSF Process Validations** lifecycle method:

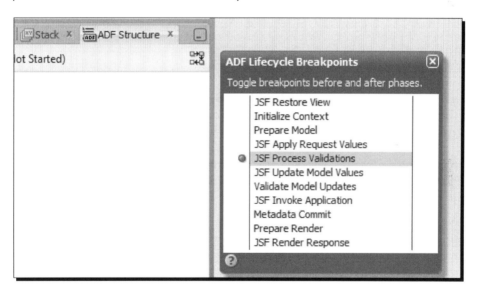

For more information, please refer to the following link:

```
http://docs.oracle.com/cd/E35521_01/web.111230/e16182/web_testdebug.
htm#BABHEGBI
```

The Metadata Services framework

The Oracle Metadata Services framework is used to provide customization features for ADF users in an ADF web application. Users have the ability to customize the way a web application is presented to them. The customer can add more custom features at runtime using **Metadata Services** (**MDS**).

For example, in the following screenshot, the base document for the page is displayed with customization for User1 and without customization for User2, at the same time:

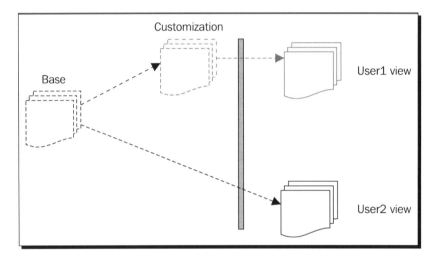

Customization layers

Customization is applied on layers at the application stage. MDS stores all the customization information in its repository and this customization information is separated by layers within MDS.

For example, a single site can have many customization layers such as industry, healthcare, financials, operations, and so on. Within these layers, you can have another set of layers, such as admin, users, customers, support, and others, based on the user role and the view that has to be customized for each of these roles. In order to support customization within JDeveloper, we will have to start JDeveloper as a customization developer. This can be changed by using the **Switch Roles** option from the **Tools** menu. The CustomizationLayerValues.xml file will have the design-time layer information retrieved by JDeveloper as shown in the following code snippet:

```
<cust-layers  xmlns=
  "http://xmlns.oracle.com/mds/dt">
```

```
<cust-layer name="industry" id-prefix="i">
  <cust-layer-value value="financial"
    display-name="Financial" id-prefix="f"/>
  <cust-layer-value value="healthcare"
    display-name="Healthcare" id-prefix="h"/>
</cust-layer>
<cust-layer name="site" id-prefix="s">
  <cust-layer-value value="headquarters"
    display-name="HQ" id-prefix="hq"/>
  <cust-layer-value value="remoteoffices"
     display-name="Remote" id-prefix="rm"/>
</cust-layer>
</cust-layers>
```

Customization classes

Customization classes are used to define customization for layers. These classes will evaluate the current context and return a string result, which is used to locate the customization layer.

Customization classes are defined in the `<cust-config>` element in the `adf-config.xml` file, as follows:

```
<cust-config>
    <match path="/">
    <customization-class name=
        "com.mycompany.IndustryCC"/>
    </match>
</cust-config>
```

The customization class will look like the following:

```
public class IndustryCC
  extends CustomizationClass {
  private static final
    String DEFAULT_LAYER_NAME = "industry";
  public IndustryCC() {
  }
  public CacheHint getCacheHint() {
    return CacheHint.ALL_USERS;
  }
  public String getName() {
    return mLayerName;
  }
```

```
public String getIDPrefix
   (RestrictedSession sess, MetadataObject mo) {
      return new String ("I");
}
public String[] getValue
   (RestrictedSession sess, MetadataObject mo) {
      return new String[] {"financial"};
}
}
```

The customization class is added to the MDS section of the `adf-config.xml` file, as shown in the following screenshot:

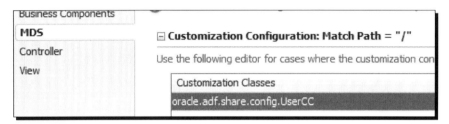

Seeded customization

This type of customization is seeded in the application development and is deployed along with the application. The customization class should be available in the JDeveloper classpath to support seeded customization.

In order to enable customization, you will have to select the **Enable Seeded Customizations** option by going to **Project Properties | ADF View**.

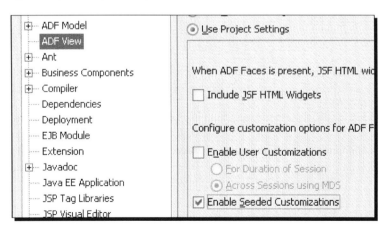

Runtime customization

Runtime customization is done for the application at runtime. The component displayed in the application needs to be customized at runtime. For example, the width of a column that is adjusted at runtime in the application is to be stored for the complete session and even across the session. For this to happen, you will have to set the `CustomizationAllowed` attribute to `true` for these components and set the **Enable User Customization** option in the **ViewController** project properties.

For more information, please refer to the following link:

`docs.oracle.com/cd/E35521_01/web.111230/e16182/customize.htm#CFHBABEB`

The Active Data Services framework

The **Active Data Service (ADS)** framework is a server-side push framework that allows UI information to be refreshed, with the value as a particular interval of time. The ADF Faces components that support the Active Data Service framework are `activeCommandButton`, `activeImage`, `activeOutputText`, `table`, `tree`, and `treeTable`.

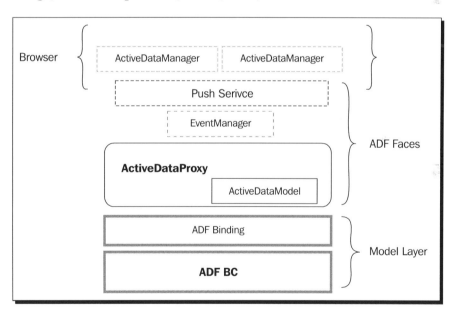

The ADS framework

The ADS framework consists of the following interfaces:

- ◆ `ActiveDataModel`: This interface is responsible for starting and stopping active data. This will keep track of the active data's event ID as well.
- ◆ **Event Manager**: This interface listens and raises a push event for the active data. It manages and retrieves the active data.
- ◆ **Push Service**: This interface transmits the active data to the client for a refresh.
- ◆ **Active Data Manager**: This interface delivers the active data to the client. It handles multiple client interfaces using a shared channel.
- ◆ **Active Data Proxy**: This interface listens to the data change event and delegates to JSF models.

Modes of data transport

There are three modes of data transport that are used in updating the information in the UI layer. They are the `Streaming`, `Polling`, and `Long Polling` modes.

- ◆ `Streaming`: Through this mode, only one data change request is sent to the client and it is always open. The data change event occurs and the client is notified with a partial response and the associated component is refreshed with the data.
- ◆ `Polling`: The application will poll for a refresh event at specific time intervals. At each interval, the event occurs to notify the client with the changes.
- ◆ `Long Polling`: A request is sent to the client and the response is returned only if the data change event occurs.

The ADS configurations are done in the `adf-config.xml` file. Some of the settings included are `<transport>`, `<polling-interval>`, `<keep-alive-interval>`, and `<latency threshold>`.

A more detailed explanation on Active Data Services can be found at the following link:

```
http://docs.oracle.com/cd/E35521_01/web.111230/e16182/adv_ads.
htm#BEIDHJFD
```

WebLogic server configurations

It is better to learn some configurations related to the WebLogic server so that we will be in a position to find issues related to deployment, and analyze the issues related to the server. We will see some of the basic settings that are very useful for debugging issues in an ADF web application.

Domain

The WebLogic domain is the logical place where all the servers, including the admin server, are located. The domain is like a home for all servers and clusters and will include configurations that will directly affect the settings in the servers.

For the integrated server, a domain named `DefaultDomain` is automatically created. The **Domain Configurations** section in the **Admin** console is used to configure domain-related settings. Some common settings of interest are **Production Mode**, **Log File Location**, **Log File rotation directory**, **Security**, and **Control**, among others. You have the power to start and stop the servers and clusters by using the **Control** section of the **DefaultDomain** configurations.

The managed server information, such as SoaServer, or WebCenter Spaces, is also maintained and monitored in the same domain. The domain can have information about a managed server, as well as control over it.

Servers

The default server, which is the admin server, is a part of WebLogic's domain `DefaultDomain` in the integrated server. The server will host all the applications deployed to it. The server also has the shared libraries deployed to it to support the ADF application at runtime. Some common settings for the servers are **Listen Address**, **Listen Port**, **Login Timeout**, **Monitoring**, and **Control**.

The URL for the admin console for the integrated server would be `http://127.0.0.1:7001/console`.

Deployments

This section is used to deploy the EAR or WAR file to the server. The entire EAR file, WAR file, and also the shared library deployed to the server are listed in this section. You can install, update, and delete the archives and libraries from the deployment console, as shown in the following screenshot:

The Security realm

The `Security` realm is the place where security-related settings are configured for the application. The default realm called `myrealm` will have the providers, key store, roles, policies, authentication, authorization, and credential mapping configured for the application.

Data sources

The data source section is important in configuring the database connection information and maintaining the connection pool as well. The **Java Database Connectivity (JDBC)** data source is listed in this section, and the application will look up the **Java Naming and Directory Interface (JNDI)** tree and request a database connection from the data source. The data source should exactly match the data source used for the application. Some common configurations for the data source are URL, driver class, and JNDI name, among others.

Diagnostics

This is the place where the logfiles are configured for collecting and analyzing information. The WebLogic Diagnostic framework is responsible for maintaining the logfiles, the diagnostic modules, images, and archives, among others.

Creating an extension

ADF allows you to create an extension or a plugin that will work with JDeveloper 11*g*R2. For example, we might create a plugin in JDeveloper that will allow the user to open the Model or ViewController project file in Notepad.

The extension development is based on a standard called **Open Services Gateway Initiative** (**OSGI**). More information about OSGI can be found at `http://www.osgi.org/Main/HomePage`.

You can download the Extension SDK from Oracle by going to **Help | Check for Updates**. The URL to download the Extension SDK is as follows:

`http://www.oracle.com/ocom/groups/public/@otn/documents/webcontent/131167.xml#oracle.jdeveloper.esdk`

The Extension SDK API URL is as follows:

```
http://docs.oracle.com/cd/E16162_01/apirefs.1112/e17493/toc.htm
```

The extension.xml file

The `extension.xml` file is the backbone for all extensions that are added to the JDeveloper IDE. All the extension information is defined in this file. Now we will see how to create a basic extension project and run it.

Time for action – creating and running an extension

We can create an extension by using the following steps:

1. Select **Extension Project** from the **Extension Development** section under **Client Tier**. Make sure you have the Extension SDK downloaded using the **Check for Updates** option.

2. Provide the information as displayed in the following screenshot:

3. You will now have the `extension.xml` and `MANIFEST.MF` files created for the project. The `MANIFEST.MF` file will only provide the version information.

4. Right-click on the extension and click on **Deploy to Target Platform**. Subsequently, click on the **Run Extension** option. A new JDeveloper will open up with your extension added to the IDE.

5. Verify the extension added to the JDeveloper IDE by going to **Help | About | Extension**.

6. Open the **First Sample** example provided in the *Extension SDK samples* to explore more on creating extensions.

What just happened?

We created a new extension for the JDeveloper. The newly created extension will only display the information about your extension in the **Extension** section. The Extension SDK samples contain many examples to start exploring extensions.

Pop quiz

Q1. Which of the following is an option in an entity object for performance tuning?

1. Retain the association accessor
2. Cascade delete
3. Update batching
4. Both 1 and 2
5. Both 1 and 3

Q2. MDS allows the user to customize the application at runtime.

1. True
2. False

Q3. _____ and _____ are the two options available to store the state of the application using passivation.

1. **File** and **Database**
2. **Cloud** and **Database**
3. **MidTier** and **File**
4. **Database** and **Cloud**
5. None of the above

Q4. The _____ element is used to define the data transportation mode for ADS.

1. `<transport>`

2. `<transport-control>`

3. `<latency>`

4. `<threshold>`

5. `<transport-latency>`

Summary

Let us recap what we learned in this chapter. We learned about the advanced topics in an entity object, view object, and application module. We have learned about the state management in an application module. We learned about some complex usages of task flows and managed beans. We also learned to debug an application. Finally, we learned some performance tuning for ADF.

Pop Quiz Answers

Chapter 1, Installing and Configuring JDeveloper IDE

Pop quiz

Q1	3
Q2	2
Q3	2
Q4	Connections and descriptors
Q5	5

Chapter 2, Getting Started with ADF

Pop quiz

Q1	3
Q2	Top down and bottom Up
Q3	3
Q4	1
Q5	3

Chapter 3, Understanding the Model Layer

Q1	3
Q2	3
Q3	1
Q4	Application module
Q5	1

Chapter 4, Validating and Using the Model Data

Q1	Collection and UniqueKey
Q2	3
Q3	2
Q4	1
Q5	3

Chapter 5, Binding the Data

Q1	3
Q2	4
Q3	1

Chapter 6, Displaying the Data

Q1	2
Q2	3
Q3	1
Q4	4
Q5	3

Chapter 7, Working With Navigation Flows

Q1	Unbounded and bounded
Q2	5
Q3	1
Q4	4
Q5	4

Chapter 8, Layout With Look and Feel

Q1	5
Q2	1
Q3	4
Q4	3
Q5	4

Chapter 9, Implementing Security

Q1	4
Q2	1
Q3	3
Q4	3
Q5	4

Chapter 10, Deploying the ADF Application

Q1	1
Q2	4
Q3	1
Q4	4

Chapter 11, Advanced Features of ADF

Q1	5
Q2	1
Q3	1
Q4	1

Index

inlineStyle 159
partialSubmit 159
partialTriggers 159
rendered 158
styleClass 159
visible 159

Property Inspector pane 29
property sets 257
pseudo classes, ADF skinning framework
about 207
drag and drop 207
inline editing 208
message 208
right to left 207
standard 207

Push Service interface 282

Q

query components
about 163
af:query 163

QUERY_MODE_SCAN_DATABASE_TABLES
mode 263

QUERY_MODE_SCAN_ENTITY_ROWS mode 263

QUERY_MODE_SCAN_VIEW_ROWS mode 263

Query Optimizer
about 263
ALL_ROWS mode 263
FIRST_ROWS mode 263

Quickstart wizard 12

R

RANGE_PAGING_AUTO_POST mode 263
RANGE_PAGING mode 263
RangeSize option 262
Range validator 105
readOnly property 160
Recently Opened Files pane 24
records
inserting 134

RefreshCondition item 143
Regular Expression validator 106
remove() method 118, 119
removeRowWithKey method 131
rendered property 158
Required property 160

resource bundle
about 258, 259
list 259
properties 259
XLIFF 259

Resource palette
catalog, creating 26, 27

Resource palette window 26
resources
permissions, adding for 225-227

Retain Association Accessor Rowset option 256
return element, Data Controls palette 132
roles
about 230
assigning 231-233
creating 231-233
Customization Developer 17
Database Developer 17
J2EE Developer 17
Java Developer 17
Studio Developer 17

rollback() operation 81
root_menu.xml file 269
Router activity
about 183
default-outcome property 183
expression property 183

RowFetchLimit option 262
RowSet.closeRowSet() method 264
Rowsets
working with 264

rows property 160
Run Manager 28
runtime customization, Metadata Services
framework 281

S

Save Point Restore activity 183
script expression
adding 113, 114

Script validator 106
SCROLLABLE mode 263
searchRegion item 144
Secret property 160
security, ADF application deployment
about 245

V

validateEntity() method **117**
validate() method **259, 260**
validateModelUpdates method **197**
validation
  about 97, 127
  creating, steps 102
validation execution **111**
validation rules
  about 99
  attribute-level validation 99
  entity-level validation 99
  transaction-level validation 100
validator tags **170**
value property **160**
varStatus property **168**
view accessors **264**
View activity
  about 186
  adding, to task flow 187
view criteria, Data Controls palette **132**
view layer **32**
View layer, ADF architecture **34**
view link
  about 77
  adding, to application module 81, 82
  creating, between EmpVO and DeptVO 77-79
view object
  about 71
  types 72, 73
  uses 71
view object collection, Data Controls palette **129**
ViewObjectImpl class **118**
view object options, ADF business components
  about 92
  General 92, 93
  Query 93, 94
view objects
  advanced features 262
view objects, classes
  view definition 118
  view object 118

view row 118
Visibility options, task flow
  Library Internal 190
  URL Invoke 190
visible property **159**

W

Web Application Archive (WAR) **239**
weblogic-application.xml file **244**
WebLogic server **238**
WebLogic server 10.3.5.0 **238**
Weblogic server configurations
  about 282
  data sources 284
  deployments 284
  diagnostics 285
  domain 283
  Security realm 284
  servers 283
WebLogic server deployment
  about 247
  integrated server 247
  standalone server 250-252
weblogic.xml file **222, 244**
WebPageTemplate.jspx file **152**
Webservice data control **268**
WebSphere **238**
web.xml file **222, 243**
Wild card activity **188**
Windows
  system requisites, for JDeveloper 8
workspace
  creating, for employee directory
    application 37, 38
wrap property **160**

X

XMLMenuModel feature **269**

Thank you for buying
Oracle ADF 11gR2 Development Beginner's Guide

About Packt Publishing

Packt, pronounced 'packed', published its first book "*Mastering phpMyAdmin for Effective MySQL Management*" in April 2004 and subsequently continued to specialize in publishing highly focused books on specific technologies and solutions.

Our books and publications share the experiences of your fellow IT professionals in adapting and customizing today's systems, applications, and frameworks. Our solution-based books give you the knowledge and power to customize the software and technologies you're using to get the job done. Packt books are more specific and less general than the IT books you have seen in the past. Our unique business model allows us to bring you more focused information, giving you more of what you need to know, and less of what you don't.

Packt is a modern, yet unique publishing company, which focuses on producing quality, cutting-edge books for communities of developers, administrators, and newbies alike. For more information, please visit our website: www.PacktPub.com.

About Packt Enterprise

In 2010, Packt launched two new brands, Packt Enterprise and Packt Open Source, in order to continue its focus on specialization. This book is part of the Packt Enterprise brand, home to books published on enterprise software – software created by major vendors, including (but not limited to) IBM, Microsoft and Oracle, often for use in other corporations. Its titles will offer information relevant to a range of users of this software, including administrators, developers, architects, and end users.

Writing for Packt

We welcome all inquiries from people who are interested in authoring. Book proposals should be sent to author@packtpub.com. If your book idea is still at an early stage and you would like to discuss it first before writing a formal book proposal, contact us; one of our commissioning editors will get in touch with you.

We're not just looking for published authors; if you have strong technical skills but no writing experience, our experienced editors can help you develop a writing career, or simply get some additional reward for your expertise.

Oracle ADF Enterprise Application Development— Made Simple

ISBN: 978-1-849681-88-9   Paperback: 396 pages

Successfully plan, develop, test, and deploy enterprise applications with Oracle ADF

1. Best practices for real-life enterprise application development

2. Proven project methodology to ensure success with your ADF project from an Oracle ACE Director

3. Understand the effort involved in building an ADF application from scratch, or converting an existing application

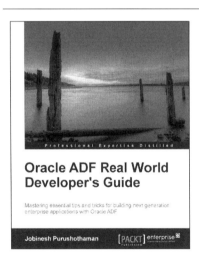

Oracle ADF Real World Developer's Guide

ISBN: 978-1-849684-82-8   Paperback: 590 pages

Mastering essential tips and tricks for building next generation enterprise applications with Oracle ADF

1. Full of illustrations, diagrams, and tips with clear step-by-step instructions and real-time examples.

2. Get to know the visual and declarative programming model offered by ADF.

3. In depth coverage of ADF business components and ADF binding layer.

4. Teaches you the ADF best practices and fine-tuning tips.

Please check **www.PacktPub.com** for information on our titles

Oracle Information Integration, Migration, and Consolidation

ISBN: 978-1-849682-20-6   Paperback: 332 pages

Over 60 recipes to create rich Internet applications with many exciting features

1. Learn about integration practices that many IT professionals are not familiar with

2. Evaluate and implement numerous tools like Oracle SOA Suite and Oracle GoldenGate

3. Get to grips with the past, present, and future of Oracle Integration practices

Oracle APEX Best Practices

ISBN: 978-1-849684-00-2   Paperback: 298 pages

Accentuate Oracle APEX development with proven best practices

1. "Oracle APEX Best Practices" will get you started with Oracle APEX for developing real-world applications that perform and maximize the full potential of Oracle APEX

2. You will also learn to take advantage of advanced SQL and PL/SQL along the way

3. Combines the knowledge of Oracle Apex Experts -- Alex Nuijten, Iloon Ellen-Wollf, and Learco Brizzi

Please check **www.PacktPub.com** for information on our titles

3722678R00192

Printed in Germany
by Amazon Distribution
GmbH, Leipzig